Windows® 7: The Best of the Official Magazine

A real-life guide to getting more done

PUBLISHED BY
Microsoft Press
A Division of Microsoft Corporation
One Microsoft Way
Redmond, Washington 98052-6399

Copyright © 2010

Future and/or Microsoft cannot accept any responsibility for errors or inaccuracies in such information. Readers are advised to contact manufacturers and retailers directly with regard to the price of products/services referred to in this book.

Library of Congress Control Number: 2010921008

Printed and bound in the United States of America.

1 2 3 4 5 6 7 8 9 WCT 5 4 3 2 1 0

Distributed in Canada by HB Fenn and Company Ltd.

A CIP catalogue record for this book is available from the British Library.

Microsoft Press Books are available through booksellers and distributors worldwide. For further information about international editions, contact your local Microsoft Corporation office or contact Microsoft Press International directly at fax (425) 936-7329. Visit our website at **www.microsoft.com/mspress**. Send comments to **mspinput@microsoft.com**.

All images in this book are supplied by Jupiter Images (UK) Ltd (www.jupiterimages.com) or Future Publishing Ltd.

With grateful thanks to the following people and organizations for their contributions to the content of this book:
Peter Boston, Philip Collie, Lynn Cormack, Cliff Evans, Linda Jones, Patricia Kenar, Dave Law, Jake Ludington, Mark Moran, Gavin Reynoldson, Alun Rogers, Alison Schillaci, SouthPeak Games, Barrington Harvey Press, Nike +iPod, PrimaSoft PC, Inc.

Acquisitions Editor: Juliana Aldous
Developmental Editor: Sandra Haynes
Project Editor: Rosemary Caperton
Operations Editor: Jo Membery, Future Publishing
Art: Seth Singh & John McAllister, Future Publishing
Cover design: twist creative • seattle
Deputy Editor: James Stables, Future Publishing
Editor-in-chief: Adam Ifans, Future Publishing

Body Part No: X16-03275

Windows 7: The Best of the Official Magazine

Welcome...

to your comprehensive guide to Window 7. The team behind
Windows: The Official Magazine – the only Windows magazine
approved by Microsoft – has compiled this book to show you how the
new operating system can simplify yet enrich every element of your life.

Introduction

Security... simplicity... discovery. You can have it all with Windows 7. If you're not using your computer to its full potential, or you're concerned about convoluted procedures or letting your PC defenses down, then fear no more! Windows 7 protects and performs like no operating system before it. This book takes you on a complete tour – from personalizing your desktop to organizing your workflow or family life to creating a home movie for your loved ones to treasure. Find out how Windows 7 really can assist and improve every area of your life...

Get Started

May we introduce you to Windows 7. Get to grips with setting things up exactly how you want them and catch a first glimpse at just some of the features that the operating system has to offer. You'll soon want to get going...

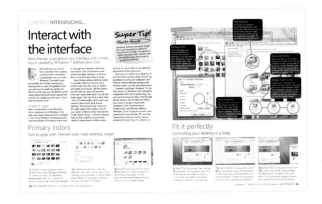

Explore

Once you've become more familiar, you'll want to see how diverse the operating system can be. Find out more about how Windows 7 can help to organize your life and, in turn, make you more productive – and creative – whether you're using your PC in an office or home environment.

Do More

This is where the fun starts. You've got to grips with the system, now it's time to start embarking on some really useful, and entertaining, projects. Your PC is not just for work (although it can help there, too!) – it can help you to host a party, find your family history, and so much more...

Contents

Get Started

Explore

Contents

Contents

Do More

Contents

Get Started

It's time to switch on and discover the user-friendly features of Windows 7

Chapter 1 **Introducing...**

Chapter 2 **Your first hour**

"Wow"

12

reasons why you'll love Windows 7

A guide to the most outstanding elements
in this latest Microsoft operating system

1 The interface looks amazing

☐ The Windows Aero interface manages to be both eye-catching and unobtrusive. Much of this is down to the Aero Glass transparency effects on window borders and menus. There's a whole bunch of great effects, such as Flip3D, which shows every running application in a scrollable 3D stack of windows. And you can quickly make all windows transparent simply by hovering your mouse over the Show Desktop bar in the right-hand corner of the Taskbar – great if you want to check files or gadgets on your desktop.

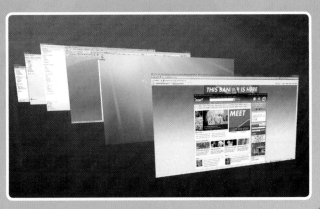

2 Access your home media anywhere

☐ If you're out and about a lot and don't want to take your music, video and photos with you, Windows 7 allows you to access all the files stored on your home PC wherever you are. Provided you've got an internet connection, you can access them using Remote Media Streaming in Windows Media Player 12. You need to have Windows 7 on the home PC with your media stored on it, and Windows 7 on the PC you want to access the files from. Then, on both computers, allow media sharing so that the files can be shared.

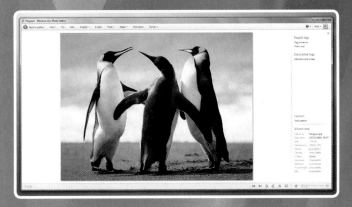

3 Foolproof to set up

☐ To install Windows 7: insert DVD, press Install now, turn brain off. The set-up process in Windows 7 is no more taxing than installing a game, and no longer stops halfway through to ask you an asinine question about which currency symbols to use at which times.

4 Speed up in a flash

☐ Windows 7 offers an easy way to eke more life out of a laboring PC, and all without taking the side off the case. ReadyBoost is an instant adrenaline infusion, and all you have to do is plug in a ReadyBoost-compatible flash drive or digital camera memory card. Because these can read and write data very quickly, they can act as surrogate memory, so the PC can do more at once without grinding to a halt. Windows 7 also supports multiple memory sticks, for an even greater increase in speed.

SPEED UP You decide how much space on your USB drive to assign to ReadyBoost

(5) Windows Media Center can be built in

Windows Media Center is now a component part of the Windows 7 Home Premium and Ultimate editions. Its advanced from-your-own-sofa television recording, scheduling and time-shifting capabilities mean that, for many of us, all other forms of recording TV and movies will quickly become obsolete. It's also a great way of managing a bewilderingly huge music and photo library – again, all from sedentary comfort.

ENTERTAINMENT TIME Windows Media Center turns your PC into an easy-to-use, complete home entertainment system

(6) All you need for top class gaming

Windows 7 is an excellent choice when you want to play games. The gaming experience has been improved in Windows 7 with the new Games Explorer – accessible in the Start menu. You can view games that come with your PC in one area and also see ones that you've added yourself. Games that you install will automatically receive updates through Games Explorer, along with other information, such as how long you've been playing a game and achievements you've gained. The Performance Index tool checks out the hardware in your system and assigns a number that you can compare to the one on the back of the game box. If your PC's number is equal or better, you can play it.

(7) Parental controls

At last, you can ease back on some of the worry about what your little rugrats are up to on the computer. Windows 7 has a collection of very straightforward ways to keep non-patronizing tabs on your kids' computing, such as setting strict time limits on how long they can use the PC for, what age rating of game they're allowed to play, or restricting specific sites and types of site so they can't ever clap innocent eyes on them. This is all easily and simply tied into the individual User Accounts that you can create and set up with Windows 7, not only providing a personal space for your children, but a space that you can place responsible limits on as well.

(8) Desktop gadgets

Those handy little gadgets in Windows Vista have been given an overhaul for Windows 7. The Windows Sidebar has been taken out and replaced with desktop gadgets. So now you can put your gadgets wherever you like on the desktop. Headlines from websites, your inbox, the local weather, a TV guide, a photo gallery, a notepad, Sudoku – pretty much everything that you care to mention has a 'gadget' made for it. Microsoft has created a handy gallery of gadgets so it's easy to browse, select and install what you need.

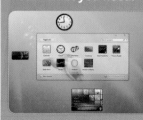

MOVEABLE MENU Gadgets can be now be dragged around the desktop to suit your workspace

(9) Supremely fast file searching facilities

The new operating system has a constantly updated database, which keeps tabs on every file as it's created, changed or deleted. Whenever you type in a search term (whether it's a filename, the sender of an email, name of a song, or a million other possibilities), the results will be presented instantly, as you type.

(10) Mobile computing

Available in Premium editions, the Windows Mobility Center puts efficient laptop power usage at the heart of Windows 7. There are three configurable power plans that enable users to opt for different levels of performance or battery life. Alongside this, new power-saving features will make your Windows 7 laptop battery last even longer, such as an adaptive display that dims the brightness of your screen if you've gone away to make a cup of tea.

(11) The best networking

To make everyone's life easier, a new Network and Sharing Center has been introduced. It provides a visual breakdown of your network, where you can check the connection status, view network devices and the PC, as well as troubleshoot problems. This data is provided via the Network Map that lets you see instantly if the network can find the internet, and provides a summary of all this information. For problems, the new Network Diagnostics and Troubleshooting provides easy-to-understand reports and advice. Windows 7 is also designed to work with the newest wireless networks and offers the latest in security support for WPA2. So it's easier and safer to use in conjunction with wireless hotspots. Windows 7 also comes with View Available Network, which makes it easy to see what networks are available when you want to connect to the internet, and it's now easier to connect to them too.

(12) Windows 7 Touch

Now there's an easier way to use your PC – if you've got a touchscreen monitor or laptop, you can navigate Windows 7 using the power of your finger, so there's no need to ever use a mouse and keyboard again. Pull up or down to scroll open windows, double-tap on one of the many large icons in Windows 7 to open a program, or drag and drop files without breaking a sweat. There's also support for multi-touch – a more advanced type of touchscreen where you can use more than one finger to make it even easier to control what's on screen.

Get ready: Action stations!

Windows 7 brings you the Action Center – your one-stop spot to keep the system running smoothly

Windows 7 introduces the freshly minted Action Center, to help manage your system and troubleshoot problems, and it can be customized to suit your computing expertise.

You can find Windows 7 Action Center in three ways: click the icon on the right-hand side of your taskbar; type 'Action Center' into the search function on the Start menu, or go to **Start → Control Panel → System and Security → Action Center**. Here you'll find system maintenance and security information, troubleshooting and recovery options, Windows Update and notifications.

When you open Action Center, you'll find any security and maintenance issues highlighted by colored bars. A red bar is high priority; a yellow bar indicates tasks that you might want to resolve (anything from recommended maintenance to helpful advice on fixing driver issues).

On the right-hand side of the Security and Maintenance headings you'll see an arrow, click on this to expand or collapse the section. Expanding the section shows the various elements that you need to manage. For example, in the Security section you'll find Network Firewall, Windows Update, Virus Protection and other security related concerns.

You don't need to open Action Center to check for issues, it will notify you when there's a problem. Simply hover your mouse over the icon in the notification pane of the taskbar (bottom right) to see new messages.

While Windows 7 offers more control over notifications (see 'Notification control' below), it's best to stick to the recommended level while you get to know your shiny new operating system.

At the bottom of the page you'll see two hyperlinks, one for Troubleshooting and one for Recovery. Clicking on **Troubleshooting** will take you through to another pane that lists everything from Programs to System and Security. The **Recovery** button gives you the option to resolve a problem by restoring your computer to a state where it worked properly. You can even quick link through to Windows Update, Backup and Restore and Windows Program Compatibility Troubleshooter directly from Action Center.

Notification control

How to manage Action Center messages

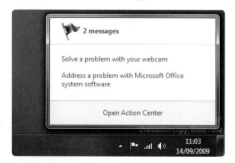

1 AT THE BAR The Action Center notification icon is displayed in the taskbar by default. You'll find messages about security and maintenance settings and Windows Update.

2 MAIN PANE Left-click on the icon, then **Open Action Center** to get to the main pane. Select **Change Action Center settings**. You can now turn your messages on or off for each section.

3 MANAGEMENT While you're getting to know Windows 7, it's a good idea to keep the default settings. As you get more experienced, you can remove them when you feel more comfortable.

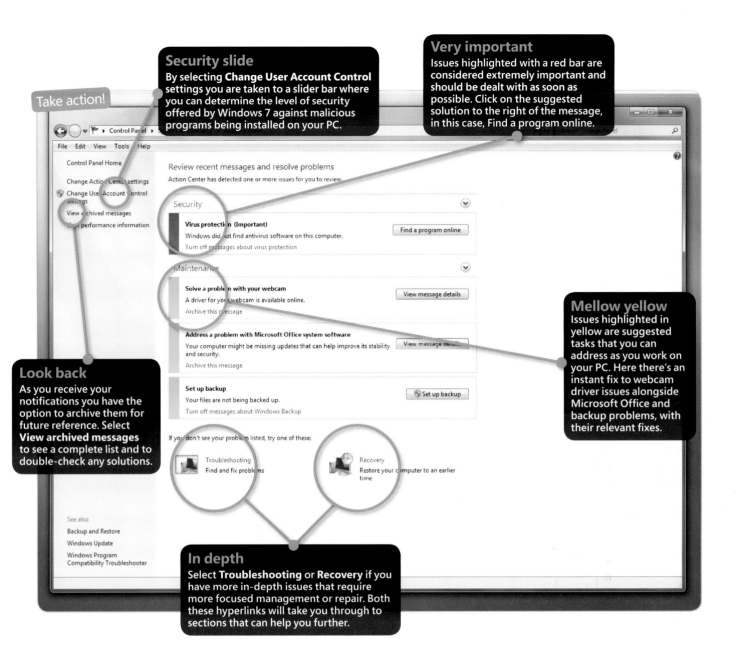

Take action!

Security slide
By selecting **Change User Account Control** settings you are taken to a slider bar where you can determine the level of security offered by Windows 7 against malicious programs being installed on your PC.

Very important
Issues highlighted with a red bar are considered extremely important and should be dealt with as soon as possible. Click on the suggested solution to the right of the message, in this case, Find a program online.

Look back
As you receive your notifications you have the option to archive them for future reference. Select **View archived messages** to see a complete list and to double-check any solutions.

Mellow yellow
Issues highlighted in yellow are suggested tasks that you can address as you work on your PC. Here there's an instant fix to webcam driver issues alongside Microsoft Office and backup problems, with their relevant fixes.

In depth
Select **Troubleshooting** or **Recovery** if you have more in-depth issues that require more focused management or repair. Both these hyperlinks will take you through to sections that can help you further.

4 CLEAN SLATE To keep your taskbar tidy, you can remove the Action Center icon. Click **Start → Control Panel** and change the view to Small icons/All Control Panel Items.

5 SHOW OR NO SHOW Click on **Notification Area Icons**; the first icon is Action Center. Here you can choose to keep the icon and notifications, lose them both or only show notifications.

6 CUSTOMIZE While you're here, you can make other adjustments to your notification taskbar. Handy if you're monitoring several applications at once. When you've finished, click **OK**.

Interact with the interface

New themes, a gorgeous new interface and a multi-touch capability, Windows 7 defines your cool

Microsoft has put a lot of time and effort into creating a product that is eminently customizable. You can tailor Windows 7 to match your personality and moods, turning your desktop into a visual smörgåsbord that you just want to reach out and touch. Which, by the way, you can thanks to the vastly improved touchscreen experience. It gives new credence to the term, "can't keep my hands off it"!

Shake it, baby

Aero, introduced to us by Windows Vista, continues on in Windows 7 but with some tasty improvements. Available in the Home Premium, Professional and Ultimate editions it introduces new ways to manage your desktop. While the style factor, such as animations and translucent glass windows, is obvious there is more to Aero than its looks...

Aero Shake reduces desktop clutter in seconds. When you've too many screens open at once, click on a pane and shake your mouse. All the screens but the one you want will instantly minimize. Want them back? Just do the shake again. The next trick is Aero Peek – this is immeasurably useful when you need to take a quick look at your desktop. Simply move your mouse to the right edge of the taskbar and all your open windows will go transparent. Finally, there's Snap – a window resizing feature that's ideal for anyone who needs to keep several windows open at once, or has to refer to two different documents at the same time.

Now you can control your desktop, it's time to make it pretty using Themes. Say goodbye to boring old wallpapers and hello to instant desktop backgrounds, window colors, sounds and screensavers.

It doesn't end there. Windows 7 is the first version of Windows with completely integrated multi-touch technology. You can use it to browse online, flick through photo albums, shuffle files and folders and zoom in to get a closer look. Available in the Home Premium, Professional and Ultimate editions, Windows Touch is easy to use and, once paired with a touchscreen PC, you'll be amazed by what you can do. Just be prepared to lose hours to creative fun!

Primary colors

Get to grips with Themes and make desktop magic

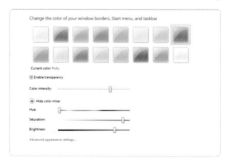

1 THEME In Personalization, select a theme by hitting **Change the theme**. To create your own, click **Desktop Background**, select your picture, its position and timings, then **Save Changes**.

2 COLOR Go to Window Color and select your color. You can adjust their intensity using the slider or click on **Show Color Mixer** to manipulate brightness, hue and saturation. Click **Save**.

3 SOUND Choose sounds for various activities from a pre-recorded list, recording and playback. To save, right-click **Unsaved Theme** under My Themes, then click **Save Theme**.

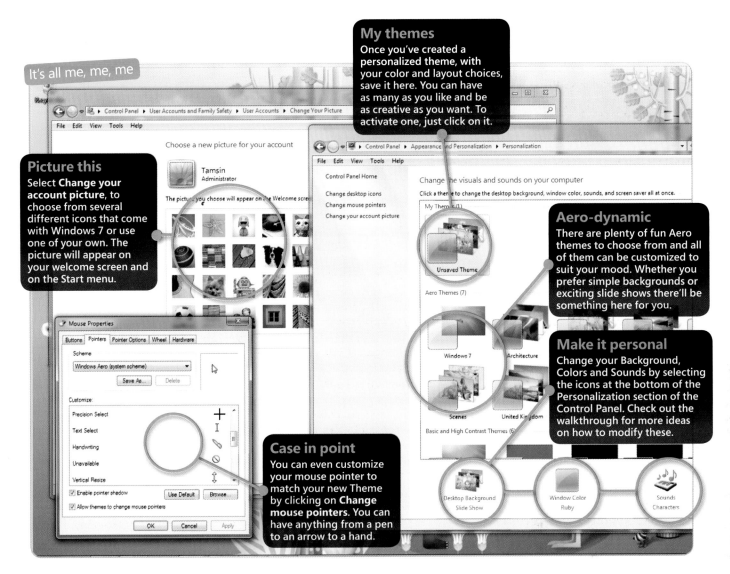

It's all me, me, me

My themes
Once you've created a personalized theme, with your color and layout choices, save it here. You can have as many as you like and be as creative as you want. To activate one, just click on it.

Picture this
Select **Change your account picture**, to choose from several different icons that come with Windows 7 or use one of your own. The picture will appear on your welcome screen and on the Start menu.

Aero-dynamic
There are plenty of fun Aero themes to choose from and all of them can be customized to suit your mood. Whether you prefer simple backgrounds or exciting slide shows there'll be something here for you.

Make it personal
Change your Background, Colors and Sounds by selecting the icons at the bottom of the Personalization section of the Control Panel. Check out the walkthrough for more ideas on how to modify these.

Case in point
You can even customize your mouse pointer to match your new Theme by clicking on **Change mouse pointers**. You can have anything from a pen to an arrow to a hand.

Fit it perfectly
Controlling your desktop is a Snap

1 TAKE IT UP To activate Snap, click on the pane of the document and lift it to the top of your screen to open it in full screen. An outline will appear showing you where it is going to go.

2 TAKE IT DOWN To reduce the size of the document, drag it to the bottom of the screen and it will snap back to its original position. It takes some practise but soon you'll have it down perfectly.

3 SIDE BY SIDE To snap documents side by side, click on the pane and drag the document to the left or the right. When the outline pane appears release, then repeat for the second document.

Jump start

Windows 7 introduces some exciting new features and customization options for the taskbar and Start menu

You are about to be amazed by the impressive new features in Windows 7 and how much they will change your user experience. From Jump Lists to Libraries and taskbar management, you can customize Windows 7 to suit your personal style.

There are quite a few fantastic new features designed especially for the Start menu and taskbar, and the first of these is Jump Lists. These are lists of the most recent items you've used, such as websites or documents or folders, arranged according to the programs you used to open them. By pinning these to your taskbar or Start menu you can have instant, easy access to the things you use most regularly.

Libraries are another clever invention; instead of organizing your files into different folders you can use Libraries to sort them according to type, no matter where they are stored. When you first open your libraries you'll find four default collections: Documents, Music, Pictures and Videos, and you can add your own as you go. Customize these by adding them to the Start menu or changing the way they look. You can pin Windows Explorer to your taskbar to put your Libraries a mere click away.

While we're visiting the Start menu, we may as well have a look around inside... The search box that sits at the bottom of the bar is a quick and easy way of looking for items. It will start searching for files, folders, programs and email messages as you type and display them according to category. Many familiar links have been removed, such as the Connect To button and Recent Items. You can pop these all back if you want; it's all about you and your working style.

The taskbar has also undergone surgery and looks fantastic. Its transparency opens up your desktop and the buttons do more than just show you what programs you have working. You can customize the way these appear, but in default view they sit as unlabeled icons that offer you a preview as you hover the mouse over them. It is incredibly useful if you have a stack of multiple items (such as websites) open at the same time and need quick access.

Pinning items and controlling how they appear is extremely easy to do and they can be changed whenever the mood strikes you. On the right side of the taskbar, you'll find the notification area. Again, you get to decide how many notifications appear (see page 8) and which ones get precedence.

By deciding which Jump Lists appear on your taskbar and which on your Start menu, alongside carefully managed notifications and icons, you can already see how your desktop has become far tighter and richer.

Now it's time to style Windows 7 up in your own version of chic efficiency. ⊞

Jump Lists sorted

Managing your Jump Lists is truly simple

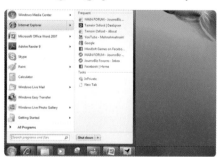

1 JUMP LISTS To view a Jump List item (such as a recently opened website), go to **Start**, point to a pinned program, then click the arrow next to the program. To open the item, just click on it.

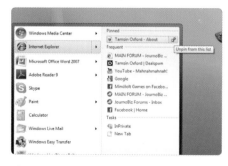

2 PIN IT Go to the program's Jump List, point to the item, click on the pin icon; it will move into the Pinned Icons box. To unpin it, click the pin icon next to the item in the Pinned Icons box.

3 A DRAG You can pin to the Jump List by grabbing an icon or shortcut from the Start menu or desktop and dragging it to the taskbar. To move an item from a Jump List, just drag it to a new location.

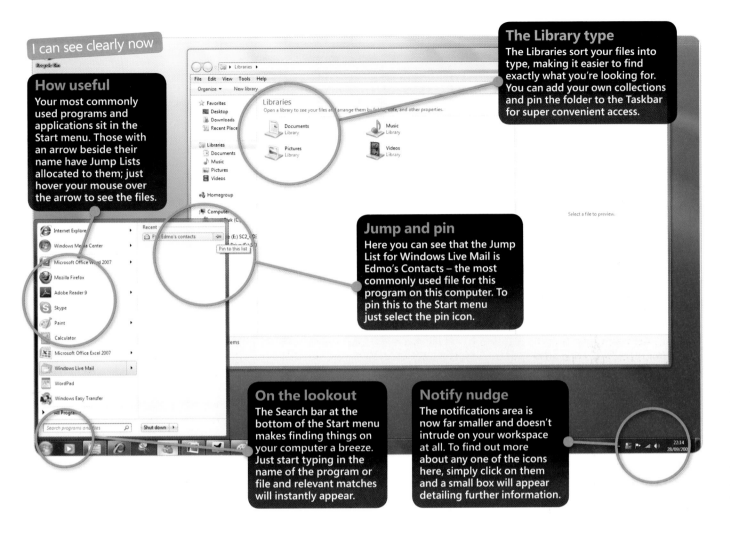

I can see clearly now

How useful
Your most commonly used programs and applications sit in the Start menu. Those with an arrow beside their name have Jump Lists allocated to them; just hover your mouse over the arrow to see the files.

The Library type
The Libraries sort your files into type, making it easier to find exactly what you're looking for. You can add your own collections and pin the folder to the Taskbar for super convenient access.

Jump and pin
Here you can see that the Jump List for Windows Live Mail is Edmo's Contacts – the most commonly used file for this program on this computer. To pin this to the Start menu just select the pin icon.

On the lookout
The Search bar at the bottom of the Start menu makes finding things on your computer a breeze. Just start typing in the name of the program or file and relevant matches will instantly appear.

Notify nudge
The notifications area is now far smaller and doesn't intrude on your workspace at all. To find out more about any one of the icons here, simply click on them and a small box will appear detailing further information.

Start menu magic
Start as you mean to go on and make Windows 7 work for you

1 START SWITCH To move the Start button, right-click an empty space on the taskbar, uncheck 'Lock the taskbar', then click on an empty space and hold the mouse to drag it to another edge.

2 CLEAR VIEW To start afresh, go to **Control Panel → Appearance and Personalization → Taskbar and Start Menu**. In the Start Menu tab, uncheck the 'Store and display...' box. Click **OK**.

3 GET IT RIGHT To add or remove items on the right pane of the Start menu, hit **Customize** from the Start Menu tab, then choose the items you want to appear. Click **OK**.

Device control at your fingertips

Managing your hardware need not be a chore thanks to the improved design and options included in Windows 7 Device Manager

If one of the main reasons behind your move to a new operating system is to benefit from a better rapport between your PC and gadgets like your cell phone or MP3 player, you've made the right choice with Windows 7. The Windows 7 Device Manager helps you assess hardware issues and manage updates, drivers and settings. Device Manager can change advanced settings, uninstall devices and troubleshoot pesky problems. And it's all really easy to sort!

When you first install Windows 7, you're going to want to add all sorts of essential peripherals and sometimes you'll need to repair driver issues or install updates, and even remove old hardware. This is where the Device Manager comes in.

Go to **Start → Control Panel → System and Security → Device Manager**. If you're running your PC with an administrator password it will ask you for this now. The devices displayed here are essentially external ones that you've connected to your PC and can include anything portable like your mobile phone, MP3 player or hard drives.

If you only need to check items like your printer, fax machine or monitor, you can access these by going to **Start → Devices and Printers**. But the Devices

and Printers section won't show information about hardware inside your computer or speakers and peripherals connected through a serial port or the less common PS/2. For those kinds of enquiries, go to Device Manager.

Fear not

Before you attempt to make major changes to your settings and drivers, it's worth noting that Device Manager has a valuable function that enables you to restore settings if disaster occurs. The roll-back function restores your PC to a point when everything was working perfectly. Just in case you make a change for the worse, of course.

Getting to know you

Hardware problems can be frustrating, so get on top of them asap!

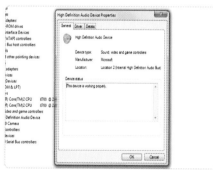

1 WARNING BELLS Any items that carry the yellow warning icon are not working properly. In Devices and Printers, right-click the device or computer with the warning icon and then click **Troubleshoot**.

2 PATIENT PLANNING Wait patiently for Troubleshoot to diagnose the problem. This can take several minutes, but will provide you with key information so you can address it. Just follow the instructions to fix your hardware.

3 UPDATE A DRIVER If you have a device that isn't working efficiently then it probably isn't running its latest driver. Download the driver from the manufacturer's site then open up Device Manager to begin installation.

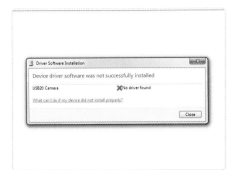

4 LEARNER'S LICENSE Scroll down until you come to the device that you want to update then double-click the device name. Go to the Driver tab, click **Update Driver**, then follow the on-screen instructions to install.

5 PRINTER ISSUES If you're having problems with your printers, this information will be displayed in Devices and Printers. To install a printer, update drivers and manage settings, go to **Start → Devices and Printers**.

6 DRIVER RESET If your problems get worse or the driver causes your hardware to stop working then you can restore the previous version. Go to Device Manager and double-click the category listing your device driver.

7 ROLLING OVER Once you've selected the device, click the Driver tab and select **Roll Back Driver**. If this button is dimmed then you either need to log on as administrator or there is no previous version of the driver installed.

8 TURNED OFF If a piece of hardware isn't working, it's a good idea to make sure it's turned on. Go to Device Manager and then double-click the category where your hardware is located to open the tree and find your device.

9 TURNED ON Right-click the sound card or processor that you want to check and you'll either see the option to Disable it or Enable it. Click **Enable** and then test your device – hopefully this will resolve your issue.

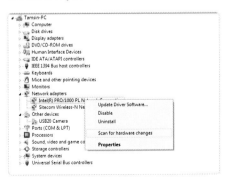

10 DEVICE DETAILS Device Manager gives you an instant view of your hardware's important information. To assess the driver status, its working status and more, double-click the relevant icon to open its window.

11 DRIVER DETAILS If you want to see more info about your current drivers, click on **Drivers → Driver Details** to open up a new window with all the details. You can also check that it has a digital signature for safety reasons.

12 SCAN IT If you want to assess newly installed hardware or check your system is working properly, right-click on a category then click **Scan for hardware changes.** The system will run a check and alert you of any issues.

Take note, and get creative

The improvements in WordPad, Paint and Sticky Notes make a world of difference in Windows 7

Let's start with Sticky Notes. These clever devices, introduced to us by Windows XP Tablet Edition, have evolved to become a lot more useful and customizable. You can format their color, text format and size with a single click and you can flip through your notes and collapse them quickly and easily. Those with a touch screen or tablet PC will be happy to hear that Sticky Notes support pen and touch input, and you can switch between these two modes whenever you want. Once you've jotted down your notes for that novel of yours, it's time to open up the freshly squeezed WordPad.

WordPad has been a part of Windows for a long time, but this new facelift will have everyone appreciating just how useful it can be. The ribbon interface, the strip across the top of the window that was introduced as part of Office 2007, has been included in the new WordPad, making accessing features and managing documents far more efficient.

WordPad has also been fitted out with more formatting options, such as highlighting, line breaks, colors and bullets. This program has evolved from simplistic word processing to a useful tool that will help you to create, and manage, stylish documents.

In addition to the word processing features, WordPad also has Paint integrated into its design. This gives you the ability to include rich formatting and graphics, plus you can link to objects, such as pictures or other documents.

To access Paint through WordPad, select the **Paint** icon and the program will instantly open up. A matching image to the one you create in Paint will appear within WordPad, as the two programs are completely in sync.

Paint has also experienced some excellent changes, making it far more intuitive. The large Paste icon is a huge improvement, as is the inclusion of the Ribbon interface. The digital brushes have more choices, the image menu makes image manipulation far easier and there are more shape selections and more realistic effects. Once you've spent time playing around with WordPad, Paint and Sticky Notes, you'll wonder how you ever lived without them.

The artist's palette

Express yourself with a fresh new lick of Paint

1 FIND IT Go to **Start ➔ All Programs ➔ Accessories ➔ Paint**. Once open, you'll see the features located in the ribbon at the top of the window, grouped together according to function.

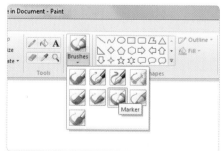

2 BRUSH IT Go to Brushes, select the brush type, then click **Size** to determine the thickness of the brush stroke; in Colors, click **Color1** and then drag the pointer to paint.

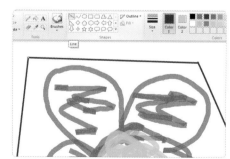

3 LINE IT Drawing straight lines can be tricky with a mouse or finger... go to **Shapes ➔ Line** to select your line then choose color in the Color 1 tab. To draw, just drag your pointer across the area.

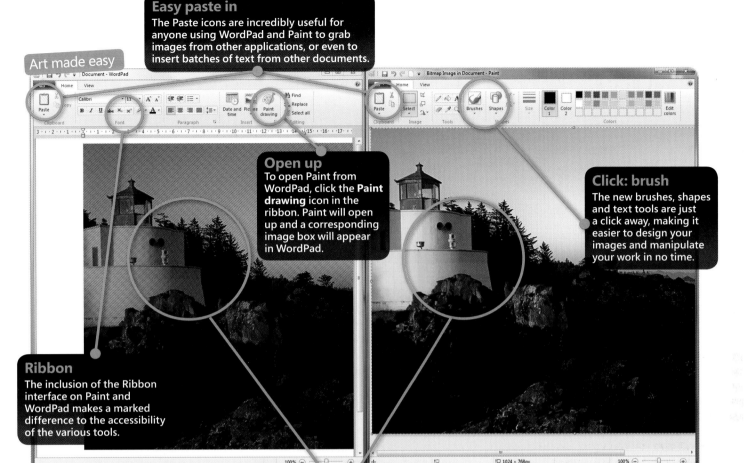

Art made easy

Easy paste in
The Paste icons are incredibly useful for anyone using WordPad and Paint to grab images from other applications, or even to insert batches of text from other documents.

Open up
To open Paint from WordPad, click the **Paint drawing** icon in the ribbon. Paint will open up and a corresponding image box will appear in WordPad.

Click: brush
The new brushes, shapes and text tools are just a click away, making it easier to design your images and manipulate your work in no time.

Ribbon
The inclusion of the Ribbon interface on Paint and WordPad makes a marked difference to the accessibility of the various tools.

Reflection
As you edit the image in Paint, the changes will be reflected in WordPad. To adjust image size to match the layout of your document, use the image size tools in Paint until it matches perfectly.

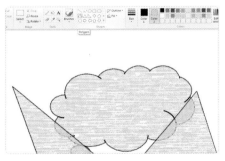

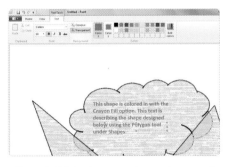

4 FILL IT To fill, go to **Tools → Fill**; choose the style, then go to color in **Colors → Color 1** to choose your outline color. To fill the background just select **Color 2**, then right-click the area to fill it.

5 SHAPE IT Use ready-made shapes by going to Shapes and choosing one, or go to the Polygon shape to create your own custom figure. To change the outline style, go to **Shapes → Outline**.

6 TEXT IT A picture paints a thousand words, but it's nice to explain... Go to **Tools → Text tool**, then drag the mouse where you want text. Adjust font, size, style under **Text Tools → Text → Font**.

Introducing Windows 7

Discover the new features of Windows 7, and personalize the settings to your liking

The first time you load up Windows 7, you might not think that much has changed since its predecessor, Windows Vista, but you'd be mistaken. Although on the surface Windows 7 hasn't been radically altered, there are many great new features.

As the previous pages have shown, the Taskbar now becomes the place to launch your programs. Once you've got a few programs open, just hover the mouse over the icons and a thumbnail preview window will pop up to tell you what's open. An additional user-friendly feature is Jump Lists. When you right-click a program icon, a menu will appear giving you the option to open old files you've been working on or websites you've recently visited, along with the ability to quickly change settings.

Many other things in Windows 7 have been made easier to use, but before you start delving into all the new features, your first port of call needs to be Windows Update. It's always worth checking if there are any new downloads available to keep your PC running at its best. Updates are typically set to install automatically via the internet.

If you've bought a new PC with Windows 7, and you still have your old PC running an older version of Windows, you'll probably want to import your old files and settings. The Windows Easy Transfer route makes this easy – find out more on page 200. Over the course of installing and transferring, you'll notice many system options are now behind a security prompt, flagged with a shield icon. Click through the prompt (or enter your password) to continue. It can be a chore during the early stages but they become less frequent, and your PC is safer as a result. You can change how many notifications you receive by clicking the small flag icon on the Taskbar, selecting **Open Action Center → Change User Account Control Settings** and adjusting the slider to suit, although it's recommended you leave it at its default setting for security reasons.

For advice, click **Start → Help and Support** in Windows. You can also find further guidance at the website for *Windows: The Official Magazine* – www.officialwindowsmagazine.com.

The Get Started five-minute guide...

Everything you need to know about personalizing Windows 7

1 CHANGE VIEW Right-click the desktop background and select **Personalize** to pick a new background or why not try one of the new Aero Themes to really give your desktop a spruce up.

2 CONNECT If using a wired network connection, just plug the Ethernet cable to your PC. For a wireless network, type 'Set up a connection or network' into the Start menu and follow the steps.

3 PROTECT There are lots of viruses lurking about on the internet, so before you start surfing, get a good anti-virus program. Go to http://go. microsoft.com/fwlink/?LinkID=140669.

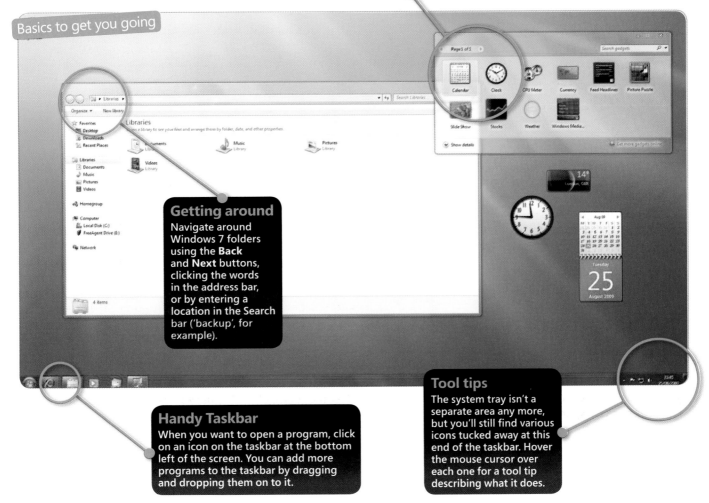

Gadgets galore

Windows 7 doesn't display any desktop gadgets by default, so you'll need to add them by right-clicking the desktop and selecting **Gadgets**. If you want more, click on **Get more gadgets online**.

Basics to get you going

Getting around

Navigate around Windows 7 folders using the **Back** and **Next** buttons, clicking the words in the address bar, or by entering a location in the Search bar ('backup', for example).

Handy Taskbar

When you want to open a program, click on an icon on the taskbar at the bottom left of the screen. You can add more programs to the taskbar by dragging and dropping them on to it.

Tool tips

The system tray isn't a separate area any more, but you'll still find various icons tucked away at this end of the taskbar. Hover the mouse cursor over each one for a tool tip describing what it does.

4 SHARE IT Create an account for each individual that uses the PC. **Start →
Control Panel → User Accounts and Family Safety → User Accounts →
Manage another account**.

5 ADD GADGETS To make your desktop really useful, you can add gadgets to it. Right-click the desktop and select **Gadgets** and then just drag and drop each gadget anywhere you like.

6 BACK UP Now you've got your PC running, you don't want to lose any files, so schedule regular backups. Type 'Backup and Restore' into the Start menu, hit **Enter** and click **Set up backup**.

Join the Library

Now that you're familiarized with Windows 7, it's time to start exploring all the nooks and crannies of customizing this good-looking operating system

 You've switched on your Windows 7 PC, so now it's time to become acquainted with your shiny new operating system. As well as looking radically different to Windows XP, Windows 7 works differently, too. In this section, you'll find your way around the interface and discover how you can tweak it to fit your own particular preferences.

What's new

The first thing you'll notice when you run Windows 7 is the lack of icons on the desktop. Then you'll spot the large taskbar, which is now far more customizable. Another big difference is the introduction of the Libraries folder, which can be found next to Internet Explorer on the Taskbar. The icon is your first portal to Windows Explorer from the desktop. Opening the folder for the

first time will bring up a window containing Documents, Music, Pictures and Videos folders. Not to be confused with the User folder (which still exists from Windows Vista), the Libraries folder allows you to make collections of different folders in one easy accessible place. You can add more folders to the existing Library or create a new library.

Explore

There are some subtle changes to the Windows Explorer interface. Most notably the Menu bar; this now adapts depending on the highlighted file or folder in question. For example, an image file will have options such as Preview, Burn or Share on the Menu bar. The left-hand navigation pane has also changed, and is far more comprehensive. All the quick links you need are there – including files that get the highest use – but the layout is far cleaner.

User access

As you continue your new voyage into Windows 7, subtle differences from Windows Vista may start to become apparent. Take User Account Control, for example. The UAC still exists but the default setting has changed. You will now only be notified when the computer makes changes to your PC and not when you do, much like Windows XP.

Should you wish to increase the level of User Account Control, simply navigate to **Control Panel → User Accounts and Family Safety → User Accounts** and adjust the setting using the level-slider. To make your life even easier, you may wish to adjust the way in which you interact with Windows. Should you need narration when typing, or need to optimize the computer for issues with poor eyesight, then go to **Control Panel → Ease of Access → Ease of Access Center** for more settings.

LIBRARIAN When launching Windows Explorer from the taskbar, the Libraries folder is the first window you see. It features the most common locations found in your user profile folder

In real life...
Intuitive input

 Adam Ifans, Editor, *Windows: The Official Magazine*
By its nature, the default interface requires a good degree of hand-eye coordination. New users or anyone with a physical impairment may find it necessary to adjust the basic input controls. This could be as simple as slowing down the mouse, changing the size of on-screen text or requesting Visual Notifications rather than audio ones. Thankfully, Windows 7 is fully set up for any of these options, and more.

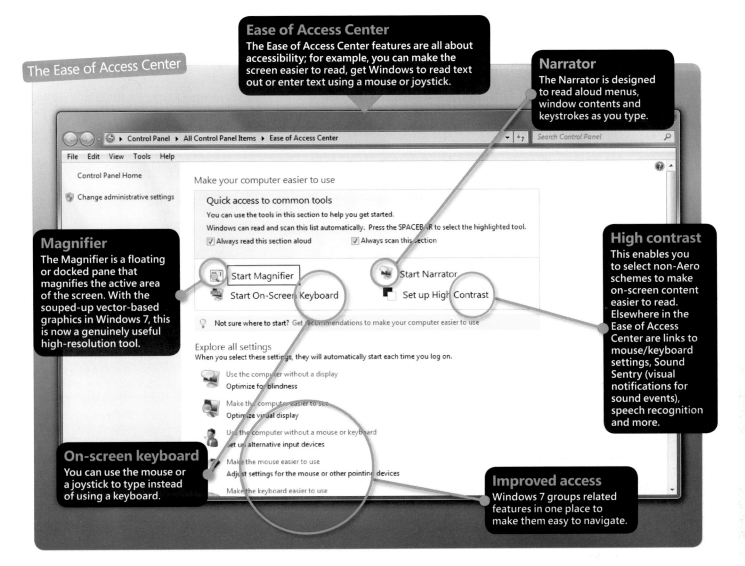

The Ease of Access Center

Ease of Access Center
The Ease of Access Center features are all about accessibility; for example, you can make the screen easier to read, get Windows to read text out or enter text using a mouse or joystick.

Narrator
The Narrator is designed to read aloud menus, window contents and keystrokes as you type.

Magnifier
The Magnifier is a floating or docked pane that magnifies the active area of the screen. With the souped-up vector-based graphics in Windows 7, this is now a genuinely useful high-resolution tool.

High contrast
This enables you to select non-Aero schemes to make on-screen content easier to read. Elsewhere in the Ease of Access Center are links to mouse/keyboard settings, Sound Sentry (visual notifications for sound events), speech recognition and more.

On-screen keyboard
You can use the mouse or a joystick to type instead of using a keyboard.

Improved access
Windows 7 groups related features in one place to make them easy to navigate.

Introducing the Address bar

It hides more power than you might imagine, so use it wisely...

Windows 7 uses 'breadcrumb' navigation. Look at the contents of the address bar (see right)... System and Security is to the right of the Control Panel, the current location, indicating their relationship: the System and Security menu is located within the Control Panel.

To open the Control Panel, point at the name in the Address bar – it glows blue – and click. The window then changes to Control Panel and you'll find yourself in the heart of your system. The breadcrumb

address bar now shows Control Panel. To get back to the System and Security window, click the back arrow left of the address bar. It's essentially a web browsing approach, with address bar breadcrumbs, hyperlinks and arrows.

If you point at the arrow between any two connected entities in the Address bar, you get a drop-down menu providing links to key features within the parent. If you click the arrow at the far left of the address bar, you can trace through the hierarchy and jump to key locations, including your

NIFTY NAVIGATION The Address bar is now an interactive navigational tool, with clickable buttons and drop-down menus

user profile and libraries. Finally, you'll see a search box beside the address bar. Search is everywhere in Windows 7, so finding files or programs is always quick and easy.

The Start menu

What's really on the menu with Windows 7? It's time to hit Start and see what's on offer

Super Tip!

(Take control)

You get plenty of options to make your Start menu work the way you want it to. Just right-click **Properties** ➔ **Customize** to peruse the choices.

 It's time to hit the Start button – the gateway to the Start menu itself. Unlike Windows XP and Windows Vista, the Pinned Programs section is now on the taskbar. This retains permanent links to programs while the rest of the left menu updates dynamically. Pinned Programs comes with a Windows Media Player link by default, but you can add other programs here by right-clicking it and selecting **Pin to Start menu or taskbar**. You can also drag and drop folder shortcuts here.

In Windows 7, the left side of the menu displays the programs you've used most recently, with the most commonly used programs at the top. A subtle change from Windows XP – where the menu displayed only the most commonly used programs – but an important one: how often have you installed a new program in Windows XP then waited an age for it to appear on the Start menu? That's when you might resort to pinning programs, but the Windows 7 approach pretty much guarantees Start menu shortcuts are more relevant to your current habits.

On the other hand, it could be a giveaway that you've been playing games instead of working, so you may prefer to deactivate this! Right-click the **Start** button, select **Properties** and uncheck **Store and display a list of recently opened programs**. You can do the same for recently opened files, too.

Dynamic updates

The All Programs menu has had a much-needed facelift. In previous versions of Windows, All Programs spawned a fly-out menu that took over the desktop. In Windows 7, All Programs opens within the left side of the Start menu with a vertical scroll bar. When you click a folder icon within All Programs, it expands the contents of the folder in a drop-down list, so the Start menu always updates dynamically. Click the **Back** button at the bottom of **All Programs** to return to the Start menu view.

On the right side of the menu you'll find shortcuts; nothing too radical here, apart from dropping the word 'My' from 'My Computer' and 'My Documents'.

The Start menu can be customized by right-clicking the **Start** button, **Properties**, then **Customize** in the **Start Menu** tab. For instance, you can convert the Control Panel to a menu rather than a link. Here, because the link is the right side of the Start menu, you do get a fly-out menu. You can also ditch the Windows 7 menu's behavioral pattern completely by reverting to a Classic – Windows XP – menu style.

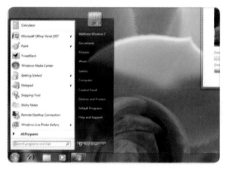

NEW, IMPROVED Start looks a bit like it did in Windows XP but it behaves in a very new way

Search is central

The basics are as important as the clever stuff...

The Start menu hooks you up to Search Everywhere and Search the Internet options. The former launches a standard search window; the latter fires up Internet Explorer and conducts, by default, a Bing web search. Switch between them with the arrow keys. Given the overwhelming integration of search within Windows 7, you might expect a permanent search field. However, if you hit the **Windows** key or click the **Start** button, a live cursor appears in the search field, so you can type your search terms. Using the Windows key as a search button tells you something about the importance of search within Windows 7.

MAKE ROOM The All Programs menu displays on the left of the Start menu, leaving the desktop clear

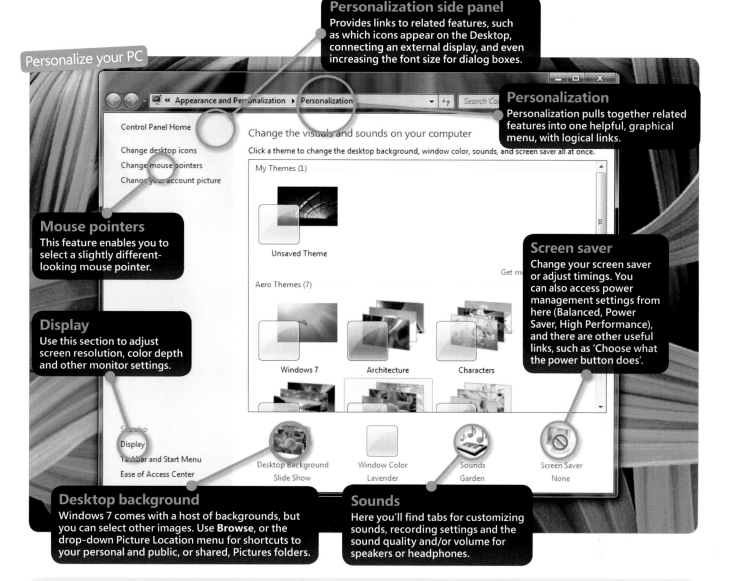

Personalize your PC

Personalization side panel
Provides links to related features, such as which icons appear on the Desktop, connecting an external display, and even increasing the font size for dialog boxes.

Personalization
Personalization pulls together related features into one helpful, graphical menu, with logical links.

Mouse pointers
This feature enables you to select a slightly different-looking mouse pointer.

Screen saver
Change your screen saver or adjust timings. You can also access power management settings from here (Balanced, Power Saver, High Performance), and there are other useful links, such as 'Choose what the power button does'.

Display
Use this section to adjust screen resolution, color depth and other monitor settings.

Desktop background
Windows 7 comes with a host of backgrounds, but you can select other images. Use **Browse**, or the drop-down Picture Location menu for shortcuts to your personal and public, or shared, Pictures folders.

Sounds
Here you'll find tabs for customizing sounds, recording settings and the sound quality and/or volume for speakers or headphones.

Windows Themes

Add a little extra color into your life through a new theme...

You can adjust the transparency of windows in the default Glass theme and also change the overall tint. Both color changes and transparency effects can be previewed live just by clicking on the appropriate boxes and moving the transparency slider to suit your taste.

If you find that your computer struggles with transparency, or if you just don't like it, uncheck the **Enable transparency** check box. You'll now have flat windows but the same overall look, feel and color scheme.

Incidentally, if Windows 7 has decided on your behalf that your PC lacks the graphical oomph to run Glass, you cannot force it to try.

You may think that Themes should be part of the Windows Color and Appearance section, but it's not used that often as Windows 7 has a whole section dedicated to its brand new Themes. You can select high-contrast modes to make on screen text more legible, so it makes sense to keep the Themes out of the way in favour of frequently-used features.

GOOD LOOKING The Aero theme looks great but you don't have to go transparent

Those handy little gadgets

Now desktop gadgets are more customizable and useful than ever before

It's time to take a closer look at the desktop gadgets included in Windows 7. These gadgets put fun and informative tools – like pictures, news and weather – right on to your desktop. Now, however, Sidebar has been removed, so they are free to sit anywhere on your screen. You can

Building your collection

Add, remove and control gadgets

Adding a gadget to your desktop is easy. Just right-click on your desktop, go to Gadgets and select **Get More Gadgets Online**. Download your gadget, then return to the Gadgets control panel. Right-click on the gadget icon and select **Install**, then double-click it or drag it on to your desktop once it's installed.

If you want more information about a gadget before installing it, click on it then select **Show Details** at the bottom of the gadget control panel.

To remove a gadget, close it by selecting the X icon or right-click on it in the gadget control panel and select **Uninstall**. To keep your gadgets on top of your open windows, right-click them and select **Always On Top**.

resize and customize them to suit your personal preferences. Brilliant!

When you first boot up Windows 7 there are several gadgets that are included, such as Clock, Calendar, Stocks and Feed Headlines. Check these out by going to the Start menu, typing 'gadgets' into the search bar and then clicking on **Desktop Gadget Gallery**. If you want to install one of these on to your desktop, just drag it from the Desktop Gadget Gallery to wherever you want it on the desktop.

Under the hood

The Feed Headlines gadget can be customized to display news headlines from whichever source you like, and it's extremely useful for a snapshot glance at world events. If up-to-date news is essential to your work then this gives you instant access. Feed Headlines uses RSS feeds, XML feeds, syndicated content and web feeds provided by your chosen host. To change your feeds, right-click the gadget then select **Options** to choose from a list of available feeds. See opposite for how to add your own feeds or turn to page 113 for more on RSS.

If you need easy access to international times then the Clock gadget is the one for you. To change the name, time zone and appearance, just click on the **Options** button on the right side of the gadget. You can have multiple versions of the same gadget so, for example, three or four clocks from different time zones can sit on your screen simultaneously.

The Slide Show displays a series of images on your computer, and by clicking on the **Options** icon, you can choose what pictures you want to appear, transitions between pictures and for how long the images are displayed. There are plenty of choices for the transition effects – like checkerboard, fade and wipe – and you can even shuffle the pictures.

If you get addicted to gadgets, there are plenty available for free online that you can download at the click of a button. From flight information to shopping and the latest in fashion, there's a gadget for you. To see the wide variety of gadgets online just go to Start, type 'gadgets' into the Search box and select **Get More Gadgets Online**.

or turn to page 113 for more on RSS.

Super Tip!

Gadgets be gone

If you go a bit 'gadget crazy', it's as easy to hide them as view them. Just right-click the desktop, point to View, then click **Show desktop gadgets** and uncheck the box.

GREAT GADGETS The standard gadgets can make a big difference to your working experience.

Need a feed? It's easy to add more

Get the most from Feed Headlines by subscribing to the RSS feeds you want

When you first open Feed Headlines and click on the **Options** tab, you'll find that there are very few feeds immediately available. The list of feeds you see in your menu is reflective of all the feeds in your Internet Explorer 8 feed subscription list, so if you've just installed Windows 7, there will only be the

default options available. It may look like you can't add any more, but there's a simple way to increase the number of feeds you have...

Subscribe to new ones by going to the websites that have feeds you want to follow, clicking on the orange RSS icon in the navigation bar and selecting the feed. This will take you

to a page that gives you the option of **Subscribe To This Feed**. If the RSS icon does not turn orange, the site does not offer any feed options. Once you've subscribed, go back to your Feed Headlines gadget, click on **Options** and your feed will now be in the Display this feed menu. Up-to-date info on tap...

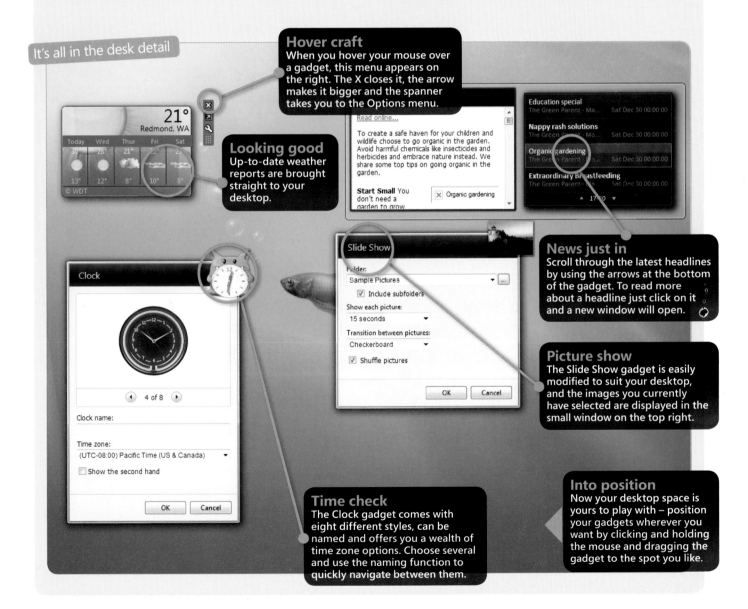

It's all in the desk detail

Hover craft
When you hover your mouse over a gadget, this menu appears on the right. The X closes it, the arrow makes it bigger and the spanner takes you to the Options menu.

Looking good
Up-to-date weather reports are brought straight to your desktop.

News just in
Scroll through the latest headlines by using the arrows at the bottom of the gadget. To read more about a headline just click on it and a new window will open.

Picture show
The Slide Show gadget is easily modified to suit your desktop, and the images you currently have selected are displayed in the small window on the top right.

Time check
The Clock gadget comes with eight different styles, can be named and offers you a wealth of time zone options. Choose several and use the naming function to quickly navigate between them.

Into position
Now your desktop space is yours to play with – position your gadgets wherever you want by clicking and holding the mouse and dragging the gadget to the spot you like.

Explore

Once you're acquainted with what's on offer, you can really start working Windows 7 to your advantage

Keeping your system safe and secure online

Windows 7 offers the most protected Windows platform yet, giving you the ultimate in PC peace of mind

Security might not seem as sexy as the new Windows superbar, with its Jump Lists and preview panes, but it's one of the most important reasons for upgrading from an older operating system.

When Windows XP was designed, most of us didn't have always-on broadband connections – and then when we got them, assorted net nasties were quick to go on the attack. Websites attempted to install malicious software, spammers created avalanches of infected emails, and if you connected an unprotected PC to the internet, it would be full of damaging infections in a matter of minutes. Microsoft did its best to thwart the attacks, but no sooner did it fix one problem than another one simply popped up in its place...

Self-protection

Not all the problems came from outside, though. If you're a fan of gory PC gaming, you'll be vividly aware that some games aren't suitable for young children. And, as anyone who uses the internet knows, offensive and utterly unsuitable content is only ever a few clicks away. As more and more of us have moved our PCs from a small study room to the main front room, the need for parental controls has grown.

In Windows 7 there are seven key tools that keep your system safe and secure: Windows Action Center, which enables you to control a whole host of options including security; User Account Control (UAC), which stops software (and other users) from doing things without your permission; Parental Controls, which keep the kids safe and keep the system safe from your kids; Windows Defender, which hunts and kills malicious software; Windows Firewall, which is designed to stop anything dodgy getting on your system in the first place; Windows Backup which is improved so you can keep backups of individual folders, files or libraries to another drive or the network; and last but not least, BitLocker, which keeps your private files private. Together they offer rock-solid security and peace of mind. Over the next few pages you'll discover how to use them to keep you – and your system – safe.

In real life...
Safe and snug

**Nick Odantzis,
Section editor,
*Windows: The
Official Magazine***

Windows 7 helps to allay a host of typical PC fears. It's such a well thought-out system that protects on all counts. From first lines of defense, such as the Firewall, to phishing alerts to customizable Parental Controls, there's an omnipresent approach that encompasses all areas of Windows itself, your life online and the information stored on your PC.

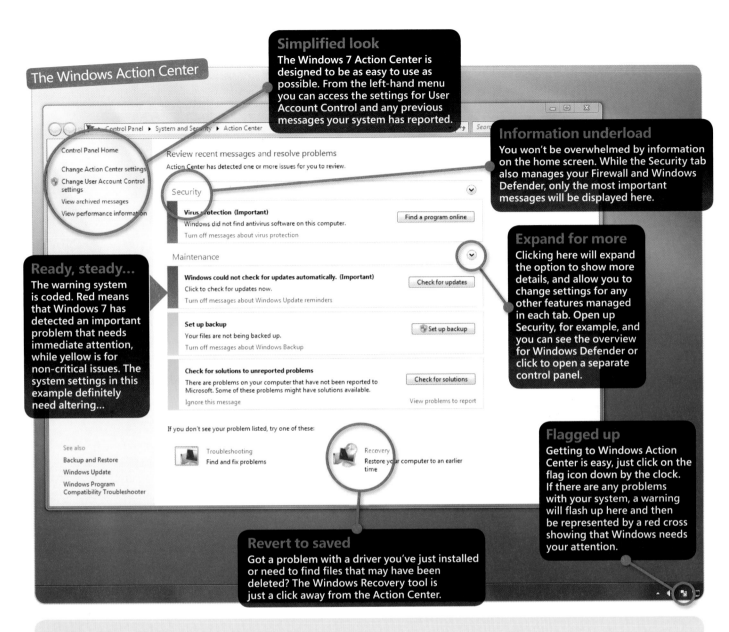

The Windows Action Center

Simplified look
The Windows 7 Action Center is designed to be as easy to use as possible. From the left-hand menu you can access the settings for User Account Control and any previous messages your system has reported.

Information underload
You won't be overwhelmed by information on the home screen. While the Security tab also manages your Firewall and Windows Defender, only the most important messages will be displayed here.

Ready, steady...
The warning system is coded. Red means that Windows 7 has detected an important problem that needs immediate attention, while yellow is for non-critical issues. The system settings in this example definitely need altering...

Expand for more
Clicking here will expand the option to show more details, and allow you to change settings for any other features managed in each tab. Open up Security, for example, and you can see the overview for Windows Defender or click to open a separate control panel.

Flagged up
Getting to Windows Action Center is easy, just click on the flag icon down by the clock. If there are any problems with your system, a warning will flash up here and then be represented by a red cross showing that Windows needs your attention.

Revert to saved
Got a problem with a driver you've just installed or need to find files that may have been deleted? The Windows Recovery tool is just a click away from the Action Center.

Microsoft Security Essentials

Cliff Evans, Head of Security and Privacy, Microsoft UK

"The increasing sophistication and criminality of malware attacks means that consumers must take sensible precautions to protect themselves.

"Many of today's attacks are designed specifically to steal personal information to commit crimes such as identity fraud. To protect themselves, consumers should ensure that they have all the latest updates installed, avoid opening emails and attachments from unsolicited addresses and run anti-malware software package.

"Microsoft Security Essentials (www.microsoft.com/Security_Essentials) is a no-cost anti-malware service that provides real-time protection, helping to protect a validated genuine Windows PC from viruses, spyware and other malicious threats.

"In addition to up-to-date anti-malware, and a firewall turned on, consumers should also ensure Windows Update is set to automatic and that they receive Microsoft updates. We would also recommend consumers install Internet Explorer 8 due to a number of built-in security features. For example, the new SmartScreen filter will help you stay safe by protecting against deceptive and malicious websites."

Stop spyware with Windows Defender

Protect your PC from unwanted programs and malware with the help of this vigilant tool

In some ways owning a PC is like owning a pet – it takes a lot of looking after. If left to its own devices it could get into all sorts of trouble. This is where a guiding hand comes in useful and, as part of Windows 7, you get Windows Defender, a program that will help you and your PC defend against malicious or unwanted programs.

You've probably heard of spyware and adware, which are programs that sneak on to your system and snoop on your personal data, blast you with adverts and generally fill your PC with nonsense. They're often hard to detect and difficult to remove, which is why Windows Defender is so handy. It does two important things – it gets rid of

unwanted programs from your PC, and it stops them getting into your system in the first place. You can launch Windows Defender by typing 'Defender' into the Search bar in the Start menu.

Fully integrated

Windows Defender works with Internet Explorer 8 to help you decide whether new software should or should not be installed; it provides always-on protection that monitors key system locations and watches for changes that signal the presence of spyware.

It works by combining a number of useful and very clever strategies. Superior scanning and removal technologies use up-to-date spyware definitions created by Microsoft, with

help from Windows Defender users who submit reports of potential new spyware.

At all stages, Windows Defender is simple to use and comes with preconfigured settings to help you set up a stable platform and then continue to stay secure. An improved user interface gives you more control over your software. Common tasks such as scanning, blocking and removing unwanted software are easier than ever, and a Software Explorer helps you understand which software and services are running on your computer and stops or disables 'rogue' software. Windows Defender automatically handles many common tasks and interrupts or alerts you only in the case of serious issues that require immediate action.

Windows Defender

Secure your system against spyware and other internet nasties

1 LAST SCAN When you launch Windows Defender, it tells you when it last scanned your system. If you want Windows Defender to scan automatically, click **Tools** in the toolbar.

2 OPTIONS The Tools and Settings screen enables you to see what software's running and what files are quarantined. Want to check the scanning settings? Click on **Options**.

3 SELF-DEFENSE Windows Defender will check for updates then scan your system at 2am every day. If you want to change the time, use the fields for **Frequency** and **Approximate Time**.

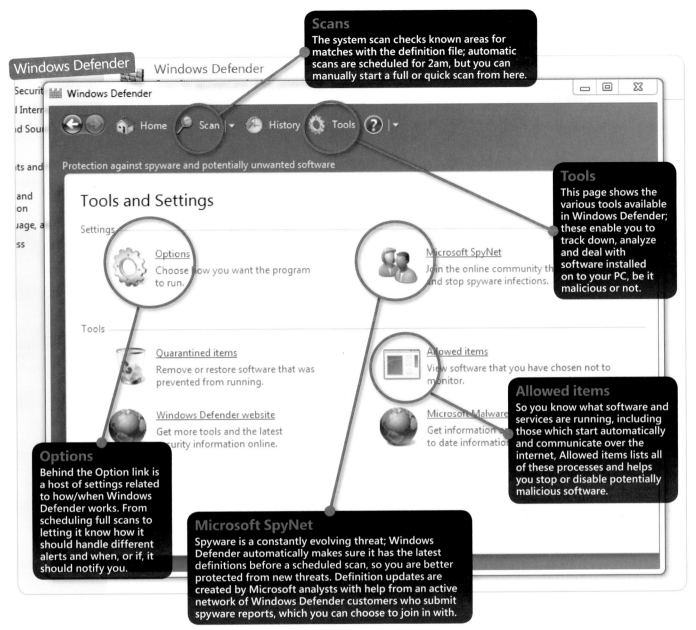

Scans
The system scan checks known areas for matches with the definition file; automatic scans are scheduled for 2am, but you can manually start a full or quick scan from here.

Windows Defender

Windows Defender

Securit...
d Intern...
d Sour...

ts and...

and
on

uage, a...

ss

Windows Defender

⬅ ➡ | 🏠 Home | 🔍 Scan | ▾ | 🕐 History | ⚙ Tools | ❓ | ▾

Protection against spyware and potentially unwanted software

Tools and Settings

Settings

⚙ **Options**
Choose how you want the program to run.

👥 **Microsoft SpyNet**
Join the online community th... and stop spyware infections.

Tools

🗑 **Quarantined items**
Remove or restore software that was prevented from running.

🌐 **Windows Defender website**
Get more tools and the latest ...curity information online.

🖼 **Allowed items**
View software that you have chosen not to monitor.

🌐 **Microsoft Malware...**
Get information a... to date informatio...

Tools
This page shows the various tools available in Windows Defender; these enable you to track down, analyze and deal with software installed on to your PC, be it malicious or not.

Allowed items
So you know what software and services are running, including those which start automatically and communicate over the internet, Allowed items lists all of these processes and helps you stop or disable potentially malicious software.

Options
Behind the Option link is a host of settings related to how/when Windows Defender works. From scheduling full scans to letting it know how it should handle different alerts and when, or if, it should notify you.

Microsoft SpyNet
Spyware is a constantly evolving threat; Windows Defender automatically makes sure it has the latest definitions before a scheduled scan, so you are better protected from new threats. Definition updates are created by Microsoft analysts with help from an active network of Windows Defender customers who submit spyware reports, which you can choose to join in with.

4 MORE POWER Real-Time Protection (on by default) checks on crucial elements of Windows and warns of attempts to change them; only disable if using another anti-spyware package.

5 ON-DEMAND Scan at any time by clicking **Scan** in the toolbar. The process takes a few minutes because it peers into every corner of your PC to make sure you're spyware-free.

6 THE NEWS Once the scan has completed, Windows Defender will tell you the results. If your PC is free from nasties, you'll see the 'Your computer is running normally' message.

Prevent hackers with Windows Firewall

Keep hackers at bay and arm yourself against online attacks with this simple but thorough defense system

The news is rife with how another hacker has attacked some computer system in the world. It's not as if these hackers are physically attacking systems, they're attempting to gain access via the internet. To stop this sort of malicious attack, the Windows Firewall is a critical first line of defense.

You might be wondering how it's possible for someone to gain access to a computer over the internet. In order to communicate with other computers, PCs have various ports – so, for example, chat software might use one port, file sharing software another, network printing yet another, and so on. Ports are a bit like real-world doors – if you don't keep them locked, there's always the

possibility that an unwanted intruder will sneak in. Windows Firewall addresses the problem by locking any ports you're not using, and by doing so it can prevent some of the nastier kinds of online attacks from affecting your PC. It's switched on by default and you can see its settings by going to **Control Panel → System and Security** and clicking on **Windows Firewall**.

Properly configured, the Windows Firewall can stop many kinds of malware before they can infect your computer or other computers on your network. Windows Firewall, which comes with Windows 7, is turned on by default and begins protecting your computer as soon as Windows starts. The Windows Firewall Control Panel is designed to be

easy to use, with several configuration options and a simple interface.

In Windows 7, the Firewall is more advanced than ever, and it's designed to be less intrusive too. You should notice fewer warnings and requests for authentication, and yet you'll be safer. The Windows Firewall not only allows programs that you've explicitly authorized to access the internet but monitors them for strange behavior. For example, if a component of Windows that is designed to send network messages over one port on your PC tries to send messages by way of a different port due to an attack, Windows Firewall can stop that message leaving your PC, thereby preventing the malware from spreading to other users.

In real life...
Putting a block on your open ports

Adam Ifans, Editor, Windows: The Official Magazine

For the majority of the time you won't be troubled by Windows Firewall, but there might be the odd occasion when you'll have to delve a little deeper to fix a problem or adjust the limits for a certain program.

Scroll down the main pane to **View and create firewall rules**, for a list of services and programs that have been given access through the Firewall. They're divided into Inbound and

Outbound categories. If you're having problems with a single program or service, it's possible that the Windows Firewall is blocking it. So if, say, Remote Desktop won't function, it's worth checking here to see if it has been approved. Scan the list of tick boxes and the related name, if the service/program is unchecked then tick the relevant box and see if that fixes the problem. Using the new **Add new rule** button, it's also possible to add individual programs, and restrict access for these to the local network or individual IP addresses.

EXTRA PROGRAMS You can add programs yourself, as well as configuring individual ports and restricting access to the local network or specific IP addresses

Slamming the internet front door

"If your name's not down, you're not getting in!"

1 SPLIT PERSONALITY Windows Firewall has two sets of rules – one for private networks, like the one you have at home, and one for public ones, for example using Wi-Fi in a coffee shop. The latter should be set for stronger security.

2 CUSTOMIZE SETTINGS By clicking **Turn on Windows Firewall**, you can change the top level options for each type of network. You can stop Windows connecting to public networks altogether, for example.

3 ALLOW PROGRAMS Select **Allow a program through Windows Firewall** to see a list of all programs which are currently given access to the internet. From this window, you can also add a new, previously blocked application through.

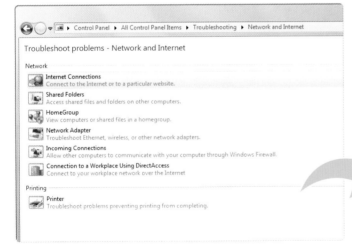

The Windows Firewall blocks certain connections; check **Notify me** so that you can override any decisions

4 FIXING THE PROBLEMS If you're having trouble connecting to the net or getting a program to work, there's a handy problem solving screen within Windows Firewall, too. Simply click on the **Troubleshoot** option and you'll find all the help you need broken down into a set of recognizable headings.

Those different settings...

The ability to vary settings in Windows Firewall is handy if you use your PC in different locations: Windows Firewall will detect which network connection you're using and use the appropriate settings to protect.

5 IN ACTION When it comes to general use, you'll probably hear nothing from Firewall – it'll just happily monitor things. If you run a new program that tries to access the internet in an unusual way, that's when an alert will be generated and you'll need to decide if the program should have access.

Protecting you and your data

Keeping files safe from prying eyes and limiting access to your PC is now easy to sort out

Super Tip!

Encrypt your drive

From the My Computer screen you can start the BitLocker set-up just by right-clicking a drive and choosing **Enable BitLocker**.

Windows XP had a major Achilles heel; by default, when you installed it, you had administrator access. As an administrator you have total control over your system, which means you can change system settings, install software and make any modifications you wish. Unfortunately that access was exploited – if you were running in administrator mode and a bit of malicious software crept on to your system, it too had administrative access, which meant it could cause chaos.

If you've ever suffered from malware then you've seen the problem in action. In Windows Vista, Microsoft introduced a new feature called User Access Control (UAC) that prevented any changes to

system files happening without explicit permission. For example, if a program attempted to install itself, a warning would flash up and you were presented with the choice to **Continue** and allow it, if you were expecting the change to be made, or **Cancel** and block it.

Stress free

This feature, which is now part of Windows 7, helps dramatically, because if any software tries to do anything at all with your PC, you'll have to give it permission. In theory, this should enable you to spot any potentially malicious activity on your computer in advance.

UAC works in two ways. If you're logged in as the computer administrator (which, as the owner of the PC, you

probably will be), system changes no longer happen silently. Instead, the UAC warning will pop up and nothing will happen if you don't click **Continue**. If you're not the computer administrator, UAC is more demanding. Instead of the Continue and Cancel buttons, you'll need the administrator password. If you don't have it, the changes won't happen.

That means that UAC doesn't just protect you from malicious software, but also from any other members of your family fiddling with your system settings, which can be almost as bad as a virus! One common complaint about UAC in Windows Vista was that it generated too many warnings and became tiresome. In Windows 7, UAC has been updated to give you control over the level of

How BitLocker works at keeping all of your

How to lock your PC so it won't boot without a USB key present

1 MISSING CHIP Normally a PC requires a special feature called a TPM chip to use BitLocker; for computers that lack this, click on **Start** and type 'gpedit.msc' into the search box.

2 CHANGE POLICY Press **Enter**, then click **Continue** if the User Account Control dialog box pops up. Click **Local Computer Policy → Administrative Templates → Windows Components**.

3 ADVANCED OPTIONS Double-click **BitLocker Drive Encryption** then **Operating System Drives**. This will bring up a set of options specific to your computer's C: drive.

OUT OF CONTROL It is possible to disable the UAC system, but it is not really advisable

reporting you want. There are four options, ranging from turning UAC off completely to requiring authorization for every change to program settings.

Data protection

A lost or stolen PC might contain sensitive information that, in the wrong hands, could be very damaging. BitLocker is designed to eliminate this threat, and you'll find it in Windows 7 Ultimate (and Enterprise). The idea behind it is simple. It uses a system called encryption to scramble the data on your hard disk; once the data is encrypted it can't be accessed by other people – even if they use hacking tools or run a different operating system. You have access, but other people don't.

Using BitLocker to lock up your PC

A handy prompt to check that you're doing the right thing

BitLocker Drive Encryption is a data protection feature available in the Windows 7 Ultimate (and Enterprise) edition, and is Microsoft's response to the problem of protecting data.

BitLocker has been designed to work with PCs that include a TPM (Trusted Platform Module) chip; if your PC has such hardware, you can log on when BitLocker is running. If you don't have a TPM chip you can still use BitLocker, but you'll need a USB flash drive. Your BitLocker password will be installed on this drive, and you'll need to insert the drive every time you boot your PC.

Although many laptops now come with TPM hardware for protecting data if they get lost, on PCs the technology is still quite rare. In the tutorial below you'll see how to use BitLocker on a PC without a TPM by using a USB key for authentication.

One improvement in Windows 7 is that you can now easily encrypt portable storage, like USB keys, with BitLocker. Without the correct password, the whole drive becomes completely unreadable.

BitLocker prevents a thief from breaking Windows 7 file and system protections or from performing offline viewing of the files stored on the protected drive.

By combining drive encryption and integrity checking of early boot components, BitLocker can provide a seamless, secure and manageable data protection solution available for both business and personal users.

START SCRAMBLING BitLocker can now encrypt portable storage by default

vital data safe and secure

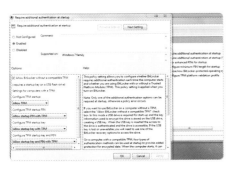

4 ENABLE USB Click **Require additional authentication at startup** and then select **Enabled**. This will allow BitLocker to encrypt boot drives without a TPM (Trusted Platform Module).

5 APPLY CHANGES Save all your changes and then start BitLocker. Find your main OS drive (usually C:) and hit **Turn On BitLocker**. Make sure you have a usable USB key plugged in.

6 THE KEY If you have no TPM present, Windows 7 will walk you through encrypting your drive with a USB lock. It will also generate a passcode – use this to gain entry if you lose the USB key.

Set up your PC so it's safe for all the family

It's great that children are so computer literate, but you still need to keep tabs on what they're up to...

 So you've secured your system against malicious online attacks, it's time to think about the children. There might be content on your computer that you don't want them to see, such as family finances or work documents. Or you might enjoy the odd game of Doom 3 but be less keen for your seven-year-old to play it.

Even if you're not sharing a system, you probably want to make sure your children don't stumble on to any unsuitable internet sites. The good news is that the Parental Control features in Windows 7 cover all of these issues, and they couldn't be easier to use.

The real worry for parents, though, is what their children use the computer for. It's bad enough that they've already borrowed 'Soldier Trainer: Attack, Attack'

from the cool kid in the playground, and are now learning marksmanship behind your back, without the added worry of what websites they're visiting and who they're talking to online.

Breathe easier

There's no substitute for sitting with your kids and teaching them to use a computer responsibly but, in the longer term, when you can't always be in the room with them, Windows 7 will let you breathe a bit more easily.

In every edition of Windows 7, you can set up monitored accounts for each youngster in your family from the Control Panel, using the Parental Controls button. From here you can create User

Accounts, within which your child can fully personalize their desktop and settings. However, what they can view, read and play is controlled by filters for games and web content that you set up.

The very young

The Web Filter option is useful for very young children, because you can make an exclusive access list of suitable sites, and limit your child's browsing to these. By default, Windows 7 lets you set parameters for games and applications that your children can use, as well as setting time limits on their account. In order to access the web filtering and activity monitor controls, you'll need an extra piece of software, like Windows Live Family Safety, that you can download from http://download. live.com/familysafety.

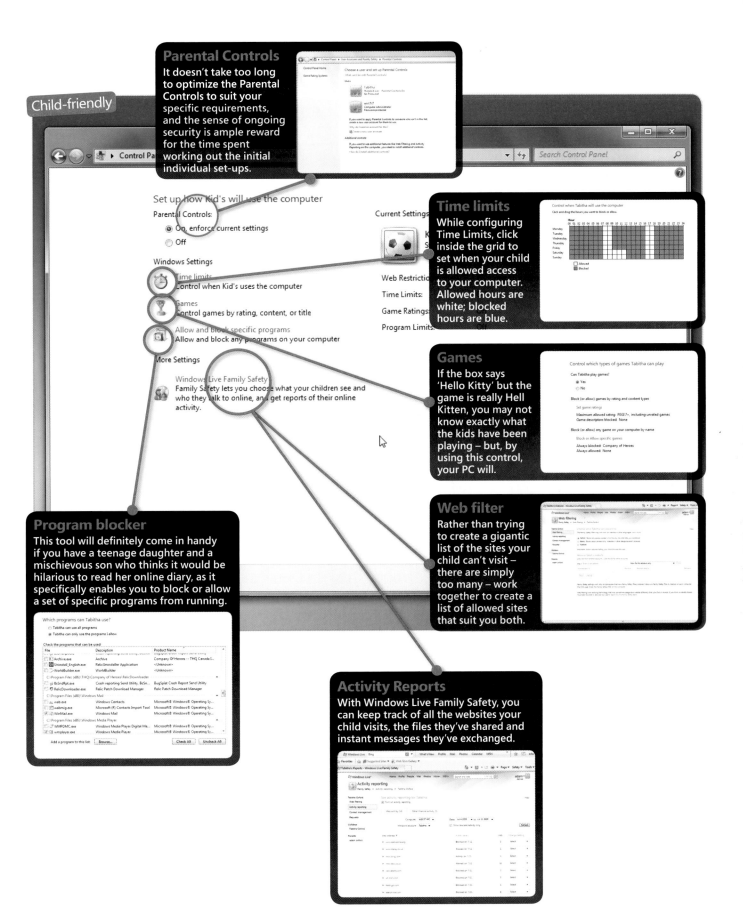

Parental Controls

It doesn't take too long to optimize the Parental Controls to suit your specific requirements, and the sense of ongoing security is ample reward for the time spent working out the initial individual set-ups.

Child-friendly

Set up how Kid's will use the computer

Parental Controls:
- ● On, enforce current settings
- ○ Off

Windows Settings

Time limits
Control when Kid's uses the computer

Games
Control games by rating, content, or title

Allow and block specific programs
Allow and block any programs on your computer

More Settings

Windows Live Family Safety
Family Safety lets you choose what your children see and who they talk to online, and get reports of their online activity.

Current Settings

Web Restriction

Time Limits:

Game Ratings:

Program Limits:

Time limits

While configuring Time Limits, click inside the grid to set when your child is allowed access to your computer. Allowed hours are white; blocked hours are blue.

Games

If the box says 'Hello Kitty' but the game is really Hell Kitten, you may not know exactly what the kids have been playing – but, by using this control, your PC will.

Web filter

Rather than trying to create a gigantic list of the sites your child can't visit – there are simply too many – work together to create a list of allowed sites that suit you both.

Program blocker

This tool will definitely come in handy if you have a teenage daughter and a mischievous son who thinks it would be hilarious to read her online diary, as it specifically enables you to block or allow a set of specific programs from running.

Activity Reports

With Windows Live Family Safety, you can keep track of all the websites your child visits, the files they've shared and instant messages they've exchanged.

Using User Accounts to protect your children

With youngsters being so computer literate, it's vital to get to grips with the comprehensive systems built into Windows 7

While the majority of children sit at a PC to carry out school research or look for innocent amusement with no problems at all, we're all too aware that an alarming number of minors receive unwanted sexual comment online or by text message, making it a worrying situation for parents. Websites like MySpace, Bebo and Facebook offer thousands of profiles – often showing a child's name, age, location and more – that can be used by undesirables.

So what's the solution? Well, whatever your opinion of social networking, the extreme popularity of websites like these means that they are likely to be a permanent fixture on the internet agenda for the foreseeable future. We need to accept that these social arenas will attract our youngsters and we need to do what we can to protect them while they're surfing for sites or catching up with friends over the internet.

Safe to surf

Tightening controls is one of the solutions, and something that various child protection agencies are working hard to bring into practise. Ideally, child safety software should be part of every new PC built today. As you'll have seen on the previous pages, one of the big advantages of Windows 7 is that it comes with built-in Parental Controls (**Start → Control Panel → User Accounts and Family Safety → Parental Controls**), which help you to limit access and make the internet a safer place. You can create an account for each child, with Parental Controls activated, and then select what restrictions to put in place. You can use the standard settings to block them from visiting certain websites or using programs, or you can create a customized list.

What's even more reassuring is that these safety measures are all so simple to set up and put into action or amend as your child matures.

Parental Controls

Keep the kids safe – and away from your secret files

1 CREATE AN ACCOUNT Log in using the administrator. Go to Control Panel and choose **Create or Manage Accounts** (link under User Accounts and Family Safety). Choose **Create an Account** from the next screen.

2 NAME IT You can create a separate account for the children to use, or one account for everyone who's going to access the PC. Just type the name of the new account on the next screen and select **Standard User**.

3 PASSWORD PROTECTED Click **Create an Account** and your child's details will appear on the overview page. Select their icon to make changes. To start with, you can change the portrait picture or add a password to the login screen.

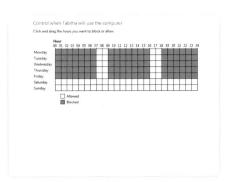

4 WEB FILTERING Clicking on **Set up Parental Controls** takes you to another account selection screen. Choose your child's account; notice the information at the bottom of the screen about Web Filtering.

5 TURN ON CONTROLS From the next page, you can activate Parental Controls – just click on the appropriate button at the top. Now you can change the first three settings for managing your children's behavior on the PC.

6 TIME'S UP The first option is to set time limits for when the account can be active. So long as your child doesn't know the password to other accounts, they won't be able to use the PC outside of the specified hours.

7 GAME OVER Windows will reference the names of any games installed with online rating systems. The second option lets you limit the games that your child can play by their official rating for suitability, like PEGI 7+.

8 MANUAL CONTROL You can also set the games you want to allow your children to play by title. Selecting the second option takes you to a screen which lists all the games currently installed on your PC.

9 PROGRAM BLOCKER Back at the account overview page, the final option is to limit which programs can be run by the account user. You can allow any installed application by clicking on the relevant button in the list.

10 GET EVEN SAFER To activate the last two features, which block certain websites and log all activity, you'll need to download an extra program. Try the Family Safety pack from http://download.live.com.

11 CHILD IDENTITY Start Windows Live Family Safety from the Start menu, and it will log you into a website where you can create a Live account for your child, enabling you to activate the **Web Filter** and **Activity Monitor**.

12 LEVELS OF ACCESS Once you've created an account, you can customize the level of Web Filtering and read activity reports. Log the child in to Live.com using the icon on the taskbar the first time the account is used.

Prime searching

Windows 7 is designed to never lose anything again, so how easy is it to find elusive files?

We've all experienced it: you need to find something in a hurry and while you can remember what it was about, you've no idea when you did it, what program you did it in, what you called it or where you put it. Considering we now store virtually our entire lives on our PCs, finding a document, video or photo is like looking for a needle in a haystack. Windows 7 solves the problem in style though.

The Windows 7 search engine is fast, flexible and incredibly effective, and if it can't find something, it probably doesn't exist! There are three ways to search: when you're browsing, you can use the Search box in the top right-hand corner of the window; the **Search** box in the Start Menu, or you can click **Start ➜ Search** to open the Search folder to carry out very complex searches.

When you type text in a search box, Windows 7 looks for any occurrence of that text – for example, if you typed 'john', it would look for files called 'john', documents containing the word 'john' and files created by a user called 'john'. You can specify searches a bit more by adding prefixes, such as:

Name: john This searches only for files whose name includes the word 'john'.
Modified: 2008 This searches only for files that were changed in 2008.

You can also use search operators such as AND, OR and NOT, as well as the greater than and less than symbols:

Summer AND Vacation – Windows 7 will show you files containing the word 'summer' and 'vacation'. Files containing just one of the words won't be listed.
Summer NOT Vacation – will come up with files that include the word 'summer' but don't include the word 'vacation'.
Summer OR Vacation – will show you files that contain either the word 'summer' or the word 'vacation'.
Summer Vacation – will only show

you files containing the phrase 'summer vacation'.
date: <01/01/09 – will only show you files created before the January 1 2009.
size: >4MB – will only show you files bigger than 4MB.

You can create very complex searches, but wouldn't it be great if you could use plain English instead? You can. Open the Control Panel, click **Appearance and Personalization** and then **Folder Options**. Now, click on the **Search** tab and then tick the **Use natural language search** box. Click on **OK**, and you can now search in plain English – so, for example, you might search for 'documents by bert 2007'. ⊞

Using the search box

Get the most from those magic boxes that pop up

1 QUICK HITS Click **Start** menu. Type your criteria in the search box; the results appear as you type. Windows 7 searches files and browsing history, but you can carry out an internet search.

2 LOCATION You can now filter searches by location. If the file your are looking for is on the web, select the Internet icon to open a search in your chosen internet search engine.

3 CHOOSE CUSTOM There are further search facilities, too. Select **Custom** to bring up the options. This window contains different locations that you can include or exclude in your search.

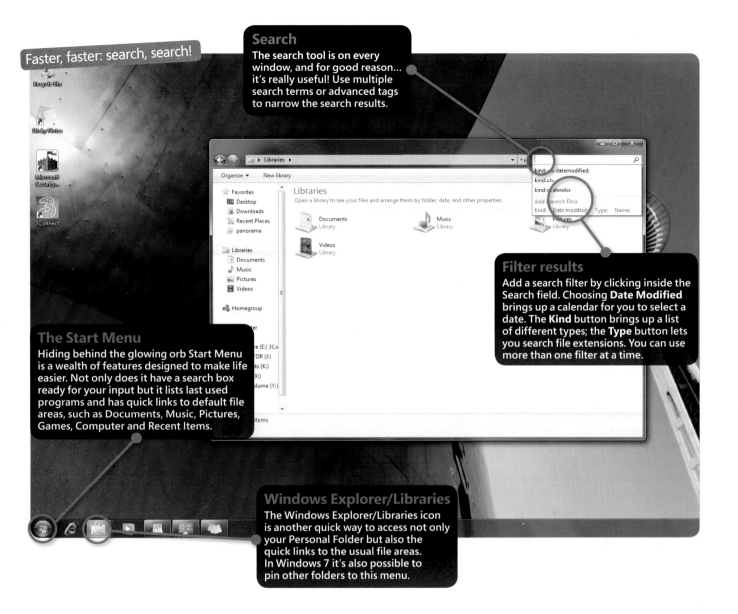

Faster, faster: search, search!

Search
The search tool is on every window, and for good reason... it's really useful! Use multiple search terms or advanced tags to narrow the search results.

Filter results
Add a search filter by clicking inside the Search field. Choosing **Date Modified** brings up a calendar for you to select a date. The **Kind** button brings up a list of different types; the **Type** button lets you search file extensions. You can use more than one filter at a time.

The Start Menu
Hiding behind the glowing orb Start Menu is a wealth of features designed to make life easier. Not only does it have a search box ready for your input but it lists last used programs and has quick links to default file areas, such as Documents, Music, Pictures, Games, Computer and Recent Items.

Windows Explorer/Libraries
The Windows Explorer/Libraries icon is another quick way to access not only your Personal Folder but also the quick links to the usual file areas. In Windows 7 it's also possible to pin other folders to this menu.

4 SAVED SEARCHES Open the Start menu and select **Personal Folder**. Here you'll find the Saved Searches folder. The Sticky Notes Connector will appear, plus any searches already saved.

5 NARROW DOWN You can select advanced search settings by clicking inside the search box. Depending on the folder you are in, you can filter results by Kind, Date Modified, Type and Name.

6 MORE OPTIONS Selecting the file of your choice will change the options in the toolbar above. The options will be relevant to the file type. Here, an image file has Preview options.

Find files quickly and easily

Go a step further to see just how powerful the Windows 7 detective team is...

When hard drives were tiny and we only saved work stuff, finding things was easy. Now, though, hard disks are huge and we stuff them with songs, photos, videos and emails – so you're asking quite a lot of your PC when you ask it to find a particular file. Hurrah, then, for the search system in Windows 7. It's bad news for U2 – *I've found what I'm looking for* would be a rotten song title – but it's great news for everyone else, because you'll never lose another file – from that important spreadsheet to those holiday snaps – ever again. As you'll discover, it's easy to make file finding even faster when you know what type of file it is or another key detail using the advanced search features.

SEARCH FASTER Windows 7 Search makes it easy to find what you're after

Limit your search to speed it up

By searching for a specific type of file you can speed up your file hunts

1 DIFFERENT FILTERS Depending on the type of file you search, Windows 7 will give you specific filter options. Searching for music files will give you options like Artist, Album, and Genre.

2 DO IT BY DATE When a search is complete, click in the Search field and select **Date modified**. A calendar appears so that you can select the date (exact or vague) the file was modified.

3 CHOOSE CUSTOM As mentioned in the previous pages, the **Custom** button offers more options. The window contains different locations that you can include or exclude in your search.

4 SHARING Another specific filter option is **Share with...** Click this and you get the option to share the file with a HomeGroup or specific people. By selecting the latter, you can add or remove people from the list.

5 FOLDER SEARCH You can limit your search to a particular folder, for when you know roughly where something is. Simply navigate to the folder you want to search and type your criteria in the search box in the top-right corner.

6 SEARCH ALL Often the file(s) you're looking for will be in obvious places. However, you might need to search your entire hard drive or a removable drive. Click **Custom**, then select **Locations** to tell Windows 7 where to look.

7 TRACK ALL THOSE TAGS Tags enable you to add extra valuable information to files, and Windows 7 can search for those tags. Click the **Arrange by:** button and select **Tags** from the drop-down menu.

8 SIZE MATTERS Narrow your searches by selecting an approximate file size. Click inside the search field and select **Size**. From the drop-down menu, you can select different file size ranging from Empty (0KB) to Gigantic (>128MB).

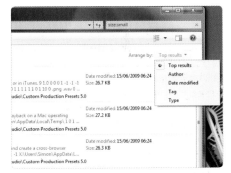

9 TOP RESULTS You can further refine your results by selecting more than one option. After selecting, say, **Size** you can then select another option like **Top results**; this option then sorts your results into order of relevance.

10 PREVIEW FILES You can see a file's contents without leaving Search. Click on **Organize → Layout** and tick the **Preview Pane** box. In the case of Microsoft Word docs, this means you can read the file without opening it.

11 SAVE YOUR SEARCH Once you've fine-tuned your search criteria, you can save it for future use by clicking on **Save Search**. Any time you want to run it, go to **Username → Searches** and double-click on your search folder.

12 PLAIN TALK In **Control Panel → Appearance & Personalization → Folder Options → Search** you can switch on natural language searching. This means you can use plain language, such as 'charges overdraft'.

Exploring the Index

The Index is a catalog of files that Windows 7 updates whenever there is the capacity to do so

When you search in Windows 7, you're not actually searching your hard disk, you're searching the Index. Obviously, this is a much faster process than looking through your entire hard disk.

The Index doesn't keep track of every single file on your computer, though. That's because your PC is packed with system files, hidden files and other components you probably never look at. Instead, the Index looks at the folders you actually use – your Home folder, your Pictures folder, and so on.

That doesn't mean you don't need to tweak the Index. You might not want it to scan your browser history, or you might keep important files in folders the Index doesn't scan. The walkthrough below shows how to customize the Index to your exact requirements. You can access the Index in two ways – from the Search folder, or by clicking **Start ➔**

Control Panel ➔ Performance Information and Tools ➔ Adjust Indexing Options (ensuring the Control Panel is in small or large icon view).

Since the invention of the PC, we've stored our stuff in the same way we'd store paperwork; we create different folders for different things and then store files in each folder. So your Work folder might have subfolders for contracts, research, letters, etc. There's nothing wrong with this method, but filing has its limits. Not everything falls into one category and one category only, and this is particularly apparent when you're storing digital photos.

Enter tags... These allow you to attach as many different terms to a file as you like. You can then search for those tags, so for example you might search for 'Fred' and 'family', or you might search for a single 'the kids' tag. With Windows 7, you can do the same with the files on your hard disk. It's effective and easy.

Tag, you're it!

Forget about old-fashioned filing – unleash the power of tagging

  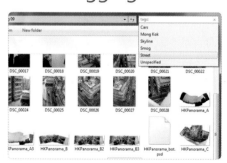

1 ADD A TAG At the bottom of the window you'll see information about the currently selected file. If you click on **Add a tag**, you can add tags to the file without having to open it.

2 TAG TEAM You can apply tags to multiple documents simultaneously, provided the files are taggable. Select the files and enter the appropriate info. Click **Save** to add the tags to all the files.

3 FAST FIND To find tagged items, click within the Search field and select **Tags**. A list of all tags is shown, so you don't even need to type in any keywords.

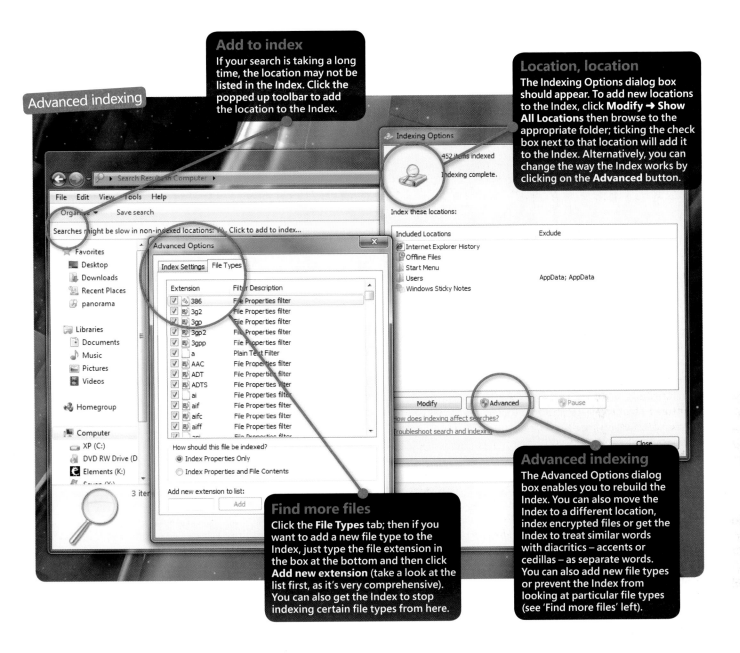

Advanced indexing

Add to index
If your search is taking a long time, the location may not be listed in the Index. Click the popped up toolbar to add the location to the Index.

Location, location
The Indexing Options dialog box should appear. To add new locations to the Index, click **Modify → Show All Locations** then browse to the appropriate folder; ticking the check box next to that location will add it to the Index. Alternatively, you can change the way the Index works by clicking on the **Advanced** button.

Find more files
Click the **File Types** tab; then if you want to add a new file type to the Index, just type the file extension in the box at the bottom and then click **Add new extension** (take a look at the list first, as it's very comprehensive). You can also get the Index to stop indexing certain file types from here.

Advanced indexing
The Advanced Options dialog box enables you to rebuild the Index. You can also move the Index to a different location, index encrypted files or get the Index to treat similar words with diacritics – accents or cedillas – as separate words. You can also add new file types or prevent the Index from looking at particular file types (see 'Find more files' left).

4 RAPID RESULTS Double-click a stacked tag to see files. This will show as a search result. Save the results using **Save Search**; search again and Windows 7 will find files with the selected tag.

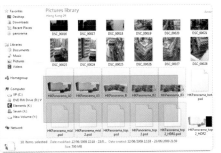

5 TAG PICTURES Tags get even smarter when used with images. If you want to apply tags to multiple images, you need to use the mouse in order to select those files you want to tag.

6 SEE MORE Right-click the bottom of the window and select large size icons for more metadata. To view/add tags, move your mouse over the stars; click on the rating you want, then **Save**.

Do things quicker in Windows 7

Are you using your PC to its full potential? Here are 11 ways to optimize the way you use Windows 7

1 Schedule
If your PC is left on when not in use, you can schedule common tasks to occur. Go to the Start Search menu, type in 'Task Scheduler' and hit **Enter**. Once the Scheduler is open, select tasks and edit the time they occur and how long they last, along with other options. The tasks you'll probably want to run most often are Disk Defragment and System Restore.

2 Integration
You can save time on reading emails and news by integrating them into your email program. Do this by downloading the latest Windows Live Mail at http://

ALL IN ONE Save time and stress by combining all your emails and feeds in one program

download.live.com. From here you can add mail accounts, send instant messages and get RSS feeds delivered.

3 Streamline
Programs or folders you use on a regular basis need to be easy to access. The desktop is the most obvious place, although desktop icons require a double

NAME DROPPING Add tags to your files to make them quicker and easier to find in future

click. An even faster way is to pin them to the new taskbar at the bottom of your screen. To add, simply drag any icon from anywhere to the taskbar. Alternatively, open the desired program, right-click the icon on the taskbar and select **Put this program to the taskbar**.

4 Synchronize devices
If you're constantly adding new songs, pictures or videos to your PC, and you want them on your MP3 or portable media player as well, then you want to set up a sync partnership. When your device is plugged in and set up, Sync Center will detect whether new files have

PERFECT HARMONY Set up a partnership to ensure your MP3 player is always in sync

been added to your PC and add them to your device. To do this, go to **Start ➜ All Programs ➜ Accessories ➜ Sync Center**.

5 Tag your files
If you've got a lot of photos or music stored on your PC, you'll want to be able to find them quickly and easily. You can tag files by left-clicking them and adding or changing the text in the bottom of the window they're open in. You can also tag multiple files by selecting them all, right-clicking one of the highlighted files, clicking on **Properties** in the drop-down menu, and selecting the **Details** tab.

6 Start up in seconds
When you shut down your PC it can take a few minutes to power down – and then even more time to start up again. You can avoid this process by using the Sleep function. Just open the Start Menu and click on the **Power** button. This will save your current session and put your PC into a low-power state. All you need to do to start it back up is click the power button on your computer's case.

7 Use the Start search
To really save time using your PC, you need to master Start search. When you've got a lot of files, programs or emails to sift through, you can find them quickly by opening the Start search menu and typing into the box. The less you type, the more options you get (for example, type 'cal' and you'll get calculator, calendar, etc). You can also save your searches, so you can find things again in a hurry.

8 Renaming files

When you've got a huge amount of files you'd like to rename, instead of altering them one by one, you can rename them all in just a few clicks. Hold **Ctrl** and left-click each file, or left-click and drag to select all the files. Then press **F2**, type in a common name to use for all the files, press **Enter** and all the files will be given the same name, with the exception of a number at the end.

9 Disable UAC

User Account Control (UAC) is the in-built security prompt designed to safeguard against potentially damaging changes. It's a great feature, but it slows you down a bit. If you'd prefer not to have it popping up, turn it off by typing 'User Accounts' into the Start menu search, and use the slider to find the best settings for you.

10 Change users

When you've got a whole family using just one computer, you'll probably have set up individual accounts. To swap between these accounts, just press **Ctrl**, **Alt** and **Delete** on your keyboard, and select **Switch user** to change.

CTRL, ALT + DEL A quick way to lock your PC while you're away or to switch between users

11 Add gadgets

You don't have to open Internet Explorer each time you want to check on the weather or look at your eBay account. Instead, use Windows Sidebar gadgets by right-clicking on the Sidebar and selecting **Add gadgets**. To get more gadgets, go to http://gallery.live.com to download and install what you want.

10 keyboard shortcuts

Control your computer at the touch of a button or two

Quit application
One of the most useful shortcuts you'll ever know. To quickly close a window, you can use this command to close them without using the mouse. When you're on the desktop, it even opens the box to allow you to shut down or restart your PC.

Copy and paste
To copy and paste text from one file to another, just highlight the text, press **Ctrl and C**, then open the second file and press **Ctrl and V**.

Rename
When you've selected an item, pressing **F2** will allow you to rename it without having to left-click it twice with a gap in between, hoping that you don't open it instead.

Auto web address
Instead of writing a whole website address (such as www.bing.com) just write the 'live' bit and hold down **Ctrl and Enter** for the 'www.' and '.com' to be filled in for you.

Cycle through windows
If you've got Windows 7 Home Premium or Ultimate, holding the **Windows** key and pressing **Tab** repeatedly will cycle through all open windows in Flip 3D. Taking your finger off the **Windows** key will open the window highlighted.

New window
If you're in Internet Explorer or a program like Microsoft Office Word, you can create a new window by using this shortcut.

Show desktop
To get to the desktop quickly, you don't have to click on the show desktop icon. Just hold the **Windows** key and press **M**.

Page refresh
Press this every time you want to refresh a page – ideal if you're waiting for an eBay auction to end.

Select all
When you've opened a folder brimming with all sorts of files, but want to quickly delete them all, or move them somewhere else, hold **Ctrl** and press **A** to select all the files in the folder.

Quick print
Whenever you need to print – be it an internet site or an open email – just hold **Ctrl** and press **P** to quickly open the print box.

And don't forget...
Start Menu
Just press the **Windows** key to open the Start Menu, and if you want to search for something, type it into the Start Menu search box.

Advanced folder tips

Once you're comfortable with using the new interface
it's time to start delving deeper into its features

Over the last few pages, you've seen how the new Windows 7 interface can help you store and track down all of your files far more easily and faster than ever before, and discovered helpful ways to work more efficiently with your files, using the basic tools and features provided by the interface. So, with the basics covered, it's time to start delving a little deeper and take a look at ways to get more from Windows Explorer and the useful features within it.

A couple of the more obvious options are available through the Organize menu. The Layout option enables you to pick and choose which areas of the standard windows are displayed. By removing different panes, you can maximize the amount of visible space available; by adding panes you can make

sure useful features are to hand. If you've used previous versions of Windows you might be wondering where the standard menu bars have gone. They are still there – they're just hidden away. As many menu bar options only need to be accessed infrequently, it's a bit of a waste of desktop space to have them permanently on show. It is possible to temporarily display the menu by pressing **Alt**, or it can be permanently displayed by choosing **Organize**, selecting **Layout** and then **Menu Bar**.

The Folder Options dialog is still available with many useful advanced options, such as being able to fix the window style and position or resetting the current window style.

Compress it

While today's hard drives have increased vastly in size, and worries about space

are no longer of so much concern, Windows 7 supports a variety of easy ways to compress files and folders so that they take up less drive space; perfect for emailing or storing files on small capacity USB flash drives. One way to do this is to right-click on a selection of files or folders and select **Send To ➜ Compressed Folder**. This creates a single compressed file of the selected files or folders, which can easily be emailed or copied to another drive.

Alternatively, there is a more permanent method, by taking an existing folder and transforming it into a compressed folder, in which everything is compressed, but still looks and acts as a normal folder. You can do this by right-clicking a folder, selecting **Properties**, clicking the **Advanced** button and ticking the **Compress contents to save disk space** tick box. ⊞

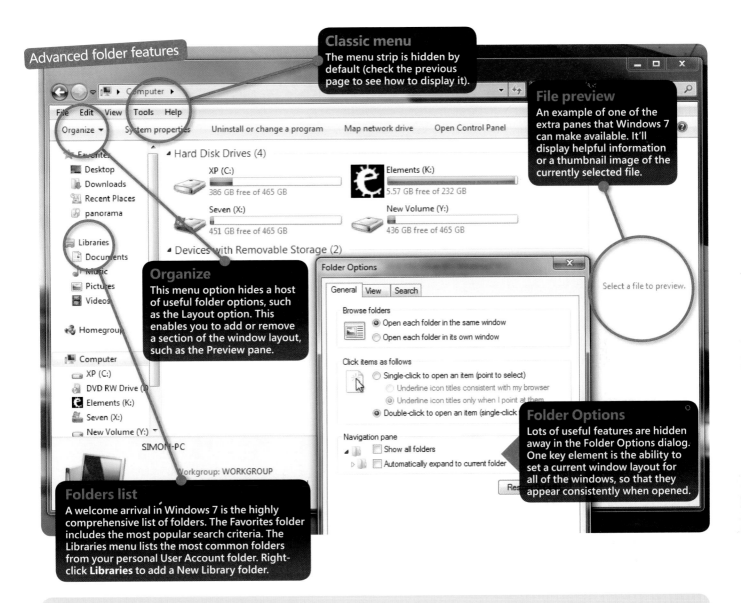

Advanced folder features

Classic menu
The menu strip is hidden by default (check the previous page to see how to display it).

File preview
An example of one of the extra panes that Windows 7 can make available. It'll display helpful information or a thumbnail image of the currently selected file.

Organize
This menu option hides a host of useful folder options, such as the Layout option. This enables you to add or remove a section of the window layout, such as the Preview pane.

Folder Options
Lots of useful features are hidden away in the Folder Options dialog. One key element is the ability to set a current window layout for all of the windows, so that they appear consistently when opened.

Folders list
A welcome arrival in Windows 7 is the highly comprehensive list of folders. The Favorites folder includes the most popular search criteria. The Libraries menu lists the most common folders from your personal User Account folder. Right-click **Libraries** to add a New Library folder.

File type management

Get a grip of your applications and the files they handle

A file is usually associated with the program that created it or the program that should open it. For example, in the case of a text document that was created in Notepad, the file will have the Notepad file type, and therefore display the corresponding Notepad icon; obviously, when you double-click it, it will open in Notepad.

Sometimes this isn't desirable

as you want to edit the file within another program. In these cases, you can either run the application and locate the document that way. Or, you can right-click the file and select **Open With**; if you can see the program listed in the menu, select it to have the file open from that program. If you select the **Choose Default Program** this opens a new dialog box. Using this you can permanently change the

FILE TYPE Choose the program that opens specific file types to save you time and effort

program that opens that type of document, so in this example it's possible to have text documents open with WordPad.

Never lose a file or photo again

Windows 7 makes backing up easier than ever, so now there's no excuse not to protect your files from corruption or deletion

Data recovery is an expensive business – assuming it's actually possible to find anything to recover. Despite this, people forget how priceless their personal files are – you can reinstall any program from the disc that came with it, but you can't magically restore an important document or vital email. The consequences of data loss are often ignored until it's too late and a precious photograph is lost forever...

In the past, data backup was a difficult and costly process, but that's all changed with Windows 7. It features a built-in backup tool that's simple to set up, supports a wide range of backup media (including CD and DVD) and can be scheduled to run automatically in the background at set intervals. In other words, it's a perfect 'set it and forget it' solution that removes any excuses for never backing up important documents, emails and other files.

Windows 7 features a built-in backup tool that's simple to set up

When it comes to backing up, you have a number of choices. You can back up to CD or DVD, although you're restricted by capacities – 650MB for individual CDs, 4.7GB (or 8.4GB if you have a dual-layer drive and compatible discs) for DVDs. The Windows 7 Backup and Restore tool will split your backup so it can be spanned across many discs, but this isn't practical if you're updating your backup regularly.

You can also back up to another location on your network, like a shared folder or a Network Attached Storage device. It's simple to set up, but that device does need to be switched on when your backup runs, and performance will depend on the speed of your network connection, particularly if it's wireless.

The easiest option is to use an external hard drive. These can be attached via a USB or Firewire port, which are much quicker than a network connection. ➡

Backing up and restoring your files

Six steps to help safeguard precious documents, photos and videos

1 SCHEDULE BACKUP Type 'backup' into the Start Menu Search box and select **Backup and Restore Center**. Now click **Set up backup**. Select whether to save to CD, DVD or external hard drive.

2 FILE TYPES Decide which types of files you want to include in the backup, such as TV shows, pictures, emails, etc. Click **Next** and then select the **Let me choose** button.

3 SELECT A FREQUENCY Choose how frequently you want to perform the backup. Obviously, the frequency will depend on how often you add to or change files on your hard drive.

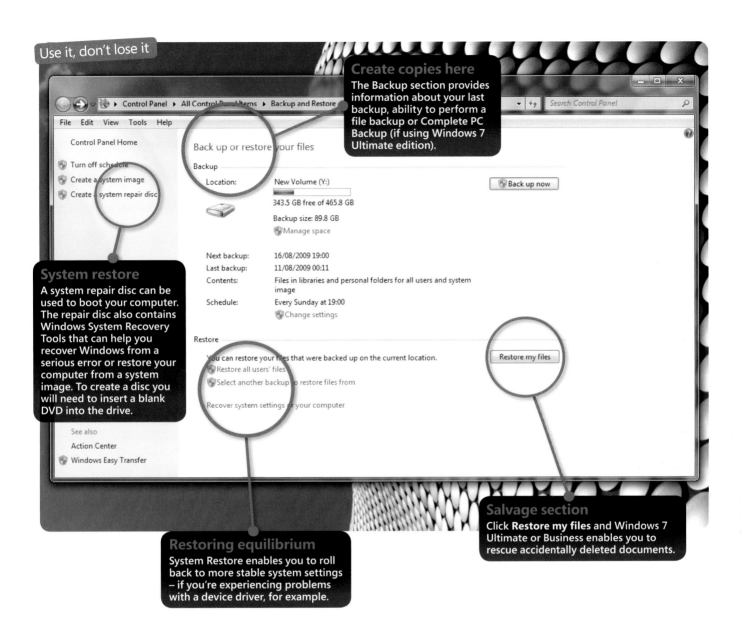

Create copies here
The Backup section provides information about your last backup, ability to perform a file backup or Complete PC Backup (if using Windows 7 Ultimate edition).

System restore
A system repair disc can be used to boot your computer. The repair disc also contains Windows System Recovery Tools that can help you recover Windows from a serious error or restore your computer from a system image. To create a disc you will need to insert a blank DVD into the drive.

Salvage section
Click **Restore my files** and Windows 7 Ultimate or Business enables you to rescue accidentally deleted documents.

Restoring equilibrium
System Restore enables you to roll back to more stable system settings – if you're experiencing problems with a device driver, for example.

4 READY, SET, GO Click **Save settings and start backup** and Windows 7 will scan your files and copy them to your backup device. If backing up to CD/DVD, you'll be prompted to insert a blank disc.

5 RESTORE FILES If you need to restore files later, plug the backup drive into your PC or put the backup DVD into the drive. Go to **Backup and Restore Center**, click **Restore Files**, and choose to restore.

6 ADD FILES Click **Manage space** to browse files on your backup drive. Select the files to restore and click **Next**. Choose whether to restore to original locations or new, then **Start restore**.

Some PCs also come with eSATA ports – external ports that work with a limited number of drives, but which offer superior performance to even USB or Firewire. Capacities vary widely; choose one with plenty of space.

A fourth option – not supported by Backup and Restore in Windows 7 –

BACK UP BUDDY Restoring backed-up files is even easier and can be a real life saver

is to backup online. Various service providers offer space, as do some security programs.

What can I back up?

The Windows 7 Backup and Restore tool backs up important files but it doesn't record system and program preferences, like desktop or Microsoft Office settings... If you're running Windows 7 Home Premium, Ultimate or Professional edition, you'll notice another option in Backup and Restore – Back up computer. This launches the Windows Complete Backup tool, which enables you to back up key files and settings that will enable you to get Windows 7 back up and running should your PC fail – your programs and preferences will be preserved, making it a far more convenient option than reinstalling Windows 7 from scratch.

For many other back-up programs you're able to pick and choose which folders get backed up, but these may not store program or Windows settings. If you don't have access to the Windows Complete Backup Tool, you'll need to install a third-party solution that will enable you to create an entire image of your hard drive. 🪟

Complete PC Backup and Restore

Ultimate Edition owners can back up their entire computer the easy way

Windows 7 doesn't just deal with backing up files, it can also make a perfect copy of your hard disk – which means if your computer runs into problems, you can get your system up and running on another PC in under 60 minutes.

Creating a Complete PC Backup works in much the same way as a normal backup, but as you might imagine it's a lot bigger; if you're using DVDs, you'll need between six and 10 blank discs for a typical system backup. You can't pick and choose what to back up, either –

Complete PC Backup makes a complete copy of your hard disk, with no exceptions or omissions.

To create a Complete PC Backup, go to **Control Panel ➜ System Security ➜ Backup and Restore**, then click on **Back Up Computer**. If disaster strikes and you need to recover your system from a Complete PC Backup, you'll need to restart your PC and hold down the **F8 key**. This brings up the Windows Recovery Environment, from which you can then select **Windows Complete PC Restore**.

Quick questions

With easy answers!

Q How do I restore my computer from a previous Complete PC Backup?
A You should boot from your Windows 7 installation disc, choose **Repair my computer** when prompted and click **Windows Complete PC Restore**.

Q I heavily edited an Office Excel file and saved over it. I now want the old version back – am I completely stuck?
A If you've been doing backups, you can simply restore the file. Windows 7 Professional and Ultimate editions have another trick, though – **Create a system image** – this creates copies of files and folders that Windows automatically saves as part of a restore point. To revert to a system image, right-click the file you want to restore, choose **Restore previous versions**, and then choose the one that you want to revert to. See the next page for further details.

Q Do system image versions take up a lot of disk space?
A System imaging only stores changes made between versions – this means the file size isn't very different.

Q Why can't I see my documents in Search results?
A If you save files on a different hard drive to Windows 7, you need to change the default Search settings to include this drive in the Search Index. Simply search for 'index' in **Control Panel** and select **Change how Windows searches**. From here you can then add and remove locations.

PC restoration made easy
Accidentally overwritten or erased a file? Windows 7 can retrieve it

If you're running Windows 7 Professional or Ultimate, you can create a system image; a complete reproduction of your system that can be retrieved should your system suffer from a unrecoverable problem. To create a system image, simply go to **Control Panel ➜ System and Security ➜ Backup and Restore ➜ Create a System Image**. As with regular file backups, you'll need a hard drive with enough room. To restore a system image that has been previously created, go to **Control Panel ➜ All Control Panel Items ➜ Recovery ➜ Advanced Recovery Methods**. The Advanced Recovery window also offers the option to reinstall Windows; to do this you'll need an original Windows 7 installation disc.

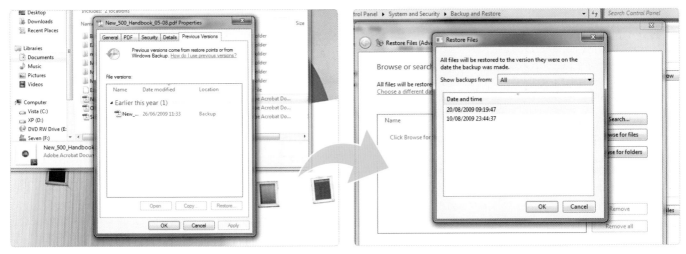

1 TIME TRAVEL Restoring a file is easy, right-click on the file to recover, choose **Properties** and go to the Previous Versions tab. A list of previous versions will appear. Click on the version you want and click on **Restore**.

2 ADVANCED RESTORE From the Backup and Restore menu, select **Restore for all users' files** to bring up the Advanced restore screen. Within this window you can filter results by date, be it from the last week, month or year.

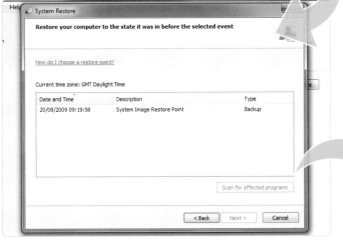

3 SYSTEM RECOVERY From the Backup and Restore menu, select **Recover system settings on your computer** to open System Restore. The System restore points are listed with a brief description and the date.

4 LAST RESORT If all else fails, go to the Backup and Restore menu, select **Recover system settings on your computer** and then **Advanced recovery methods**. Now you can choose to recover using a system image or by reinstalling Windows.

Set up your network at home in just 10 minutes

The new networking features in Windows 7 make setting up a PC connection child's play

One of the most important changes in Windows 7 is its approach to networking. Whether you're connecting to other computers or to the internet, you'll find the process of connecting, using and troubleshooting network connections much easier than in Windows XP. Some of the changes are not immediately obvious, but some of the most important changes are very visible indeed.

Over the next few pages you'll discover more about the Networking and Sharing Center, and how you can share not just documents but also entire programs with others on your network. If you've ever spent an unhappy day digging through the networking settings

of an older Windows PC only to end up giving up, you'll be delighted with the way Windows 7 does things.

Networking shouldn't be difficult – after all, a network is just a couple of computers talking to one another. However, there are lots of issues to consider. Security is a big one – you don't want just anybody wandering around your PC – but there are practicalities, too.

Are you connecting via a cable or over a wireless network? Do you want to share your media files, your folders or your printer? In older versions of Windows, setting up even the simplest network or internet connection could be a time-consuming operation, but in Windows 7 it couldn't be easier. ⊞

In real life...

Network maps

James Stables, Deputy editor, *Windows: The Official Magazine*
Home networks are getting more complex and most of us aren't network experts, so when something stops working it can be frustrating trying to track down the problem. The Network Map provides a visual report on what devices are working; if a device disappears you'll instantly see where the problem is, helping you to track it down and resolve it.

Connecting to the internet

Windows 7 provides the quickest route to the information highway

1 NO NET For a Windows 7 PC to find a connection, click on **Start ➜ Control Panel ➜ Network and Internet ➜ Network and Sharing Center.** A red cross indicates no connection is found.

2 GET CONNECTED When you run an Ethernet cable from your router to your PC, a grayed-out computer with the caption 'Identifying' appears as Windows 7 auto-detects the network settings.

3 EASY ACCESS After a short delay, the map of your network changes again. This time it shows that you're connected to the internet via your network. Click on **See Full Map** for a better look.

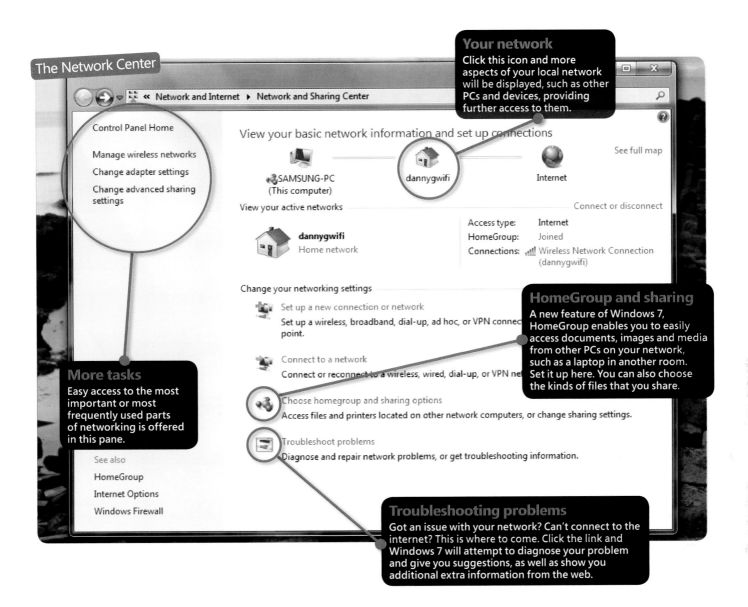

The Network Center

Your network
Click this icon and more aspects of your local network will be displayed, such as other PCs and devices, providing further access to them.

Control Panel Home

Manage wireless networks

Change adapter settings

Change advanced sharing settings

View your basic network information and set up connections

See full map

SAMSUNG-PC
(This computer)

dannygwifi

Internet

View your active networks

Connect or disconnect

dannygwifi
Home network

Access type: Internet
HomeGroup: Joined
Connections: Wireless Network Connection (dannygwifi)

Change your networking settings

Set up a new connection or network
Set up a wireless, broadband, dial-up, ad hoc, or VPN connection point.

Connect to a network
Connect or reconnect to a wireless, wired, dial-up, or VPN net

Choose homegroup and sharing options
Access files and printers located on other network computers, or change sharing settings.

Troubleshoot problems
Diagnose and repair network problems, or get troubleshooting information.

HomeGroup and sharing
A new feature of Windows 7, HomeGroup enables you to easily access documents, images and media from other PCs on your network, such as a laptop in another room. Set it up here. You can also choose the kinds of files that you share.

More tasks
Easy access to the most important or most frequently used parts of networking is offered in this pane.

See also

HomeGroup

Internet Options

Windows Firewall

Troubleshooting problems
Got an issue with your network? Can't connect to the internet? This is where to come. Click the link and Windows 7 will attempt to diagnose your problem and give you suggestions, as well as show you additional extra information from the web.

4 YOU ARE HERE At this point, you will be able to see the Network Map view, which shows that you're now connected to the internet via a gateway – in other words, your router.

5 MORE DETAIL If you click on the Network icon, Windows 7 will show more details about the network. To change your router's settings, right-click on it and select **View Device Webpage**.

6 IDENTIFY YOURSELF Like most routers this Linksys is password-protected. You'll need to enter your username and password here. By default, Linksys uses 'admin' and 'password'.

Share files and more with a home network

Connect your PCs together and share internet access, files, printers, music, video files and more

Buying your second family PC seemed such a great idea... No more queuing to use the computer. No need to wait for the kids to finish playing games before checking your email. And no "are you done yet?" when you're creating spreadsheets and they want to download MP3s.

Unfortunately, it doesn't always work out like that. Maybe the old Windows XP machine is upstairs, and only your Windows 7 PC is connected to the internet. You'll be pestered almost as much as you were before, unless you go one step further and link the two systems together in a home network.

Once your systems are connected, you'll be able to share internet access and other hardware, too. If the kids are doing homework upstairs and want to print it out on the printer downstairs, they'll be able to do so in a few clicks.

You'll also be able to quickly back up data from one system to the other – handy if you're infected by a virus or have some other kind of data disaster. And if you have young kids and want to protect them from the worst of the internet, then there are significant advantages in doing things this way. With the right combination of software and hardware you'll be able to monitor what they're doing online, block certain types of sites, even limit their access.

It pays to consider your networking options before making any expensive purchases. There are three common technologies you can use to connect your home PCs...

SECURITY MEASURES Most routers come packed with powerful security features such as hardware firewalls and intrusion detection

The first option is a conventional network crossover cable. Your PCs almost certainly have network ports already (check the manual to be sure), so all you need buy is the cable to run between them. These are widely available and inexpensive, but you will have the hassle of trailing the cable under carpet and maybe drilling through walls. The second option is to use wireless adapters, which means no need for cables at all. Much less set-up work but speeds will be reduced, perhaps considerably if the two PCs are a long way from each other. And you'll have to pay for the wireless network adapters, which vary in price depending on performance.

If those options don't appeal, then maybe you'll prefer the third: powerline networking. Here you buy an adapter for each PC, plug it into a nearby power socket and the system then shuttles data

SHARE AND SHARE ALIKE Your networked PCs appear in the Windows 7 Network window, and are only ever a double-click away

around your home's electrical wiring. While more costly, this option delivers the no-hassle convenience of wireless. With better speeds and such ease of use, it may be a justified expense.

It's all a balance between price, convenience and performance. But there's another important issue that you need to consider...

Network layout

Shared internet access is a key feature of any network, but there are two different ways of setting it up. One answer comes with Windows, and it's called Internet Connection Sharing (ICS). If your Windows 7 PC is connected to the internet, you can enable ICS then, after setting up a home network, your Windows XP PC can get online, too.

This may sound good enough, especially as ICS comes with both Windows XP and Windows 7 for free,

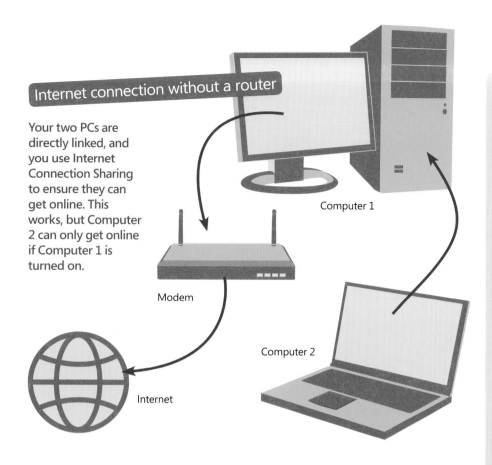

Internet connection without a router

Your two PCs are directly linked, and you use Internet Connection Sharing to ensure they can get online. This works, but Computer 2 can only get online if Computer 1 is turned on.

Computer 1

Modem

Computer 2

Internet

but there are some problems. ICS isn't always easy to configure, for instance; it doesn't support all applications (instant messaging probably won't work), and using a software solution means your

Windows 7 PC must be switched on all the time if your Windows XP system is to get online. A better solution is to buy a combined router and modem to manage the network for you. ➡

Keep it safe

Limit access to your network

■ **If you have a wireless network**, find out how to turn on security. The best method is an encryption system called WPA. This will help keep neighbors or passers-by from accessing your connection.

■ **Powerline networks** can also be accessed by neighbors; be sure to turn on security features.

■ **Routers** often come with a default password, or no password. Once set up, change this to something that's impossible for anyone else to guess.

■ **Sharing folders:** if you share the entire C drive, say, any hacker who breaks in may be able to place files in your Windows or Program Files folders, leaving you at risk of a software infection. Create a special folder like C:\MyShared and share that. Not as convenient, but safer.

Set up the Windows 7 PC
Follow the three simple steps to get networking

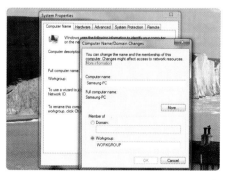

1 HARDWARE Get the network adapter working in the Windows 7 PC first (if you're using the built-in network port, skip this). Every adapter is different; read the instructions provided.

2 NAME IT Click **Start** and search for Workgroup. Choose **Change Workgroup Name**. Then in the System Properties window, select **Change...** and go for a general name, like a place name.

3 SHARE No router? Click **Control Panel → Network & Sharing Center → Change Adapter Settings.** Right-click the connection, **Properties → Sharing.** Select both boxes, hit **OK** then restart.

HIGH-SECURITY Buying a router for your network improves security and makes it much easier to share internet access

With this option, you connect the PCs to the router, instead of to each other, and then they're both able to get online, even if the other's switched off.

Routers can help improve your PC security, too. They typically include powerful hardware firewalls and intrusion detection systems, perfect for keeping hackers out of your system.

Surprisingly, routers shouldn't add much to the cost of your network. Two basic wireless adapters will cost around $60; a basic wireless router and single wireless adapter lifts this to $100. The easier set-up means it's a price well worth paying for many.

What to buy?
That's quite enough network theory, then – it's time to get practical. Which networking technology is right for you?

If you're looking for a fast, very cheap solution, your PCs are less than 100 feet apart, and you don't mind doing a little preparatory DIY, opt for the Ethernet cabling solution. Search on the internet to see what crossover cable you need, and establish the length required. If you hate the idea of messing around with cables, and want something cheap and easy, a couple of 54Mbps USB wireless adapters will do ($60). A PCI wireless adapter card is even more reliable, but you need to open up your PC to install it.

Budget wireless solutions might be slow, especially if your PCs are a considerable distance apart (more than 100 feet, say). If you need good performance, then a 'pre-802.11n' wireless adapter could help ($100).

You might get improved long-distance results from powerline networking, though, which uses your home electrical wiring to transmit data. These vary in capacity and price, so search for a deal.

If you're willing to spend a little more to get the best system, the ideal option would be a router with built-in modem. It doesn't work out too expensive as you don't need a network adapter for your main PC. Again, a price comparison site can lead you to the bargains.

Don't choose solely on price, though. This can lead you to older kit that may not be compatible with Windows 7, so read the small print carefully before parting with your cash.

First steps
You've found the technology that suits, and set it up with the instructions provided. So what now?

A good place to start is by sharing a folder. On the Windows XP system, create a new folder called something like C:\Shared. Right-click that, select **Properties → Sharing**, click on **Share...** At this point, you need to make a note of your PC's name – if you don't know it, go to **Control Panel → System and Security → System**.

Setting up the Windows XP PC
Just tell it where to look and you'll be surfing in no time

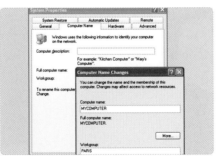

1 INSTALL Connect your chosen network adapter to the Windows XP computer. If you've gone for a wireless adapter, give it the same wireless network ID that you entered on the Windows 7 system.

2 NAME Click **Control Panel → System → Computer Name → Change**; set the Workgroup name (same as the Windows 7 PC) then close and restart the PCs. Connect to the internet and open a browser on the XP system.

3 CONNECT If IE wants to dial your old connection, click **Tools → Internet Options → Connections** and select **Never dial a connection**. If you still can't connect, check out the Troubleshooting advice opposite.

Now go to the Windows 7 PC, click **Start → Computer**, then press **Alt** and click **Tools → Map Network Drive**. Enter the computer name, followed by the folder name (\\XP_PC_NAME\Shared), and a new Explorer window should appear. That is the C:\Shared folder on the XP system, and you can drag and drop files to and from it just as though it was on your own hard drive.

You can share folders and printers on the Windows 7 PC, too, so they're available from the XP system. Access the Windows 7 Network and Sharing Center (**Control Panel → Network**) and turn on whatever you need in the Sharing and Discovery section (printers will probably need to be reinstalled before they can be shared).

It's not all about working, though. If you're running Windows Media Player 11 or later on the XP system, then launch it, click **Tools → Options → Library → Configure Sharing**, select the icon for your Windows 7 PC and click **Allow → OK**. Select **Computer → Network on the 7 PC** and you'll now see a Media icon; double-click on that, and you'll be able to use the network to access any music, pictures or video you have stored on your XP system's Media Player library.

It's an impressive feature list, especially as the technology is getting more and more reasonably priced – so what are you waiting for? Buy an adapter or two, set up your home network, and start getting the most out of your PCs. ⊞

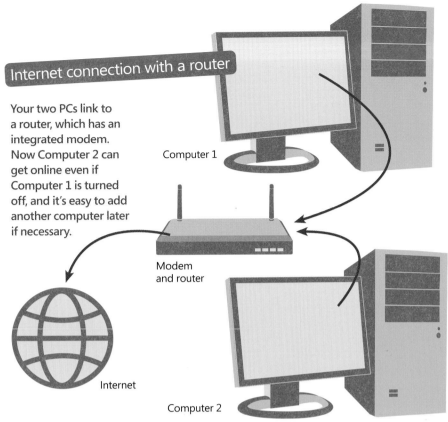

Internet connection with a router

Your two PCs link to a router, which has an integrated modem. Now Computer 2 can get online even if Computer 1 is turned off, and it's easy to add another computer later if necessary.

Computer 1

Modem and router

Internet

Computer 2

NET AID The Network and Sharing Center has tools to get your network up and running

Got a problem with your network?

If the network doesn't seem to be established, try one of these fixes

■ **Networks are fussy** If yours isn't working, turn both systems off and on. Go to the Windows 7 PC, click **Start → Network**; you should see at least one icon for each PC.

■ **No luck?** Right-click or double-click on the network system tray icon; wireless drivers will often tell you if they've detected a system.

■ **Check settings** The Windows workgroup name must be the same on both PCs. Wireless adapters must have the same network ID (SSID).

■ **Disable firewalls** Disconnect from the internet, then disable any firewalls. Make sure your firewall monitors the internet connection, but leaves your network alone.

■ **Computer Browser service** Make sure this is running on Windows XP (**Start → Run → services.msc**) and that TCP/IP is set up. Click **Control Panel → Network Connections**, right-click **Local Area Connection** and select **Properties**; choose **TCP/IP, click Properties**, then **Obtain an IP address automatically**. Close both PCs and restart.

■ **Still no good?** Windows 7 has a network setup wizard. In the Network and Sharing Center, choose **Set up a new connection or network**. Choose to **Set up a wireless ad hoc (computer to computer) network**. Make sure the Network Location Type is set to Private, not Public, so the Windows XP PC can access your files.

Connect, share and update

If you've more than one PC it's time to get connected – Windows 7 makes it easier than ever

Super Tip!

Sharing media

Windows 7 can detect and share media with all manner of devices, including the Xbox 360 and other Window 7 PCs. Find out more about sharing with an Xbox 360 on page 93.

Networking multiple computers has many advantages. It enables different users to share files and applications, as well as share a single internet account. Setting up a network can be as simple as

ENABLE ENTRY If you want users on your network to edit your files, give them access

plugging in a few cables and, once done, you're soon able to gain the benefits of sharing files and resources.

There is, quite rightly, a certain level of paranoia associated with networks and the internet in general. The trick with networking is to take a less-is-more approach and limit access to the bare minimum. For example, if people only need to view the files in your Public folder but don't need the ability to edit them, it makes sense to limit their access accordingly, so you should use the Network and Sharing Center to give read-only access rather than full access.

Conversely, you're not limited to just sharing the Public folder. If File Sharing is switched on in the **Network and Sharing Center ➜ Advanced sharing settings**,

you can share any folder by right-clicking on it in Windows Explorer and going to the **Share with...** option. Even with this level of access, it's still possible to add passwords to specific folders to limit availability.

Working together

Windows 7 also offers ways to make sharing files easier with its new Sync Center. This handy feature enables you to work on files while you're away from a network or while the shared PC is powered down; any changes made can then be synchronized once the shared files are available again. Follow the walkthrough opposite to see how this can be activated and how you can take full advantage of it.

What is HomeGroup?

The easy sharing technology at the heart of Windows 7

HomeGroup makes it simple to share your music, pictures, video and even printers over your home network. Sharing items with your HomeGroup means that you're ensuring your media is only shared with trusted computers on your home network.

The HomeGroup is protected with a password, and you'll always be able to choose what you share with the other machines in the group. Media is shared in the form of libraries, and only those who belong to the HomeGroup can see the shared

libraries – if a friend visits and connects to your network, they won't be able to see the libraries unless you enable them to do so. If a computer is a member of a HomeGroup, all the users on that machine will have access to the shared libraries.

To work with HomeGroup, computers must all be running Windows 7. HomeGroup also only works on networks set to the Home network location. Find out more about setting up your own HomeGroup on page 66.

SHARE WARE HomeGroup means that you can opt to share your media libraries and printers with your home network

Connecting to another PC

Access other PCs and synchronize amended files

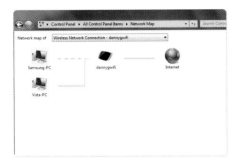

1 HELLO In the Network and Sharing Center, click **See Full Map**. In addition to the internet connection, the desktop PC can see the laptop. Right-click the other computer and click **Open**.

2 EASY EXPLORE Here you're looking at the laptop, or at least the bits that the laptop's owner has given permission to look at. In this example, you can browse the Public and Printers folders.

3 SEE FILES Double-click **Public**. If you've got read-only access you'll be able to open and copy files; if you've got full access you can edit or delete files or copy files from your hard disk.

4 WAIT A BIT You can ensure these files are always available, even when you're not connected. To do this, go back one step, right-click on **Public** and click **Always available offline**.

5 SIMPLE SYNC Open **Sync Center** from the Control Panel or search for it. You'll see that there's an entry already in there – **Offline Files**. Double-click the icon to see more.

6 OFFLINE BROWSING Here you can see the folder is synchronizing. Once it's finished, the folder will be available at all times – in this case, the Public folder on the laptop.

7 CHANGES The laptop is no longer connected but the files are available. By using the local copy of the laptop files changes will be applied to the originals when the files are synchronized.

8 UPDATE Return to **Sync Center**. Above Offline Files you'll see **Sync** – which synchronizes files immediately, and **Schedule** – which enables you to sync files at specified times.

9 OPTIONS Network and Sharing Center → Advanced sharing settings provides further options – limit access to your public folders, password-protect files, or even turn off sharing altogether.

Networking know-how

Windows 7 makes it easy to set up a home network, and also to troubleshoot any problems

There's nothing quite so effective as the topic of networking to make people's eyes glaze over at a party and have them mentally pacing the number of steps between you and the nearest escape route.

Thankfully, Windows 7 can free you from the complex, mundane tasks that make you feel like you're working as an unpaid system administrator for your household! It will let you get on with enjoying the benefits of having your own home network – like listening to the music stored on your desktop PC upstairs while you're relaxing in the lounge with your laptop to hand downstairs (see the guide below for what you need to do to achieve this).

The slick Network and Sharing Center in Windows 7 makes it easy to see at a glance how your computer is connected to others, and makes it simple to highlight any problems that are stopping the data getting through.

Great leap forward

A key network area that Windows 7 now directly tackles is wireless networking, possibly one of the best technological advances ever made for the portable PC, meaning you can stay connected on your laptop no matter where you are in the house; the kitchen, the living room or even the bathroom should you wish – just watch out for water!

Provided your kit isn't more than a few years old, then getting set up is remarkably simple. If your laptop has an Intel Centrino badge on it, then you've got everything that you need already built into the computer. Other laptops also have built-in wireless connectors – the easiest way to check is to open the Network and Sharing Center and then click **Change adapter settings** from the list on the left-hand side. If you see an entry for a Wireless Network Connection, then you're good to go.

Finally, you'll need a wireless router, which enables your computers to connect to one another, but also helps them share a broadband connection. Once up and running, Windows 7 will spring into action. The main stages from connection to solving problems are covered in the following pages.

Set up media sharing in five minutes

Share music and videos with other people on the same network

1 NETWORK DISCOVERY In the Network and Sharing Center, click **Advanced sharing settings** (left). You'll find options to fine-tune how your PC can share its files and media.

2 MEDIA STREAMING Make sure **Network Discovery** is on, then scroll down to Media Streaming and ensure that **Media Streaming** is on, then click **Choose Media Streaming Options...**

3 NAME IT Choose a name for your Media Library. This is what other users on your network will see. Ensure 'Media Programs on this PC and remote connections' is set to **Allowed**.

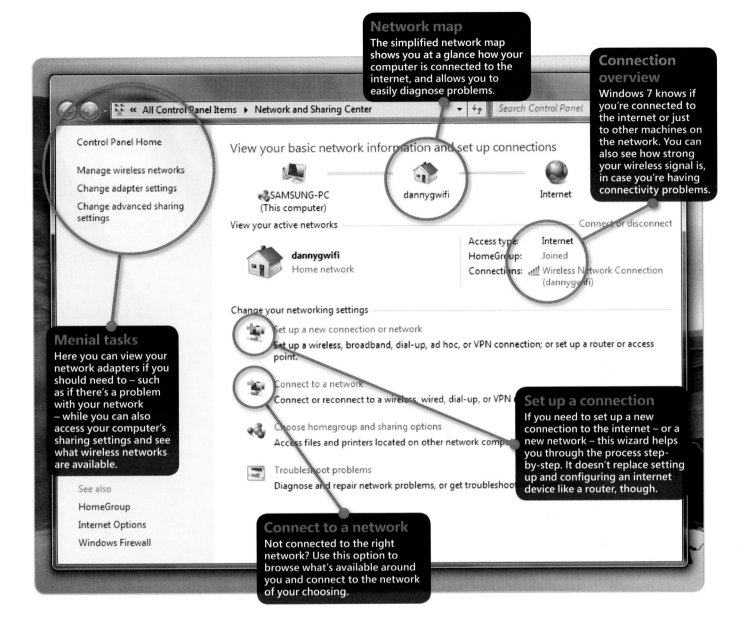

Network map
The simplified network map shows you at a glance how your computer is connected to the internet, and allows you to easily diagnose problems.

Connection overview
Windows 7 knows if you're connected to the internet or just to other machines on the network. You can also see how strong your wireless signal is, in case you're having connectivity problems.

All Control Panel Items ▶ Network and Sharing Center — Search Control Panel

Control Panel Home

Manage wireless networks

Change adapter settings

Change advanced sharing settings

View your basic network information and set up connections

SAMSUNG-PC (This computer)　　dannygwifi　　Internet

View your active networks — Connect or disconnect

dannygwifi
Home network

Access type: Internet
HomeGroup: Joined
Connections: Wireless Network Connection (dannygwifi)

Menial tasks
Here you can view your network adapters if you should need to – such as if there's a problem with your network – while you can also access your computer's sharing settings and see what wireless networks are available.

Change your networking settings

Set up a new connection or network
Set up a wireless, broadband, dial-up, ad hoc, or VPN connection; or set up a router or access point.

Connect to a network
Connect or reconnect to a wireless, wired, dial-up, or VPN

Choose homegroup and sharing options
Access files and printers located on other network compu

Troubleshoot problems
Diagnose and repair network problems, or get troubleshoot

See also

HomeGroup

Internet Options

Windows Firewall

Set up a connection
If you need to set up a new connection to the internet – or a new network – this wizard helps you through the process step-by-step. It doesn't replace setting up and configuring an internet device like a router, though.

Connect to a network
Not connected to the right network? Use this option to browse what's available around you and connect to the network of your choosing.

4 CHECK HOME Hit **Choose Homegroup and Sharing options**. Ensure the Libraries you want to share are checked, and that **Stream my pictures**... is also checked.

5 SWITCH OVER Move to the other computer you want to listen to music from. Open up the Network window. Look for the music and film icon next to a machine name and double-click it.

6 PLAY AWAY In Media Player, you'll now see the other computer listed below your Library. Click on it, and you can navigate through the media files as if they were stored on your own PC.

Hooking up to a wireless network

Connecting to the internet via a wired cable couldn't be easier, but what about wireless?

Wireless networking promises a world of leisurely internet access; media beamed direct to your living room, and instant communication with friends, family and colleagues. The reality is close to this, but it's not always as easy to connect to your wireless network as it should be.

Now, though, it is easy to connect to the networks you need, thanks to Windows 7. There's also support for Wi-Fi Protected Setup (WPS); designed to simplify the process of configuring security when connecting to a wireless access point or router by simply entering a PIN provided with the device.

Improved dialogs make it easier and faster to find and connect to legitimate wireless networks, with warnings provided for insecure connections. The Network Map shows where and what wireless devices are part of your network, and the new diagnostic tools make it far clearer to source problems and, in turn, fix them.

The hard stuff

The terminology involved with wireless networking can get a little confusing, but it's worth demystifying the most common terms. The wireless system uses standard radio waves to send data, but faster versions have since appeared. Each version is called '802.11' followed by the letter a, b, g or n; with latter letters being newer, faster and, of course, more expensive versions.

Thankfully, newer versions are compatible with previous ones. As it stands, 'a' and 'b' are outdated, while 'g' is being superseded by the latest 'n' standard, which offers faster speeds and a greater working distance.

Obviously, one of the main concerns with wireless networking is security. At the very least you should use a system called WEP. It'd be preferable to use the more recent WPA, or the even more robust WPA2 security system that all recent routers will offer. This involves setting the router with a password. Any computer trying to connect will have to supply this password as well, otherwise it will be denied access.

Using a wireless network

Get your PCs connected wirelessly in just six simple steps

1 VIEW NETWORKS Click on the network icon – shown as a bar chart like icon – and you'll see a list of available networks. Hovering over a network name will display more information.

2 STAY PROTECTED This computer is in range of its own network as well as others. Check if they are protected and how strong their signals are. Choose the one you want and click **Connect**.

3 ENTER THE KEY If the network is secure, you'll then be asked to enter the PIN (if you have a compatible router) or security key before you can get a connection. You need this to connect.

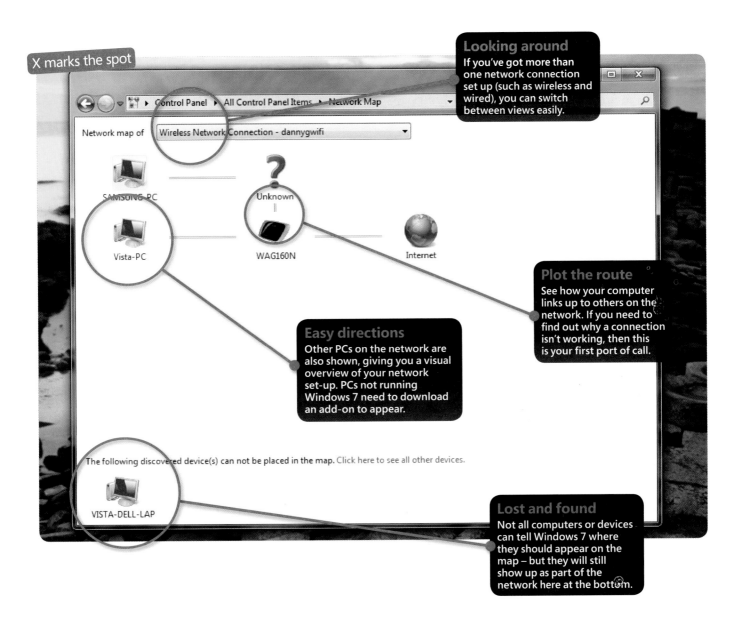

X marks the spot

Looking around
If you've got more than one network connection set up (such as wireless and wired), you can switch between views easily.

Control Panel ▸ All Control Panel Items ▸ Network Map

Network map of | Wireless Network Connection - dannygwifi ▾ |

SAMSUNG-PC

Unknown
||
WAG160N

Internet

Vista-PC

Plot the route
See how your computer links up to others on the network. If you need to find out why a connection isn't working, then this is your first port of call.

Easy directions
Other PCs on the network are also shown, giving you a visual overview of your network set-up. PCs not running Windows 7 need to download an add-on to appear.

The following discovered device(s) can not be placed in the map. Click here to see all other devices.

VISTA-DELL-LAP

Lost and found
Not all computers or devices can tell Windows 7 where they should appear on the map – but they will still show up as part of the network here at the bottom.

4 YOU'RE CONNECTED You'll then see a successful connection to the chosen network (in this case, local and internet access). You need to specify the network location first time round.

5 ANY PROBLEMS? If you have any problems connecting, right-click on the icon and select **Troubleshoot Problems** from the pop-up menu. This will take you to a Diagnostics window.

6 CHANGE SETTINGS If you need to change any saved network settings, you can do this from the **Network and Sharing Center**. You can also change the network location from here.

HomeGroup networking

Take the hassle out of sharing files and media with other computers in your home

HomeGroup is the key networking feature in Windows 7 that enables you to share your music, videos, pictures and documents without having to spend lots of time configuring your machines. Windows 7 adds a new Share with... menu that enables you to send individual files to other machines in your HomeGroup, and HomeGroup enables you to share hardware devices such as printers, too.

HomeGroup is intended to be a secure system and is password protected. You can also choose to make your files read only, so other machines can explore but not overwrite your content. Should you forget the HomeGroup password Windows 7 gives you, you can go back

and view this on the machine you originally set up the HomeGroup on.

You can only be connected to a single HomeGroup at any one time (though you can leave the HomeGroup if you need to join another). If you connect to a different network using your HomeGroup machine, the HomeGroup screen will display 'The HomeGroup is not available because you're not connected to the home network'.

Join in everyone

HomeGroup only works with Windows 7 – computers running older versions of Windows will not be able to take part in HomeGroup. You can only *create* a HomeGroup in the Home Premium, Professional or Ultimate Editions, but

you can join one with any version of Windows 7. Note that for HomeGroup to work you must have specified your network is of the 'Home' type when you first connected. If not, you can change this setting in the Network and Sharing Center. Your computers will also need to be on the same workgroup too, but generally this won't be a problem – in **Control Panel → System**, click **Advanced system settings**. You should see the Workgroup listed as WORKGROUP.

Once set up, you can find HomeGroup in Windows Explorer's Navigation Pane on the left-side of the Explorer window – launch this using the Explorer icon on the taskbar. HomeGroup is designed to be a simple, hassle-free way of sharing files across your home PCs.

Creating and joining HomeGroups

It's easy to set up a HomeGroup – and for other computers to join

1 **CREATE** Search for HomeGroup in the Start menu or go to the Network and Sharing Center. Under network details, you'll see HomeGroup: **Ready to create**. If one exists, it will tell you.

2 **FIRST UP** If this is the first machine in the HomeGroup, the wizard will ask which files to share. This examples shows media, such as Photos and Videos have been selected, but not Documents.

3 **PASS** The system generates a password to enable other machines to join. This is no substitute for having a password protecting your wireless network – your router should be secure.

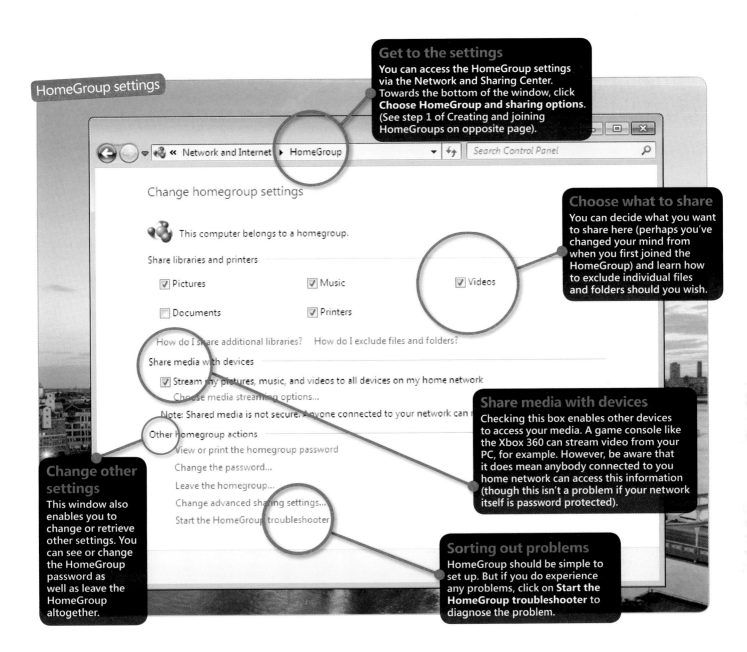

HomeGroup settings

Get to the settings
You can access the HomeGroup settings via the Network and Sharing Center. Towards the bottom of the window, click **Choose HomeGroup and sharing options**. (See step 1 of Creating and joining HomeGroups on opposite page).

Change homegroup settings

This computer belongs to a homegroup.

Share libraries and printers

☑ Pictures   ☑ Music   ☑ Videos

☐ Documents   ☑ Printers

How do I share additional libraries?   How do I exclude files and folders?

Share media with devices

☑ Stream my pictures, music, and videos to all devices on my home network

Choose media streaming options...

Note: Shared media is not secure. Anyone connected to your network can

Other homegroup actions

View or print the homegroup password

Change the password...

Leave the homegroup...

Change advanced sharing settings...

Start the HomeGroup troubleshooter

Choose what to share
You can decide what you want to share here (perhaps you've changed your mind from when you first joined the HomeGroup) and learn how to exclude individual files and folders should you wish.

Share media with devices
Checking this box enables other devices to access your media. A game console like the Xbox 360 can stream video from your PC, for example. However, be aware that it does mean anybody connected to you home network can access this information (though this isn't a problem if your network itself is password protected).

Change other settings
This window also enables you to change or retrieve other settings. You can see or change the HomeGroup password as well as leave the HomeGroup altogether.

Sorting out problems
HomeGroup should be simple to set up. But if you do experience any problems, click on **Start the HomeGroup troubleshooter** to diagnose the problem.

4 JOIN IN Other Windows 7 computers joining the network will be asked if they want to join the HomeGroup. Once prompted for the password (step 3), they will be asked what content to share.

5 EXPLORE Connected machines can browse for files in the HomeGroup in Windows Explorer. You automatically get access to printers connected to any other computer on the same HomeGroup.

6 LIBRARY Windows 7 Libraries collate content from multiple places, and can collate images across a HomeGroup, irrespective of original location. The other PCs will need to be switched on.

Move files between your PC and your smartphone

Windows 7 makes it easy to synchronize your contacts and files with your smartphone

With Windows 7 you can transfer files from your computer to your mobile device manually, but a far better option is to use the built-in Sync Center to automatically update your device whenever you connect it to your PC.

If you're using the 2007 Microsoft Office System, this can synchronize all manner of documents and data between the two devices, enabling you to take your emails, to-do list, notes, calendar, contacts and much more with you wherever you go. You can then make changes to them on your device and have the updates synchronized back with the originals, for when you're back at your desktop computer.

Smartphones are now commonplace, with many being able to send and receive email, browse the web, take notes and play back media – as well as make calls! Windows 7 supports all manner of smartphone devices, but this particular tutorial uses a Windows Mobile 6.1 phone – like the HTC Touch Diamond shown here – to connect up to a Windows 7 PC.

Windows Mobile phones offer all the functionality of a smartphone with the familiarity of the applications you find on your PC – Office Mobile gives you Word, Excel and PowerPoint, while Internet Explorer gives you your favorite sites at your fingertips. Finally, Outlook Mobile means you can take your email, calendar and contacts with you.

CONNECT & SYNC The HTC Touch Diamond is one of a new generation of smartphones

Connecting via Bluetooth

Forget about cables, connect wirelessly!

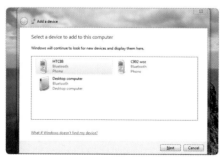

1 INSTALL THE DEVICE In the control panel, go to **Set up a new Bluetooth device**. Ensure that Bluetooth is enabled on your mobile phone. Windows 7 will then scan for Bluetooth devices.

2 ENTER THE CODE Select your device from the list and Windows 7 will connect to it. You'll need to accept the connection via your phone and enter a code to pair up the devices.

3 DRIVER INSTALL Once the device is connected it will install appropriate drivers. You'll be able to share data between your PC and phone and perform other tasks, like using your phone as a modem.

Synchronize files with your smartphone

Move files and other data between your PC and your phone

1 INSTALL YOUR HANDSET With many phones, including Windows Mobile handsets, you'll have to install software. This enables you to set up your phone with your computer correctly. You can choose which applications to install.

2 THE CENTER You can use Windows 7 Sync Center. Within this, click on **Set up new sync partnerships** to introduce Sync Center to your device. Click this and, with many phones, you'll be shown your phone's memory to sync with.

3 DEVICE CENTER On Windows Mobile phones, you're shown this window instead of continuing through Sync Center. This enables you to set up the device and configure with Office Outlook to exchange email and data.

4 MANUAL MOVING Whether it's a Windows Mobile phone or not, most mobile phones show up in My Computer and you can browse through the files on them. Click on **Start →Computer** and you'll see your device on the list of drives and devices. Double-click on the icon to see your storage options.

There are some types of file that Sync Center won't send; the good news is, manual transfers are easy

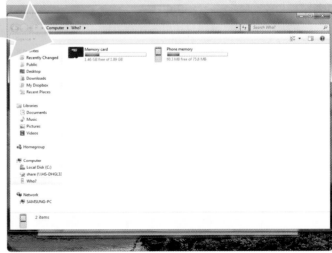

Media on the move

As the power of mobile devices increases, you're able to do even more with them. Most are more than able to handle video playback, meaning that not only can you take your phone with you, but your media as well!

5 TRADITIONAL TRANSFER Usually there are two different types of memory, your smartphone's internal storage and its storage card. To copy files to either location, simply drag and drop. You can also double-click on a folder to look at video, music or photo files on your phone.

Simple ways to organize your photo collection

What's the point of having the world's best photograph if you can't find it and share it? Well, Windows 7 offers the perfect solution

The digital camera revolution has freed us from the tedium and expense of developing film. In doing so, it has given us the power to fire off as many shots as we like until we get that one great picture that perfectly captures a mood, reveals a person's character or creates an image just the way we envisaged it.

Taking great photos still isn't easy but with trial, effort and patience you can do it. Finding them on your hard drive, on the other hand, can be a lot tougher.

Even if you periodically clear out your hard drive by archiving all your images on to DVD, you'll soon find that you're

up to 25GB of disk space in your Pictures folder, and adding more each day. That's a lot of photos to sort through every time you want to find a particular shot.

There's a number of PC programs for categorizing photos on the market but, while several of them have their good points, they all have faults – the most common being that they leave little control over which folders they're monitoring. Because of this, the browsing convenience they offer hasn't been quite enough to justify using them over Windows Explorer.

With Windows 7, however, all the tools you need for keeping track of shots and sorting them are at your fingertips. The difference is apparent as soon as you plug a camera, mobile phone or memory card into your PC. A dialog box pops up and asks if you want to

transfer the shots from your camera on to your PC. Once you've agreed to this, Windows 7 presents you with the option to add a 'tag' (or keyword) to the images you're transferring. So if, say, you've just got back from a trip to the beach and all your shots are of sand and surf, you might want to mention that.

By default, Windows 7 will then transfer all the files over to your Pictures folder, storing them in a subfolder named by the day of the transfer and the tag you've chosen – for example, the automatically generated folder might be called 'July 15 The Beach'. You'll also find that all the photos in the set have been renamed from the usual gibberish (such as 'DSC03415.jpg') to the rather more meaningful 'The Beach 1.jpg' and 'The Beach 2.jpg', and so on.

The heart of the new photography ➡

In real life...
Use the Slide Show

Nick Odantzis, Section editor, *Windows: The Official Magazine*

It's easy to overlook the Windows Sidebar Slide Show gadget as a way to view your pictures. Not only can you add your favorite pictures to it but it's a powerful tool, too – it will search subdirectories and work its way through thousands of images. If you click on a picture that takes your fancy, you can also open the view page, from which you can then edit or print. To find out more, select the gadget itself and then click on the spanner icon.

With Windows 7, all the tools you need for keeping track of shots and sorting them are there at your fingertips

WATCH THE BIRDIE Now you can brighten slightly dull images in Preview mode

ONE TOUCH Auto Adjust is a good way to bring out the colors of your image

From snap to screen
Take, transfer, tag... then browse, share and enjoy

1 TAKE THE SHOT The most important thing about creating a good photo gallery is taking a good picture in the first place. There are lots of great photography websites offering tips; visit one of them for instant inspiration.

2 TRANSFER ACROSS When you come to upload your images, a card reader is the easiest way of moving them to your PC. Failing that, plug your camera in. Windows 7 will recognize the shots and ask if you want to transfer them.

3 RAW FILES Windows Live Photo Gallery can open some kinds of RAW pictures, if the correct codec is available. If you edit a RAW file, Windows Live Photo Gallery saves your modified photo as a JPEG file.

The heart of the photography toolkit is Windows Live Photo Gallery, which monitors the contents of your pictures

4 TAG LINES Adding a tag at this point will rename your images, and will file them in a folder using the same label. You can change how Windows 7 handles the transfer by clicking on the **Options** button. Check the **Erase after importing** box to keep your camera card clean.

Retrieve lost photographs

If you delete pictures from your camera's memory card by mistake, don't worry. There are many web-based applications that can not only retrieve the data from most sources, but also deal with most file types.

5 INTO THE GALLERY Now open up Windows Live Photo Gallery. Your pictures will be there, renamed and tagged. You can do an initial sort through by rating each image from one to five stars, and then pare down your collection ready for easy browsing or sharing with others.

I AM UNDONE You can revert to the original

30 days. On the far left-hand side is the 'metadata' (hidden info) for the selected image, and you can edit information such as name, time, date and caption.

If you select more than one shot and edit the information here, Windows 7 will apply the metadata to every file selected. Most importantly, if you rename a group of files it will add a consecutive number to each one – so you can quickly change your photo library from a random collection of files with arbitrary names to photos which are

center panel for an enlarged preview, or double-click them to open in a viewing window. Shots can then be given a rating from 0 to 5, a great way to single out the best ones, without deleting anything. You can then find the best images quickly by clicking the rating you want to browse in the left-hand panel.

The suite is rounded off with some basic editing tools. What stands out about these is the ease with which you can use them. Simply click **Fix** and drag the Exposure slider to bring light to

toolkit, though, is the Windows Live Photo Gallery application. It monitors the contents of your pictures folder – and any other folders you ask it to, including those on external hard drives – and presents you with an Explorer-type thumbnail view of all the photos and videos stored there. You can alter the view to include bits of info attached to the image that are normally hidden, including the name, time taken and any tags or keywords assigned.

This is where you can really start to take control of your photo collection. The screen on the right shows a variety of sorting tools – you can sort images by name, date taken, location on the hard drive, tag, star rating, or by clicking on the **Recently Imported Items** to see only images taken from the camera in the last

You can really start to take control of your photo collection; sort images by name, date taken, location, tag, stars, etc

sorted meaningfully with usable tags.

One of the best features has to be the ability to select multiple photos and drag them over a tag in the left-hand pane – adding that tag to each shot.

Star quality

One of the most powerful sorting tools is the Star Rating. Once you've imported your images to your PC and edited the tags and names in Windows Live Photo Gallery, you can scroll over them in the

those photos that are just too dark, or hit **Auto Adjust** to have Windows Live Photo Gallery run it through the system.

That one click can transform indistinct photos into stunning family shots – perfect for those whose photography skills aren't up to scratch. And no matter how long you've been using a digital camera, there are always times when you just can't get 'the shot' and have to resort to some fixing work. Well, with Windows 7 it's never been easier.

Editing, printing and sharing...
The essential features in Windows Live Photo Gallery

1 SELECT A SHOT Once you've decided on your best shots, you can double-click on an image to go to the photo viewer, or click **Fix** from the top menu to take you straight to the editing screen.

2 PHOTO FIXES As well as a basic set of tools for altering brightness, contrast and color balance, there's a Red-eye Repair brush, and a Crop tool for cutting away unwanted background areas.

3 MAIL OUT There are several options for sharing your pictures. Click on the **E-mail** button if you want to mail the image directly to a friend. You'll be given the option of resizing it when attaching.

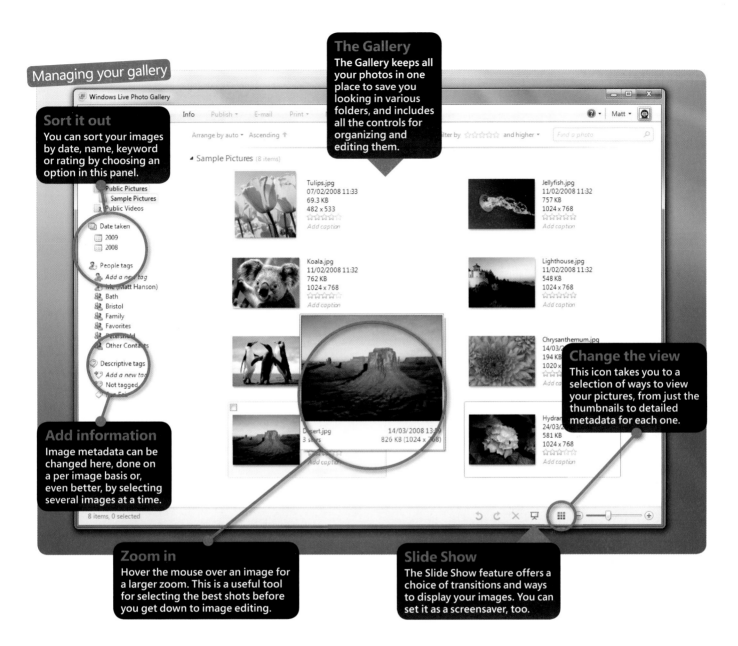

Managing your gallery

The Gallery
The Gallery keeps all your photos in one place to save you looking in various folders, and includes all the controls for organizing and editing them.

Sort it out
You can sort your images by date, name, keyword or rating by choosing an option in this panel.

Add information
Image metadata can be changed here, done on a per image basis or, even better, by selecting several images at a time.

Change the view
This icon takes you to a selection of ways to view your pictures, from just the thumbnails to detailed metadata for each one.

Zoom in
Hover the mouse over an image for a larger zoom. This is a useful tool for selecting the best shots before you get down to image editing.

Slide Show
The Slide Show feature offers a choice of transitions and ways to display your images. You can set it as a screensaver, too.

4 BURN TO DISC To create a video DVD with interactive menu that you can send to non-PC literate folk, select the images you want to include from the gallery and click the **Burn** button.

5 CHOOSE THE LOOK Windows DVD Maker offers you a choice of menu styles and backgrounds to add, as well as the option to create a slide show with backing track and customized fades.

6 TAKE CONTROL Windows Live Movie Maker (available from http://downloadlive.com) enables you to select the pic order, add music, voice-overs and video, or write your own credit sequence.

Enjoying your music with Windows 7

Why not try the best ever version of Windows Media Player? Turn your PC into an all-singing, all-dancing multimedia monster!

Windows Media Player (**Start ➔ All Programs ➔ Windows Media Player**) has been transformed in Windows 7. It's an excellent music player and organizer, and it can handle videos and DVDs, too. This section looks at how to create your own custom playlists, make CDs, copy your tunes to your PC and watch music videos without having to install or use any additional software.

Share and share alike
Windows 7 can also share your music and movies with your Xbox 360 in two ways; using Windows Media Center, and through Windows Media Player. Within Media Center, click on the arrow below

the Library button and then click on **Media Sharing**. Tick the box next to **Share my media**. If your Xbox 360 is switched on and connected to the network, it should appear as an available device. By default, Media Player shares all your media but, if you wish, you can use the Customize screen to limit the list to specific kinds of file; files with certain star ratings or files with particular parental ratings.

That's Windows 7 ready to share, so it's time to configure your Xbox 360. Choose the **Media blade** and then select **Music, Picture or Photos**. Choose **Computer**, then **Continue**, and your PC should appear in the list. Select it and you can now browse your computer's music, video and photo libraries. ⊞

NETWORK IT Sharing media with networked devices is easy with Windows Media Player 12

Playback, playlists and CD burning
Create customized lists of your favorite tracks then burn to CD

1 EASY DJ The links at the side enable you to sort your library by album, artist, etc; the Layout option (next to Search) enables you to change the way your tracks are displayed.

2 CHOOSE THE TUNES Organize your music by creating playlists. You can put together a list of your favorite songs without having to hear the tracks you don't like. Click **Create Playlist** to start.

3 ADD TRACKS You'll see a panel that asks you to drag and drop tracks over it. Browse your music collection and when you find a song you want to add, drag it over the right-hand panel.

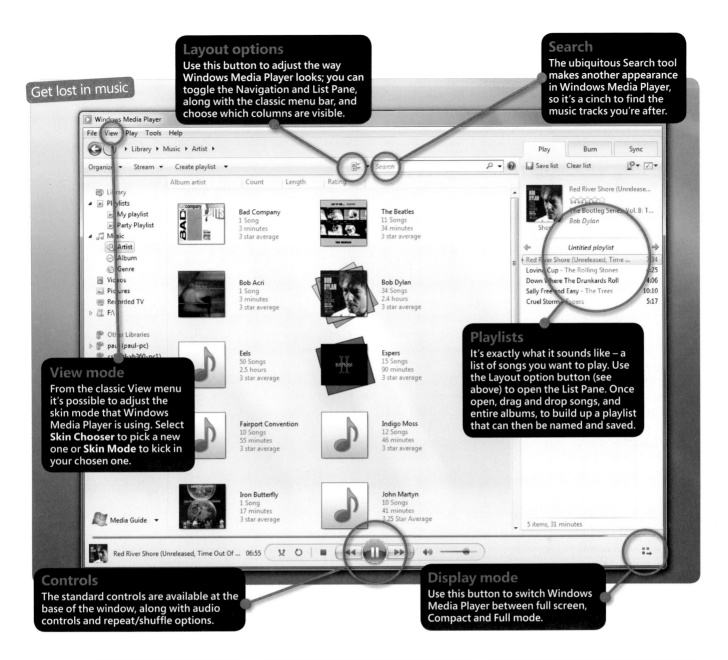

Layout options
Use this button to adjust the way Windows Media Player looks; you can toggle the Navigation and List Pane, along with the classic menu bar, and choose which columns are visible.

Search
The ubiquitous Search tool makes another appearance in Windows Media Player, so it's a cinch to find the music tracks you're after.

View mode
From the classic View menu it's possible to adjust the skin mode that Windows Media Player is using. Select **Skin Chooser** to pick a new one or **Skin Mode** to kick in your chosen one.

Playlists
It's exactly what it sounds like – a list of songs you want to play. Use the Layout option button (see above) to open the List Pane. Once open, drag and drop songs, and entire albums, to build up a playlist that can then be named and saved.

Controls
The standard controls are available at the base of the window, along with audio controls and repeat/shuffle options.

Display mode
Use this button to switch Windows Media Player between full screen, Compact and Full mode.

4 NEW VIEW Your new playlist will appear in the panel on the right, but you can change the view by clicking on the blue arrow. This will display your playlist in the main List view.

5 SEE THE SOUNDS The same arrow provides access to Windows Media Player's visualizations, which replace the display with swoopy visuals. It's particularly good in full screen mode.

6 DO DVD TOO Windows Media Player is as good with DVDs as it is with CDs. When you first go to play a DVD, you'll be asked whether to use Windows Media Player or another program.

Create playlists of your favorite tunes

Don't spend hours going through your music collection to organize an ensemble of your favorite tracks – let your PC do the hard work

Ever had one of those days when you just stare at all the music on your hard drive, uninspired by any of the albums and find it a struggle to choose something to listen to? Then the Automatic Playlist in Windows Media Player is what you need. It's a tool that takes the effort out of the selection process by creating playlists that it thinks you will like.

No, it can't magically read your thoughts and choose something depending on your mood, but what it will do is look at all the music tracks on your computer and suggest a type of playlist according to your collection. For instance, if you've got some rock music on there, it will create a playlist

with a selection of some of the rock songs in your various rock albums; or if you like a particular singer, songwriter or band, Windows Media Player will create a playlist of songs by a similar genre or artist.

To do this, open Windows Media Player, then click **Create Playlist → Create auto playlist**. To help Windows Media Player create an automatic playlist to suit your tastes, you need to add certain criteria that the music needs to match. Hit **Click here to add criteria** and you'll be presented with a drop-down list. For example, you could make Windows Media Player only include music that you have rated with four stars or more – ensuring that only your favorite tracks are added. If you're

planning an 80s themed party, set the criteria for tracks that were released in that decade.

You can also apply restrictions to the playlist, such as total running length or the amount of songs included in the playlist. Once you have set the appropriate criteria, enter a name in the Auto Playlist name text box and then click **OK**. The auto playlist will appear with the rest of your playlists in the menu on the left-hand side of the screen. You can change the criteria of any open auto playlist by clicking **Edit**. The three steps below reiterate this easy process, but if you're thinking that you'd like to share your 'mix' over the internet, check out the tutorial on the opposite page to find out how.

Create a killer playlist in minutes
Let Windows Media Player pick and choose tracks for you

1 GET STARTED Open Windows Media Player. Click **Create playlist → Create auto playlist**. A window will pop up that lets you enter the criteria of the songs you want to be included in the playlist.

2 PICK & CHOOSE Select **Click here to add criteria** to display a drop-down list. You can select by genre, band, date – even what time you usually play the track! Click **More...** for further options.

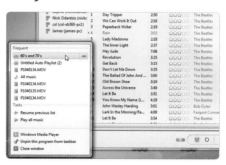

3 SAVE & PLAY Click **OK**. The playlist will now be created and added to Windows Media Player. You can access it by right-clicking the Windows Media Player icon on the taskbar.

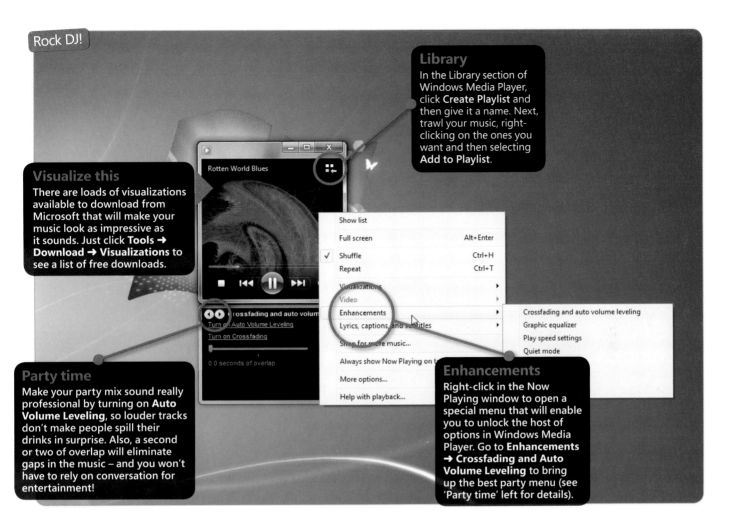

Library

In the Library section of Windows Media Player, click **Create Playlist** and then give it a name. Next, trawl your music, right-clicking on the ones you want and then selecting **Add to Playlist**.

Visualize this

There are loads of visualizations available to download from Microsoft that will make your music look as impressive as it sounds. Just click **Tools → Download → Visualizations** to see a list of free downloads.

Party time

Make your party mix sound really professional by turning on **Auto Volume Leveling**, so louder tracks don't make people spill their drinks in surprise. Also, a second or two of overlap will eliminate gaps in the music – and you won't have to rely on conversation for entertainment!

Enhancements

Right-click in the Now Playing window to open a special menu that will enable you to unlock the host of options in Windows Media Player. Go to **Enhancements → Crossfading and Auto Volume Leveling** to bring up the best party menu (see 'Party time' left for details).

Stream your music over the internet

Go public with your playlist...

1 STREAM You can share your music with other devices in the house. Or stream a playlist to a computer outside of your house over the internet, turning your PC into an internet radio station!

2 ACCESS Click **Stream → Allow Internet access to home media...** You can limit who has access to your media by linking an online ID (get a free Windows Live ID at https://login.live.com/).

3 ALLOW Click **Allow Internet access to home media**. On the PC you want to stream media to, go through the same process. Link the same online ID to both PCs to share files over the internet.

Your music, how you want it

If your radio listening is spoiled by tracks you don't like, put together a tailor-made selection of your favorites

Tired of radio DJs and their dodgy playlists? Well, you could create your own... You've probably got enough CDs to provide a range of music. If you haven't already copied your CDs to your hard drive, simply open Windows Media Player, put a CD in the drive, and it will copy your tracks over automatically.

Left to its own devices, Media Player will copy files using Microsoft's WMA file format. It's good for preserving audio quality, but there are a few players that

don't support it. For something that's sure to work on every player, click the **Rip settings** button and choose **Format ➜ MP3**. In the same menu, choose **Audio quality ➜ 192Kbps** to raise the sound quality (note that this also increases the file size).

Next, plug in your player. Click through the set-up questions (closing the **Autoplay** menu, if it appears) and the player will show up in your library – drag songs here to create your line-up. Pick tracks by flipping through the options in the left-hand menu or using

the search box. You can knock up a Greatest Hits list by clicking under Library and choosing **Create Auto Playlist**. Choose the top **Click here** link and pick a **Play Count** entry to harvest the tunes you listen to the most. Check out the previous pages for more on this.

The **My Rating** entry is a bit smarter – sorting by the star rating attached to each tune – but you've either got to set these yourself or use Media Player regularly so it can assign them automatically. Alternatively, click **Shuffle Music** for a random selection.

Make the most of your music

Creating your own selection from your favorite tracks

1 RIPPING GOOD FUN The first step is to get your music from shiny CD to capacious hard drive. Simply stick your favorite album in the drive and it will automatically begin copying the music to your My Music folder.

2 PLAYING FOR KEEPS Now create yourself a playlist with your favorite tracks on it. Just click **Create Playlist**, enter an appropriate name and your empty list will appear in the right-hand pane. Drag and drop songs, then click **Save Playlist**.

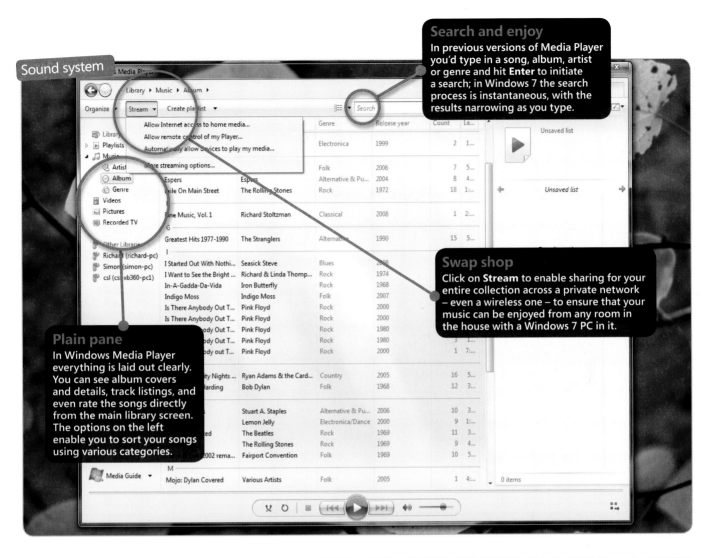

Search and enjoy
In previous versions of Media Player you'd type in a song, album, artist or genre and hit **Enter** to initiate a search; in Windows 7 the search process is instantaneous, with the results narrowing as you type.

Swap shop
Click on **Stream** to enable sharing for your entire collection across a private network – even a wireless one – to ensure that your music can be enjoyed from any room in the house with a Windows 7 PC in it.

Plain pane
In Windows Media Player everything is laid out clearly. You can see album covers and details, track listings, and even rate the songs directly from the main library screen. The options on the left enable you to sort your songs using various categories.

3 SYNCING FEELING Click the **Sync** tab and connect your MP3 player. Windows Media Player can sync with almost any USB storage device. You may get the option to name the device, then drag songs, albums or playlists over and hit **Start sync**.

4 MISSING HITS Still pining for that vital track that would complete your collection? You can buy it within the player. Click under the **Media Guide** button to choose an online music store, and have your credit card handy for registration.

Ripping yarns

Use Windows Media Player to get fast and flexible digital media playback with access to fantastic organization features

By default, Windows Media Player will turn your CDs into digital files using the Microsoft Windows Media format. This offers better compression (smaller file size) than MP3 – important if you've got a player with limited capacity or if your hard drive is filling up. However, this format isn't supported by all players, so while they work fine on PCs you can't play the files on all devices. Unless you're certain you'll never want to use anything other than Windows Media-compatible hardware and software, you might want to consider ripping your CDs in a different format. Windows Media is a perfectly good format, but MP3 is more widely supported, and you can easily change Media Player's settings to rip tracks in MP3 format.

Faster, quicker and better sounding
It's hip to rip, and Windows Media Player makes it easy too

1 GET READY Put the disc into the drive. Windows 7 may ask what program you want to use. If it does, you should select the **Play Audio CD using Windows Media Player** option.

2 DOWNLOAD DJ Windows Media Player will go online, download the track listings and artwork and rip your CD. The time it takes depends on your drive, but should only be a few minutes.

3 FIX THE FORMAT To ensure that Windows Media Player uses the correct format, click **Rip settings**, then **Format**. Click on **MP3** as this file format is compatible with most players.

4 CHANGE THE RATE Music quality is measured in 'bit rates'. With MP3s, Windows Media Player defaults to a bit rate of 128Kbps, which delivers small files but doesn't sound great. Click **Rip CD**.

5 NO PROTECTION Do you want to add copy protection to your songs; if so, you might not be able to transfer them to a portable player or your next PC? Probably not... So click **No**.

6 FIX THE LIST Your ripped CD is automatically added to your library. You can edit the artist information; select the song and click on the artist name, then type the information in.

Using Windows DVD Maker

Now you can create professional-looking video DVDs of your home movies and photos

 Creating your own playable DVD has never been easier. Using Windows Live Movie Maker Beta, you can send your footage to Windows DVD Maker; by clicking on **Output ➜ Windows Media DVD quality**, you can import it into the DVD Maker.

Obviously, you can send stills to watch as slide shows or recorded video.

You can use it as a stand-alone program too, by simply clicking on **Start ➜ All Programs ➜ Windows DVD Maker** and importing your videos manually. For the purposes of this tutorial, though, the export is done from Movie Maker. ⊞

In real life...
Pop in a slide show

**Neil Mohr,
Contributor**
*Windows: The
Official Magazine*

When you talk about Windows DVD Maker, the first thing that springs to mind is making movies, but this isn't its only ability. Equally as useful – and perhaps more practical – is the Slide Show feature. Using this, you can create photo slide shows – perfect for giving to family and friends. Instead of having to ask people to log on to online albums, they can just pop the DVD into a player and enjoy the show.

1 PUBLISH Choose **Output ➜ Windows Media DVD quality** when saving and you can import your movie to Windows DVD Maker. Save the file in an easy to find location.

2 CONTROL Open Windows DVD Maker and click **Add items**. Select your movie and then select **Add** and then **Next**. An icon displays how much space is left on the DVD.

3 MENU Windows DVD Maker enables you to add a commercial-looking menu – the main window shows what it will look like. (It's not required, but the example here shows what can be done.)

4 MENU OPTIONS Choose a menu design from the thumbnails in the right-hand panel. The main window updates automatically, so you can see exactly how your DVD menu will look.

5 SEE IT PROPERLY Click **Preview** to get a better idea of how your DVD menu will look. In this example, the footage is playing in the middle of the menu. Click **OK** to return to the editing options.

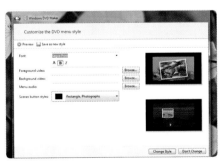

6 MENU MAKER Click on **Customize Menu** to import video or audio to personalize the menu or change button styles. Once you're happy, click **Change Style ➜ Burn** to copy to a blank DVD.

Create the perfect home movie show

Home movies can take your friends on a tour of the world, or send them straight to sleep. Make movies they'll actually want to see

Bad home movies? Shudder! They can be longer than many prison sentences, and home to multimedia's worst excesses. However, with Windows 7 you have no excuse for such nonsense. None. Go to war on bad home movies – right now!

With Windows Live Movie Maker, you immediately avoid the biggest pitfall... As it's a simple editor it focuses on the basic but fundamental things. You're not inundated with hundreds of transitions, effects and other flashy tools and, what's more, you're better off without them.

Editing in action

Let's think about a typical family vacation video. Don't worry about the PC yet – that's the easy part. Raw footage is where every project starts. The cardinal rule is: shoot everything you can, then throw out almost as much. A ruthless editor is a good editor.

Exactly what to keep will depend on your subject matter and intended audience, but you'll never go wrong by treating it as a professional project, rather than giving it a half-hearted approach. One thing to do whenever you start a new project is sit down and list anything that annoys you in other home movies you've seen and then avoid doing them, no matter what.

As an example, think of a classic roller coaster shot. The number one 'gotcha' for this type of movie is the first-person shaky-cam as someone desperately tries to keep the camcorder clamped to the side of their face. This never works. Ignoring the blurring of the world, and the nausea-enducing bounce of the camera on every twist and turn, the fact is you'll never be able to emulate the experience of being on that ride. So what do you do? Well, you do film it, but... the problem isn't the footage, it's the execution. You need to set the scene, then the action, then get the shears out at the editing stage.

First of all, the establishing shot. That should be easy enough – especially if the family is there, waving and looking nervously at the ride. Next, cut – a simple cut, nothing fancy – to the first-person camera, as a roller coaster car pulls out of the station. ➡

Welcome to the show

Add detail and a slick intro to your movie...

1 EFFECT/TRANSITION Effects work on individual clips, making them sepia-toned, blurred, or whatever you choose. Transitions link two clips – tearing, shattering and pushing the screen.

2 STAY CONTROLLED Do not overuse the transitions. One or two can add pace and look good, but any more and your film will be confusing, irritating or, worst of all, downright tacky.

3 WATCH THE SPEED Go to **Edit ➡ Trim** to switch editing modes, and drag the transition from the library. The maximum duration of the transition is the length of the second clip.

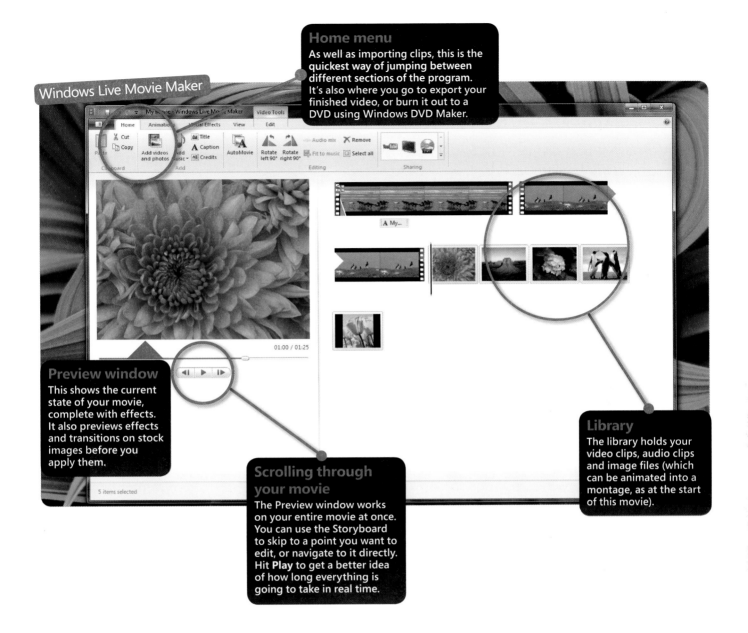

Windows Live Movie Maker

Home menu
As well as importing clips, this is the quickest way of jumping between different sections of the program. It's also where you go to export your finished video, or burn it out to a DVD using Windows DVD Maker.

Preview window
This shows the current state of your movie, complete with effects. It also previews effects and transitions on stock images before you apply them.

Scrolling through your movie
The Preview window works on your entire movie at once. You can use the Storyboard to skip to a point you want to edit, or navigate to it directly. Hit **Play** to get a better idea of how long everything is going to take in real time.

Library
The library holds your video clips, audio clips and image files (which can be animated into a montage, as at the start of this movie).

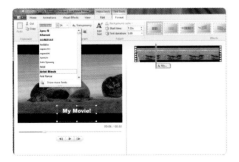

4 TITLES These are handled separately, with presets available for one-line titles, two-line titles, and a longer list of credits. You can choose the font and color of the wording here.

5 TITLE ROLE There are two title types; those that run before/after the movie, and text overlays. The former are like movie clips, and you can change how they appear on screen.

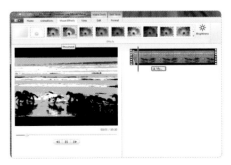

6 MIX AND MATCH Effects aren't locked to a clip, so you can stretch them out to caption a longer sequence. Any animation will only play at the start and end, rescaling as you move the clip.

Obviously, don't stick with this for too long; cut to another external shot of the roller coaster pulling away towards the big loop. When the roller coaster plummets, cut to your go on the ride. Take a first-person camera shot, showing a family member's screams, then cut back to the external. If you've got a good bit of first-person camera footage of a drop, or a turn, or a particular bit of dramatic scenery, slip it in.

Finally, cut to the family waddling uncertainly out of the gates, and get some close-up shots of reactions – cries of "Again!" or "Never again!"

Now it's a simple editing job. One transition (Cut) and one editing tool (Trim). However, when you play the video, nobody will care about the technology behind it, just the result. And believe it or not, that's the big secret of editing. Simplicity always wins out over glitz, and less really is more.

Of course, there is scope to play around with the more complicated effects as well. If you're building a montage of photos, picking a transition to go between them can look good. Even then, though, the keep-it-simple mantra applies. A page-curl may look good, but a page-curl followed by a bar-wipe followed by a dissolve followed by a shatter is overkill.

Try to stick to one effect, one editing style and one (rough) length for each segment, and the whole thing will flow. It may seem like a lot of effort for a family video, but you'll end up with movie memories you really want to watch!

Quickfire questions

Q What can I do to get better quality raw footage?

A Getting a good camera is the obvious answer, but you can improve your movies a hundred times over with a few quick tips. For the best shots, you'll need a tripod to keep the unit steady – even the steadiest hand can only hold so still. When filming, avoid the temptation to constantly zoom in and out, and keep your movements as fluid as possible to avoid giving the audience a feeling of nausea. Give your camera time to focus properly before taking footage that you plan to use. And, of course, always film far more than you need to give yourself some breathing room at the editing stage.

Q Why do I sometimes get poor-looking colors?

A When you turn the camera on, make sure the white balance function is working. Put a piece of white paper in the middle of a shot and use it to color-balance the camera. Forgetting to do this will leave your footage looking off-color, and could potentially ruin your masterpiece.

In real life...
Movie Maker

Nick Odantzis, Section editor, *Windows: The Official Magazine*

Being relatively new to the video-editing world, I was a bit hesitant about how easy I was going to find using Windows Live Movie Maker but, as it turns out, I shouldn't have been. Windows Live Movie Maker supported my old Firewire-based DV camcorder, importing the video without a problem. If anything, the limited number of options makes it easy to navigate round the interface. The timeline option is very powerful, giving precise control over the footage you've imported. After that, adding a soundtrack and creating a final DVD is simplicity itself!

Editing basic footage

Simple steps to make the most of your clips

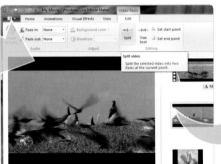

1 IMPORTING CLIPS You'll need your footage in digital format – either direct from your camera, or as a file on your hard drive. Windows Live Movie Maker supports most formats, including WMV and MPEG, but not QuickTime.

2 SPLIT UP Cut longer clips into pieces so you can use them across your project. Click the video in the main Edit pane and play it in the viewer until you get to the break point. Click **Edit → Split** to carve it into two pieces, ready to place.

3 ANIMATIONS Brighten up your video clips with animations, such as transitions, and Pan and Zoom features. If you're not sure how the effect will look, just hover your mouse over the options to preview them.

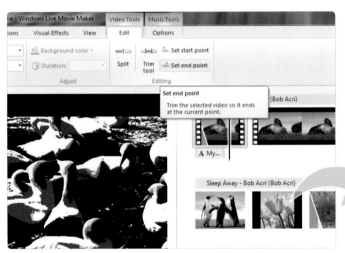

Longer movie clips will need to be cut into smaller pieces so that you can use them throughout your project

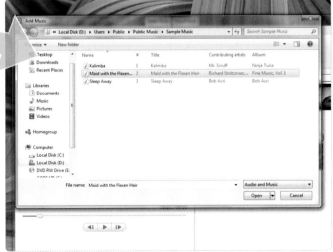

4 TRIMMING Select a clip and it will show in the Preview window. Drag the scroller to the point that you want it to start on and select **Set start point** from the Edit menu. Repeat with **Set end point**. If you don't think you've trimmed the clip exactly as you want it, simply click **Undo** and start over.

Direct and document

As it's part of the Windows Live family, you can use the same tagging and rating systems for your movies as you do with your pics in Windows Live Photo Gallery, so that your favorite clips can be found easily.

5 ADD SOUNDTRACK Adding a soundtrack is as easy as clicking **Add music**. Select your track (either an MP3 or WMA file), and it will appear in the Windows Live Movie Maker library, then just drag and drop it into your movie. You can alter the length of the soundtrack to fit the footage.

Windows Media Center

As we're putting all of our digital media on to our computers these days, it makes sense to enjoy it on them as well

Windows Media Center has been around for a while, but only for a select few; Windows XP Media Center Edition was only available to PC manufacturers, and if you wanted to get your hands on it you'd have to buy a fully-fledged Media Center PC.

Thankfully, with the Ultimate edition of Windows 7, you no longer need to shell out on shiny new hardware. That's good news – Windows Media Center is well worth having.

Big screen interface

With a typical PC, you're sat a few inches in front of the screen with a keyboard and a mouse in front of you. That's not much cop if you want to kick back and watch a DVD.

Windows Media Center gives you the best of both worlds – the power of your PC with the convenience of your TV. Instead of peering at tiny text, the

Windows Media Center interface is designed for distance, so you view it on your TV screen or on a big PC monitor. You don't need to mess around with a keyboard either – dedicated Media Center PCs come with a remote control, instead of the bog-standard PC keyboard and mouse controls.

In addition to the obvious stuff – playing your music and DVDs, showing off your photos and displaying your video clips – you can use the Windows Media Center as a digital TV recorder.

You'll find Media Center under **Start ➜ All Programs ➜ Windows Media Center**. You'll then be taken through the set-up screens; as you'll see over the next few pages, set-up is straightforward and doesn't take long, although you'll need to be connected to the internet throughout the process if you want to use some of the very desirable advanced features, such as the electronic program guide.

In real life...
Parental controls

**Adam Ifans,
Editor,
Windows: The
Official Magazine**

It's easy to lock Windows Media Center so the kids can't access inappropriate content: go to **Tasks ➜ Settings ➜ General ➜ Parental Controls** and choose a four-digit PIN code. You can now block unrated DVDs or set age limits by DVD ratings. And you can also use the Parental Controls to block access to Media Center altogether – see page 38. All of which means you'll be able to leave your children in peace using Windows Media Center without worrying about what they are watching.

Getting a perfect set-up

Follow the step by step guide and get all your media in one place

1 START SETUP Running Windows Media Center for the first time starts the set-up. Re-run it by launching Media Center, then **Tasks ➜ Settings ➜ General ➜ Windows Media Center Setup**.

2 CHANNEL PHWOAR Here, Media Center has detected 91 different channels, including digital radio stations. If you think you're in range of more, click **Scan again** to try to find them.

3 EASY INTERFACE Accessing each category is a matter of using the remote control or your computer's mouse and keyboard. Cycle through **Pictures**, **Music**, **TV** and **Tasks**.

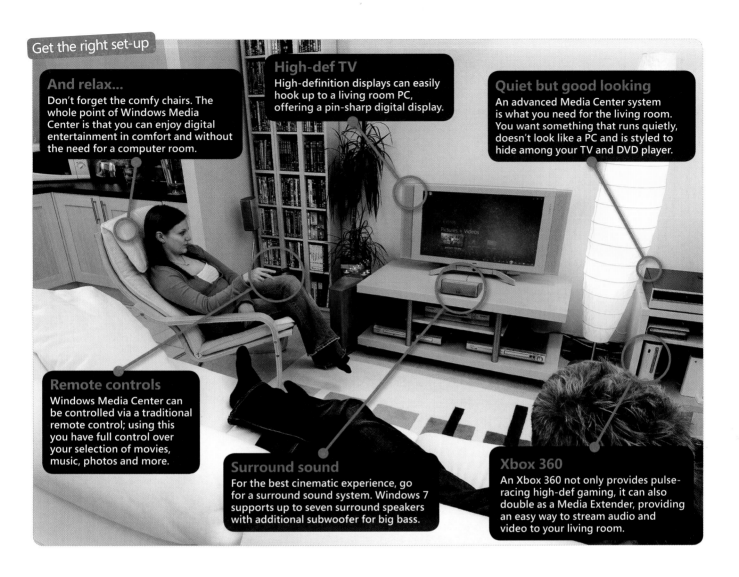

And relax...
Don't forget the comfy chairs. The whole point of Windows Media Center is that you can enjoy digital entertainment in comfort and without the need for a computer room.

High-def TV
High-definition displays can easily hook up to a living room PC, offering a pin-sharp digital display.

Quiet but good looking
An advanced Media Center system is what you need for the living room. You want something that runs quietly, doesn't look like a PC and is styled to hide among your TV and DVD player.

Remote controls
Windows Media Center can be controlled via a traditional remote control; using this you have full control over your selection of movies, music, photos and more.

Surround sound
For the best cinematic experience, go for a surround sound system. Windows 7 supports up to seven surround speakers with additional subwoofer for big bass.

Xbox 360
An Xbox 360 not only provides pulse-racing high-def gaming, it can also double as a Media Extender, providing an easy way to stream audio and video to your living room.

4 WHAT'S ON To view the guide, go to the menu and click on **TV+Movies → Guide**. You'll see listings for the available channels for the next two weeks; you can view a program by clicking on it.

5 PIC PERFECT This is the Picture Library (first option under **Pictures + Videos**). View pictures by folder, tags or date, or turn them into an on-screen slide show by clicking **Play Slide Show**.

6 MUSIC MAESTRO The music selection works in much the same way as the Picture Library; view tunes by album, artists, genres and so on. Clicking on an image opens the album.

Improving the Windows Media Center experience

By tweaking and adjusting Windows Media Center you can improve both image and audio quality

Any PC that's capable of running Windows 7 should happily run Windows Media Center, although if you're going to store a lot of music or record a lot of TV then a big hard disk is essential. Even a relatively modest music collection takes up more than 30GB of disk space, and a short TV show can be more than 100MB in size for a single episode; entire movies can vary from 700MB all the way to 4GB for full DVDs or high-definition films.

However, to get the best from Windows Media Center you'll also need a tuner card so your PC can tune in to TV broadcasts. These come in a range

of flavours – PCI or USB, single tuner or twin tuner. So what should you choose?

If you've got a standard desktop PC, a PCI card – which installs in a spare slot at the back of your PC – is a better bet than a USB one. That's because PCI cards transfer data roughly five times faster than even a USB 2.0 connection, so there's no risk of bottlenecks affecting your recordings and you won't lose a valuable USB socket either.

If you're going to be using your PC in your living room, a twin tuner card is a sensible investment. Twin tuners enable you to watch one program while recording another. On starting Windows Media Center for the first time,

Super Tip!

HD support

Windows 7 supports the latest HD optical drives by adding new icons and labels that identify HD DVD and Blu-ray drives and discs.

you can choose a custom set-up to go through all your settings. If you cancel this but need to find it later, go to **Settings ➜ General ➜ Windows Media Center Set Up ➜ Run Setup Again.** 🐱

Getting the best possible results

Fine-tune your Media Center set-up for viewing perfection

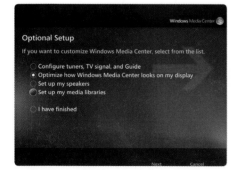

1 SET UP From the Windows Media Center setup screen, choose **Custom setup** to customize your display, sound and files. If it isn't showing, go to **Settings ➜ General ➜ Windows Media Center Set Up ➜ Run Setup Again.**

2 TV TUNER If you've set up your TV tuner, the first option will be grayed out; if not, follow the instructions at http://snipurl.com/rynp8. To set up your TV/monitor/screen, go to **Display Configuration** and follow the steps.

3 PIN-SHARP WIZARD Make sure your computer is connected to the display you'll be using – there's no point configuring the display so it looks good on your PC's screen if you'll actually be watching on a 50-inch plasma display.

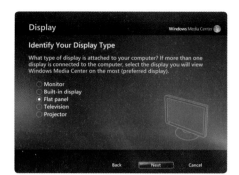

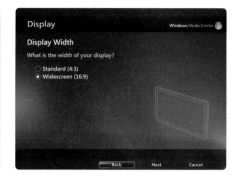

4 **SELECT YOUR SCREEN** Windows Media Center uses different settings for different displays – what looks great on a computer screen may look less impressive on a digital projector. Click on the type of display and then on **Next**.

5 **CHOOSE CABLE** Next, you need to tell Windows Media Center what kind of display to computer connection you're using. For example, if you have a standard computer monitor (or a high-def TV), it'll be DVI, VGA or HDMI.

6 **BORN TO BE WIDE** Now, do you have a standard screen (traditional 4:3 ratio, which most TV shows were made in until recently) or a widescreen (16:9 ratio, like a cinema screen)? Choose the appropriate option and click **Next**.

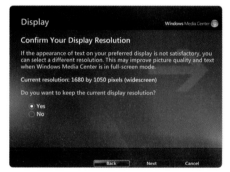

7 **WHERE IT'S AT** Windows Media Center will give you the option to keep the current display resolution or change it. Run Windows Media Center in full screen view – if you run it in a window the text may be less clear.

8 **MR SPEAKER** Back at the menu, Media Center's ready to configure the speakers. Whether listening to music or enjoying TV and movies, setting up the digital audio output properly will make a difference. Click **Next**.

9 **SOUND CHECK** To get the best set-up, tell Windows Media Center how you connect your speakers, so it can optimize the sound. Look at the back of your PC to check whether you're using audio jack or the more modern HDMI.

10 **MAGIC NUMBERS** Before adjusting audio settings, Media Center needs to know the number of speakers. If you've got a 2.1 system – that is, two speakers with a subwoofer – go for the '2 speakers' option.

11 **EAR WE GO** Media Center will now play a tone through each speaker in turn. If you don't hear the sound from each speaker, Media Center will help identify and fix the problem. If it's fine, just click on **Next**.

12 **ADD A FOLDER** Media Center looks in your Music, Pictures and Videos folders for your files. If you've stored your media files elsewhere, use the **Add Folder** option to make sure Media Center keeps an eye on it.

Get more from Windows Media Center

There's more to Windows Media Center than just watching movies and TV, check out how to find shows, enjoy slide shows and burn DVDs

It's all too easy to focus on the recorded playback side of Windows Media Center. While it's primarily thought of as a way to enjoy TV and movies there is far more to Media Center than this. Besides the newly-designed interface, its graphically-rich, remote-control driven interface enables you to navigate easily through media such as photos and movies, and it's easy to create slide shows, record entire seasons of programs and even browse the web.

One of the coolest features is that a PC with a TV tuner installed can function as a personal video recorder (PVR) to automatically record your favorite television shows. Not only does this enable you to pause and rewind live TV,

it also offers built-in support for archiving TV shows directly to DVDs.

Many of the previous technical hurdles associated with media use have been removed in Windows 7. For example, everything required to play and burn DVDs is now included as standard, removing compatibility problems of the past. Provided the minimum system requirements are met, Windows Media Center can really enhance your PC use.

Extra abilities

When you're not watching movies, Media Center can act as a perfect music station and, with its funky visualizations, it's great for providing a bit of background entertainment during parties, while the remote offers simple

mouse-free control. The same goes for the slide show feature, – this is great for showing off family pictures when the relatives come round.

The fact that Windows Media Center can be enhanced with plug-ins shouldn't be overlooked, adding all manner of features to your media enjoyment.

You can either operate your standard PC as your home media system, or you can connect it to a TV or projector for a more dedicated entertainment set-up. Alternatively, you can leave the PC in your study and use a Media Extender – such as the Microsoft Xbox 360; with this kind of device, it's possible to extend the experience – and interface – from the PC to the TV using a home network. See page 93 for details.

Finding your favorite programs

How to record shows currently on TV – and those yet to be shown

1 ADD RECORDING There isn't an option to create a new recording within **TV + Movies** of the main menu; this facility is contained as a sub-item called **Add Recording**, in **Recorded TV**.

2 SELECT SHOW Windows Media Center gives you options when searching; selecting **Search** will prompt you to enter a title or keyword to create a one-time or series recording.

3 PICK TIMES From the matches, look up the screen times. After selecting the one to record, you will be given information to help decide whether to record the show or the series.

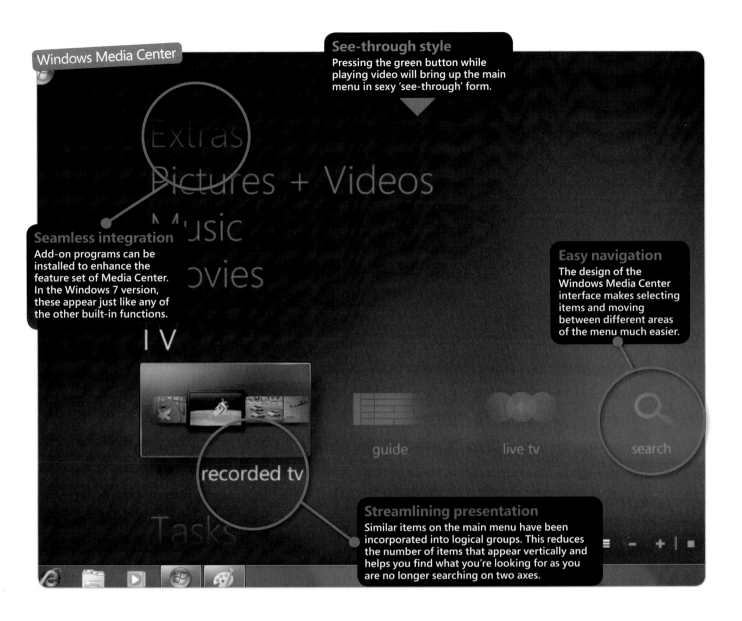

Windows Media Center

See-through style
Pressing the green button while playing video will bring up the main menu in sexy 'see-through' form.

Seamless integration
Add-on programs can be installed to enhance the feature set of Media Center. In the Windows 7 version, these appear just like any of the other built-in functions.

Easy navigation
The design of the Windows Media Center interface makes selecting items and moving between different areas of the menu much easier.

guide   live tv   search

recorded tv

Streamlining presentation
Similar items on the main menu have been incorporated into logical groups. This reduces the number of items that appear vertically and helps you find what you're looking for as you are no longer searching on two axes.

4 SEARCH GUIDE A useful feature under Search is Categories. This can act as your personalized TV guide; use this facility to get a list of all the films to be screened in a two-week period.

5 RECORDING OPTIONS On the programme screen, you get a brief synopsis, details about the screening (channel, time, etc) and the option to record one episode or the entire series.

6 YOUR OWN TIME Your program will appear in the View Scheduled List under Recorded TV; watch it when you want and, if you have a Media Center Extender, where you want.

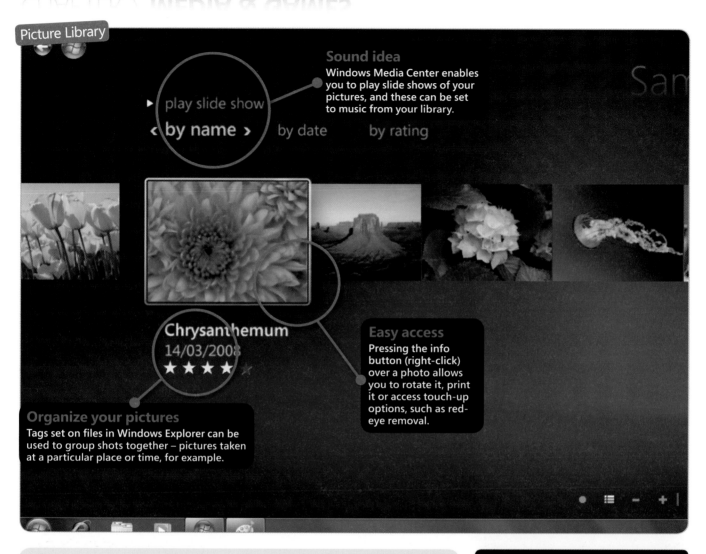

Picture Library

Sound idea
Windows Media Center enables you to play slide shows of your pictures, and these can be set to music from your library.

▶ play slide show
‹ **by name** ›   by date   by rating

Chrysanthemum
14/03/2008
★★★★

Easy access
Pressing the info button (right-click) over a photo allows you to rotate it, print it or access touch-up options, such as red-eye removal.

Organize your pictures
Tags set on files in Windows Explorer can be used to group shots together – pictures taken at a particular place or time, for example.

Windows Media Center: TV basics

Tune in for the right signal

Windows Media Center supports a range of TV signals from analog and digital transmissions, to cable and satellite using a set-top box (STB). When setting up an STB, the PC sends infrared commands to change channel. In the US, you can buy TV tuners for digital cable without an STB. Elsewhere, support varies but, in most countries, two tuners can be used at once.

If you upgraded or purchased a Windows 7 machine without TV hardware, it is easy to add on. TV Cards marked with a 'Designed for Windows 7 Home Premium or Professional' sticker are suitable.

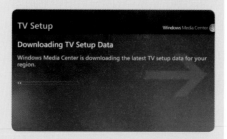

SIGNAL BOX Use this panel to tell Media Center how you receive your transmissions

UNIQUE WOW Create your own view in the new Windows Media Center music layout

Streaming from your PC to an Xbox 360

If you're lucky enough to own an Xbox 360, why not use Windows 7 to stream your movies to it?

 So then, Windows Media Center is pretty nifty, but what about accessing it from elsewhere in the house? Microsoft has devised a technology called Media Center Extender that enables you to stream media from your PC to any room in the house, and there's an extender inside every Xbox 360. Provided your Xbox and PC are networked, either using a wired or wireless network, you can use your Xbox to access your PC's music, photo and video library. And getting your Xbox to communicate with your Windows 7 PC couldn't be easier.

Super Tip!

Media Extender

With Windows 7 there is increased support for the latest types of Windows Media Center Extenders, such as new digital televisions and networked DVD players.

1 EXTEND IT To stream things from PC to Xbox 360 you'll need to configure the console's Media Center Extender. Launch Media Center, then select **Tasks → Settings**. Click on **Extender**.

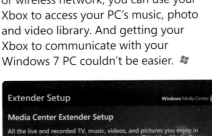

2 GET READY Before you start the set-up, switch on your Xbox 360. From the main Xbox dashboard, select the **Media** blade and then **Media Center**. Take note of the authorization code.

3 THE CODE Your Windows 7 PC will ask for a setup key, offered by your Xbox 360. Turn on the console, search for Windows PCs, and type in the code it gives you to make the connection.

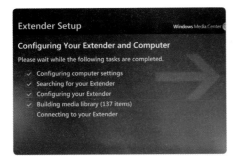

4 FINISH THE JOB Windows 7 will now configure for Xbox streaming by looking for your console, adjusting the appropriate settings and telling it where to find your music, movies and photos.

5 SEE IT You'll see a picture of an Xbox 360 in Media Center's Extenders menu. To add another, repeat the process by clicking **Add Extender**, or use the **Back** button to return to the main menu.

6 READY Your Xbox 360 will now browse the same menu system as your Windows PC. If you have installed add-ons for Windows Media Center, they will appear on the console version, too.

Play great games

DirectX is getting ever better, and if you thought PC games were eye-popping before, you ain't seen nothing yet

While there's not such a buzz surrounding the next version of DirectX – the wheels that turn the graphics in games – it's still going to be a significant leap over its previous version in Windows Vista. DirectX 11, as it's logically entitled, will make games more realistic and unlike DirectX 10 which was only available if you had Windows Vista, DirectX 11 will be available to those with Windows Vista and Windows 7.

DirectX 11 has many enhancements over its predecessor, including something the boffins call the Tesselator, a feature designed to make games look smoother and more organic, so the graphics look less blocky; some are even comparing the visuals to something you'd normally find in a movie.

DirectX 11 also been designed so that those with a multi-core processor inside their PC (such as a quad core or Core i7 processor) will get more performance.

DARK KNIGHT Batman may be in a dark, dingy warehouse, but look at the detail – ker-pow!

Of course, you'll only see the benefits of the new graphics if you've got a graphics card that can support DirectX 11.

DirectX 11 is the new kid on the block when it comes to the way games look, but what about improvements in the way we play games? Well, Microsoft has an answer, and hopefully we'll start

Get gaming in Windows 7

Windows 7 is all set for gaming – you just need to know where to look

1 USEFUL INFO In Games Explorer you'll see your system's performance rating, plus the game's recommended requirements. The **Tools** button provides access to your hardware and more.

2 ART WORKS When you install new games, Games Explorer will download the artwork and available ratings information. You can disable this by clicking **Options** in the toolbar.

3 GAME ON Good news – Solitaire's still here! You also get a bevy of other games with Windows 7, including the kids' favorite Purble Place – incomprehensible to any post teen.

seeing these enhancements sooner rather than later...

The first of these is the Microsoft Touch Pack – a series of multi-touch enabled games that take advantage of the built-in touchscreen abilities of Windows 7. You can play games using just your hands, so you can throw away your conventional games peripherals altogether, in theory. To start with Microsoft will include Microsoft Blackboard, Microsoft Garden Pond and Microsoft Rebound. So if you've got a touchscreen PC running Windows 7, you can play these three games, and – hopefully, in future – a lot more.

There's something even bigger looming over the horizon... many are hoping that Microsoft's Project Natal is going to be the next big thing in computer gaming interaction. Project Natal is a device that captures motion, allowing you to play games using body motion, rather than having to use a clumsy game controller. Unlike the Nintendo Wii, where a person's movement is detected using a hand-held device, Project Natal uses a motion sensor that sits above or below your TV, and the sensor then detects the movement of your body and translates into it gameplay action.

It doesn't track just one body either; Skeletal Mapping allows Project Natal to simultaneously track up to four people and it can even detect movement from individual fingers. This isn't all though – Project Natal can recognize you just by scanning your face, and the 'Multi-Array microphone' can not only understand what you're saying, but even sense when the emotion in your voice changes.

The Multi-Array microphone is able to locate different voices and cut down on any unwanted background noise, so you can talk to people online without having to use a headset. This means that Project Natal is truly peripheral-free.

There are a couple of videos on the website (http://www.xbox.com/en-US/live/projectnatal/) that demonstrate the potential of Project Natal. The first of these is the Ricochet demo, which shows how quickly Project Natal's sensor reacts to a person's movement.

Then there's the Lionhead demo, where a woman converses with a character on screen. The level of interaction is incredible, culminating in a scene at the end of the video where the person playing can even see themselves reflected in a pool of water.

These features are the biggies that will probably excite game players the most, but Microsoft hasn't neglected the details. The Games Explorer has been given a minor makeover, so games are split into those that are built-in and those you install yourself. Game updates will also be available through the Games Explorer window, making it easier to get the latest patches as they're released. ⊞

The future of PC gaming

Coming soon to a touchscreen near you

Touchscreen games
Games will also be able to take advantage of multi-touch, and Microsoft has already been showing off its potential with the release of the Microsoft Touch Pack, which includes three multi-touch enabled games. Then there's Microsoft's motion-sensing Project Natal, where games can be fully-controlled by using body movements.

Microsoft Rebound
It might look a bit like the original Speedball from the late 90s, but Microsoft Rebound is looking like it's going to be a hit in the 21st Century. The aim of the game is to fire your ball and destroy the opposing player; whether that's a human opponent or the computer itself. You can modify the playing fields to keep the game fresh.

Microsoft Garden Pond
OK, so it doesn't exactly sound like the most exciting game ever, but don't judge a book by appearances alone. Microsoft Garden Pond is designed for those looking for a more calming experience when they play, by making ripples in the water with swipes of your fingers in order to move origami pieces from one area of a pond to the other.

Microsoft Blackboard
Just like being back at school, without the sound of screeching nails, Microsoft Blackboard is a game of physics, where you have to create a machine on your virtual blackboard. The aim of the game is to move the balloons and balls to the finish line by rotating gears, moving seesaws and other bits of machinery.

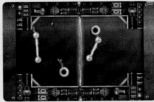

Check it

Test your PC's performance

1 THE SCORE Open the Control Panel from the Start menu; click **System and Maintenance**, then **Performance Information**. The highest score is 7.9.

2 IN DETAIL Click on the **Windows Experience Index** link; you'll see the score is set by the weakest link. So, if your memory only scores 2, that's what your overall score will be.

3 CHECK AGAIN If you want to recheck your score, close all other running programs; click **Re-run the assessment**. Windows 7 will run a series of checks and report the result.

Get ready to play

It's easy to get your games running smoothly

Some PCs don't have the ability to run the incredible light shows of DirectX capable games. But, for the first time, there is an easy way to see through the boggle of acronyms, numbers and specifications listed on the back of the game box. Built into Windows 7 is the Windows Experience Index; this scores your PC according to its capabilities, with fast, game-ready PCs scoring highly. Follow the steps (left) to check your PC's score.

Now, on games that are certified for Windows 7, you will see this number printed on the game box, so you can see at a glance if your PC will run it. Broadly speaking, if your PC scores over 4, it should run all currently available games OK. If the computer scores between 2 and 4, however, it will have trouble playing new releases; if it scores below 2, it may not run games at all.

All is not lost, however. Most new games automatically adjust themselves so they are less demanding on weaker PCs, and you can make further adjustments yourself. Just go into the graphics settings for each game and reduce the resolution and advanced lighting effects like anti-aliasing and shadows.

GAME SET You can go high for tasty graphics, or lower the settings for faster running games

STAY FRESH Run Windows Update regularly; new drivers can make a big difference

Get an easy upgrade

Boost your gaming performance in just a few minutes

Improving your PC's score can be easy. Memory can be upgraded in only a few minutes – find out what you need and how to fit it at a dedicated PC memory website. Gaming graphics are a little trickier, but not much; you can find a guide at the *Windows: The Official Magazine* website – www. officialwindowsmagazine.com/ graphics. If all your scores are low, it may be worth buying a new PC.

Some manufacturers specialize in cutting-edge gaming PCs, so think about the main use for your PC when making your purchase.

Fill a slot to make your PC hot
How to fit a graphics card in five easy steps

1 **OPEN UP** Obviously, for safety's sake, and to avoid damage, turn off the computer and unplug it from the mains before you remove the case door. You should also be aware this could invalidate any warranty, so proceed at your own risk.

2 **TAKE IT OUT** It's also advisable to take anti-static precautions – an anti-static wrist strap offers the best protection. Unclip the old graphics card from its slot – it's usually held in place by a screw but in newer PC cases, like this one, it's held by quick-release clips.

3 **SLOT IN PLACE** Fit the new graphics card by pushing it firmly into the now vacant slot and securing it in position. This can be a little tricky as you need to make sure the backplate is lined correctly. If the card needs an additional power supply, plug it in.

4 **CLOSED CASE** Make sure you screw the graphics card securely in place. At this point, you should easily be able to fasten your computer's case door back in place. Attach the monitor lead to the graphics card – it may require an adaptor – and now reattach the mains lead and power it up again.

5 **INSTALL IT** Once Windows 7 loads, the new graphics card is detected and the appropriate drivers are automatically installed, so you're now ready to play. Graphics drivers are regularly updated for improved performance, so it's worth checking the manufacturer's website for any updates.

Set up your Windows Live Mail account today

It's time to get organized, and Windows 7 is just the operating system to help you do that along with Windows Live Mail

For years, every copy of Windows came with the email program Outlook Express. It wasn't a bad program when it first came out but, over time, it became a major headache as spammers, scammers, virus writers and other net nasties tried to con people out of cash and infect systems with all kinds of unpleasantness – which is why many abandoned Outlook Express altogether. Thankfully, with Windows 7, Microsoft has offered up the rather brilliant Windows Live Mail, which is useful, secure, highly customizable and really easy to use.

For most people, email has become a crucial day-to-day tool. Because of the significance email communication now

holds for all of us, Windows Live mail is very secure – protecting vital areas and keeping information safe.

Of course, these security improvements run alongside functional upgrades, too – there's now a greatly-improved search facility that fully integrates with Windows 7 itself making it easy to track down that vital email, no matter where you may be. The reliability of Windows Live Mail is a great asset; it is capable of handling vast amounts of stored emails without any problems, meaning even the most deluged of inboxes will stay responsive.

Over the next few pages, you'll see some of the fabulous features that Windows Live Mail offers – and how to get the most out of it.

In real life...
It's the little things

**Tamsin Oxford
Contributor,
Windows: The
Official Magazine**
Windows Live Mail integrates so neatly into Windows 7 that you'll never believe you downloaded it from the web. Use the Search function in Windows 7 to track down emails, so no matter where you are in Windows 7 you can see relevant emails when you're looking for certain terms. The look and feel is chic, simple and easy to navigate.

Adding an email account
The latest generation of email is easier than ever

1 DOWNLOAD Windows 7 does not come with Windows Live Mail included, so download it from http://download.live.com. Click on **Add email account** on the link in the left column.

2 SET IT UP You'll be asked for your email address, name and password. If you don't have an email account, click on **Get a free email account**, otherwise fill in the details and click **Next**.

3 PLANET POP Enter the details of your incoming email server (usually a POP server) and your outgoing one (usually SMTP). Your ISP should have given you the information you need for this bit.

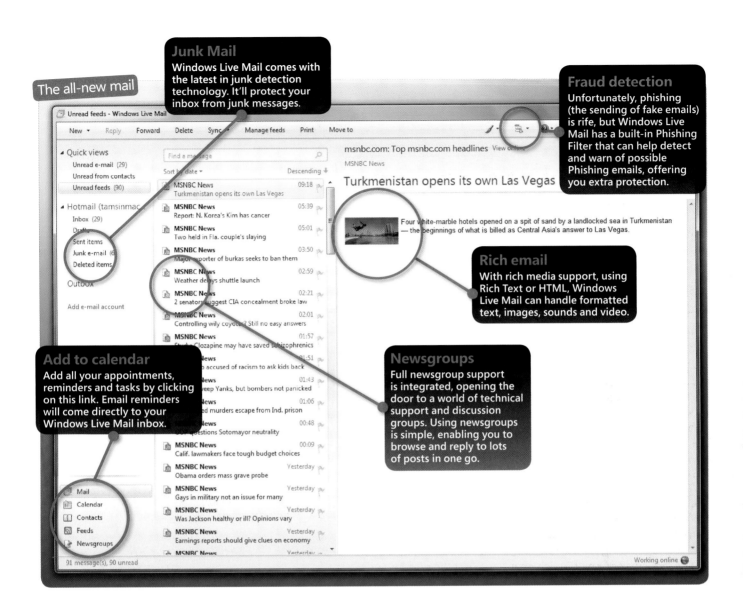

Junk Mail
Windows Live Mail comes with the latest in junk detection technology. It'll protect your inbox from junk messages.

Fraud detection
Unfortunately, phishing (the sending of fake emails) is rife, but Windows Live Mail has a built-in Phishing Filter that can help detect and warn of possible Phishing emails, offering you extra protection.

Rich email
With rich media support, using Rich Text or HTML, Windows Live Mail can handle formatted text, images, sounds and video.

Add to calendar
Add all your appointments, reminders and tasks by clicking on this link. Email reminders will come directly to your Windows Live Mail inbox.

Newsgroups
Full newsgroup support is integrated, opening the door to a world of technical support and discussion groups. Using newsgroups is simple, enabling you to browse and reply to lots of posts in one go.

4 SYNCHRONIZE Next, you'll get a bar asking you to download your mail. Select **Sync ➔ All email accounts** and Windows Live Mail will connect and download all of your latest mail.

5 TWEAK TIME You're up and running but you still need to manage your security settings to ensure that Windows Live Mail is set to your specifications. To do this, go to **Menus ➔ Safety options**.

6 ESSENTIAL INFO In Safety Options you can set the level of junk mail protection. It's recommended that you go with High; block suspicious senders, and adjust your Phishing settings.

Make sending emails a pleasure, not a chore

As good as Windows Live Mail is, you can make it even quicker and easier to use by changing its looks and its filters

Once you start using Windows Live Mail on a day-to-day basis, you may find you want to alter certain aspects to suit your needs. Fortunately, it's easy to customize.

Many changes are possible, ranging from simple things such as how emails are sorted to more radical elements, such as changing the layout of the entire application. You can also configure the Windows Live Mail interface to make it look how you want it to look.

You might not think it, but something as simple as choosing the order in which columns are displayed can make all the difference to usability. Removing some

columns or making others smaller can really help if you're having to work on a space-constricted display, such as a laptop computer.

Follow the rules

You can even tailor the filtering rules that enable you to alter how Windows Live Mail processes emails as they arrive. These rules make it easy to automatically file emails as they appear or, if you're working on a special project, to create rules to automatically look at each email based on subject or mailing list and move them to a corresponding folder.

The Windows Live Mail Message Rules is a powerful system that makes dealing

with large amounts of email far easier. It's a similar feature to that found in the full-blown Microsoft Outlook application, which goes to show how flexible it is. You're able to set rules that determine how Windows Live Mail processes emails based on content, recipient, sender and subject – either exactly or just by matching a single keyword. Then, depending whether it's a match, the rule can send the email to a specified folder (including the trash), forward it or send it on in another form. It all adds up to a faster, more user-friendly experience. The easiest way to learn about Message Rules is to create one, so follow the walkthrough… ⊞

Changing the email sort options

Filter your messages on receipt to stay on top of your mail

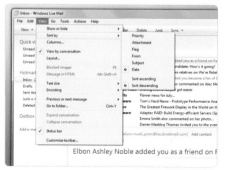

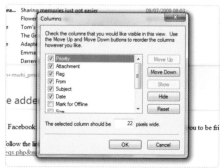

1 CHANGE THE VIEW If you don't like the default layout in Windows Mail, change it by clicking **View ➜ Layout**. You can hide elements such as the folder list or search bar, or change the location of the Message Preview pane.

2 SENSIBLE SORTING The **View By Conversation** feature groups your emails in the more traditional email layout, whereas the **Sort** function gives you control over what priorities you want to allocate to your email layout.

3 CHOOSE THE COLUMNS You can adjust your columns by going to **View ➜ Columns.** By default, the list of messages shows you whether an item is flagged high priority, whether it's got an attachment, its subject line and more.

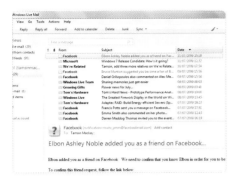

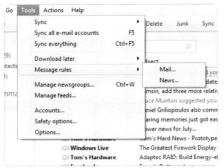

4 A CLEANER LOOK Here the layout is similar to the standard mail layout but with only a few allocated columns to make the look cleaner. You can adjust the width of the individual columns by dragging the gray lines in between.

5 THE RULES It's a big help if your email program can sort messages. The Rules feature enables you to create simple or sophisticated sorting options for incoming messages, and you'll find it under **Tools ➜ Message Rules ➜ Mail**.

6 NEW RULES To create a rule, click on the **New...** button. You can specify what Windows Live Mail should look for. For example, to filter mailing list messages by subject, tick the **Where the subject line contains specific words** box.

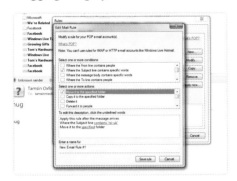

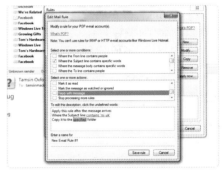

7 CHOOSE CRITERIA Specific Words is now a blue link. Click on it to choose the words Windows Live Mail should look for. The example here is looking for messages that have 'rsi-uk' in the subject line. Click **Add** and then **OK**.

8 PROCESS IT Choose what to do with your messages. If you want them filed in a specific folder, tick **Move it to the specified folder** in box 2. You'll see a link, saying **Specified**. Click on it to tell Windows Live Mail which folder to use.

9 FIND THE FOLDER To use a folder, click on the '+' sign next to Local Folders to expand the list, select the folder and click OK. If you want to create a new folder, make sure Local Folders is selected then click on **New Folder**.

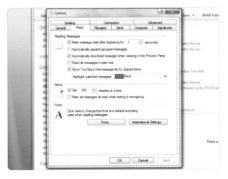

10 AND ANOTHER You can create another rule to process mailing list messages. This time, these are from a freelance mailing list so it's scanning the subject for 'freelance' and moving mail to a new folder called Freelance.

11 RUN THE RULES Once you've created your rules, click on **OK**. Check to see if the rules are doing what you want them to do. Click on **Apply Now** and a new dialog box will open with a list of all the rules you've created.

12 MORE OPTIONS Click on **Tools ➜ Options ➜ Read** to change the way Windows Live Mail treats your messages. You can read all messages in plain text and use the **Fonts** button to change the typeface.

Getting news and files with newsgroups

Newsgroups provide a wealth of knowledge and a way of sharing ideas and information – here's how to get the best out of them

Like Outlook Express, Windows Live Mail can also handle newsgroups – essentially online bulletin boards dedicated to particular subjects. Most internet service providers provide newsgroup access, and you can add your ISP's server details by clicking **Tools ➜ Accounts ➜ Add** then selecting **Newsgroup Account**. You'll be asked for the server details – something like news.myisp.com. Windows Live Mail will then download a list of all the groups provided by your ISP.

Third-party newsgroup services also offer a wider number of groups, if you really get the bug. Microsoft supports a newsgroup server of its own that's available from within Windows Live Mail. This will give you an idea of how newsgroups work and how to use them; of course the topics on offer are of a Microsoft nature.

Funk the junk

Junk email blows online via the internet, gathering in annoying piles in your inbox. While it seems like an unavoidable modern plague, you can – at least to some extent – enforce some controlling measures. Part of the trick is to use the power of Windows Live Mail junk filters.

The junk filters offer a number of protection tiers. The most obvious is the defacto junk filter, which uses advanced algorithms to separate spam. It has a number of levels of severity, up to the point where everyone is suspected.

THE VIEW Groups you subscribe to appear under Microsoft Communities in Folder List

Accessing newsgroups

Keep up to date with selected bulletin boards

1 THE LIST Windows Live Mail comes with connection details for Microsoft Communities, a collection of themed newsgroups. When you first click on the link in the folder list you're asked if you want to see a list of all groups. Click **Yes**.

2 SPOILT FOR CHOICE You'll see a list of available groups – there are plenty to choose from. Scroll through the list or use the 'Display newsgroups that contain...' field at the top of the dialog box to look for specific words.

3 CLICK TO CHOOSE When you find a group you're interested in, click on it and then click **Subscribe**. This means Windows Live Mail will automatically check this group for new messages in future. Click on **OK** when you're happy.

No more junk mail

The junk filters in Windows Live Mail keep spam mail out of your inbox

1 EASY OPTIONS Click on the Menus button in the top right-hand corner of the screen and then select **Safety options → Options**. Now you can choose how strict you want your filters to be, including deleting suspected junk mails.

2 SAFE SENDERS To make sure certain emails don't get labeled as junk, click on **Safe Senders** and **Add**. Enter individual emails or entire domains, eg '@microsoft.com' so that they will be classed as from a safe sender.

3 BUILD BORDERS You can go to the International tab and click **Blocked top-level domain list** to block emails from a particular country. You can also use Blocked Encoding to banish messages in non-English characters.

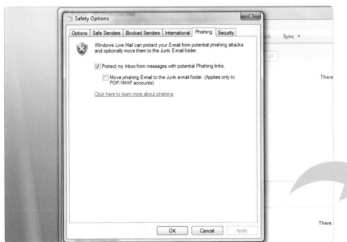

The Phishing tab provides extra security to protect you from those emails that pretend to be from your bank

4 PREVENT PHISHING The **Phishing** tab in the Safety Options dialog is a very useful extra layer of security to protect you from those emails that pretend to be from your bank or from eBay but are actually sent by identity thieves. It is advisable to tick both of the boxes in this window.

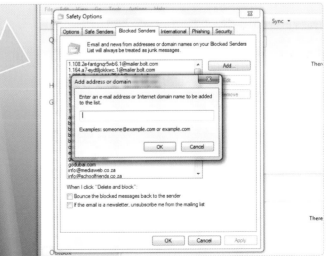

Don't give it away

Don't give your main email address too readily, as you'll just end up getting tons of junk. For example, use a second Windows Live Hotmail address for signing up for less important online services.

5 MAKE IT SAFER Another option in the Safety Options dialog is **Blocked Senders**. Here, you can input the names and addresses of people with whom you do not wish to correspond or who you know to be sending spam, thus permanently blocking them from clogging up your inbox.

Organize your life with Windows Live Calendar

With Windows 7 you can ensure you never miss another appointment. And you can organize the entire family, too

Windows 7 has been designed to help you run your life, and what better way to do this than to include the most powerful calendar to grace a Windows operating system? The Windows Live Calendar not only has everything required to organize your life, it also enables you to share and update calendars with friends, family or co-workers. To access Windows Live Calendar, go to www.windowslive.com/online/calendar and log in using your Windows Live ID.

At its heart – as you'd expect – is a flexible calendar. It enables you to view dates on a daily, weekly and monthly

basis. You can add appointments and tasks with attached reminders; helping you to organize your life – making sure you don't miss appointments, forget birthdays or generally get overwhelmed.

The program also supports multiple calendars so, if you want separate work and personal itineraries but want to access them from the same application, it's easy to arrange.

It's also possible to have your calendars published for others to see, and to subscribe to online calendars. This feature can be really useful for future planning. If you have a large family it's possible to have everyone's calendars running. And, if you're organizing a

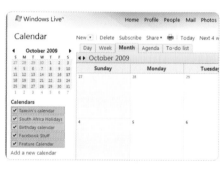

WE ARE LEGION Organize a busy lifestyle: the calendar supports multiple schedules

holiday with a group of friends or family members, you can see when everyone is free, because everyone's schedule is accessible to you.

Make a date with Windows Live Calendar

Start to organize your life the easy Windows 7 way

1 FIRST STEPS The first time you log in to Windows Live Calendar, you will need to create a new calendar. Simply click on **New** and then enter in the relevant details, such as its name and whether it is private or shared.

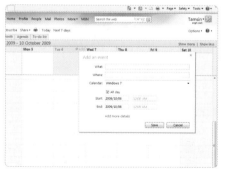

2 MAKE A DATE You can set the views as Month, Week, Day and even Agenda. To add an event, go to the Day view for that date or click on **Add** in Month or Week view. Click on **Add more details** to set reminders and recurrences.

3 NAME THE DAYS It's a good idea to have different calendars for different things – work, personal and so on. To change the name of a calendar, click on the name in the left column and change the name in the page that appears.

4 ADD MORE To add another calendar to your existing set, simply select the **Add New** button that sits below your list of calendars. Then enter the details you want and allocate it a unique color from the palette provided.

5 ADD INFINITUM There's no limit to how many calendars you can add, so create as many as you like. The tick box next to each calendar on the list in the left-hand pane means it is visible. To hide a calendar simply untick the box.

6 ORGANIZE THEM Your online calendar is eminently customizable to suit personal requirements. Go to **Options ➜ More Options** to adjust your time zone, time format, your calendar day and to select your primary calendar.

7 SHARE THEM Sometimes it's useful to be able to share your calendar with other people, especially if you are working on a collaborative project. It's simple to do – just select **Share Calendar** and follow the on-screen instructions.

8 SEE IT ALL You can toggle between Day, Month and Week views by clicking on the relevant tags at the top. You can also view according to the Agenda and To-Do list – handy if you need to see your agenda in a rush.

9 TACKLE TASKS To create your To-do list, simply click on **To-do list** and then, in the new page, **Add a to-do**. In the Options tab you can set whether or not you want the entries deleted after a certain period of time.

10 SEND IT To send your calendar as an .ics file, go to **Share ➜ Send friends a view-only link to your calendar ➜ ICS:Import into another calendar application**. Copy and paste the link into an email and send it.

11 ONLINE CALENDARS You can also subscribe to other calendars that have been published online – these could be from your friends and family, or general public calendars that list public holidays, for example.

12 MORE OPTIONS To set reminders, go to **Options ➜ More Options ➜ Set your reminder time ➜ Change how you get reminders**. The Basic/Advanced delivery options will remind you via email and/or Live Messenger.

Unlike normal calendars, Windows Live Calendar enables you to do much more than simply add appointments. You can manage tasks so that important jobs are completed to deadline.

Using the program to its full potential couldn't be easier. Once you've registered for Windows Live Calendar, you can make two types of entry – an agenda/task or a to-do. To-do's are quick, easy reminders that you can set up by simply clicking on **Add a to-do** and filling in the details.

Tasks and appointments are entered the traditional way and the Agenda option allows you to view your entries as an easily navigable list. To create a new appointment or task, click on the **Add** button and fill in the relevant information. As we are so 'time poor' these days and

too busy to fiddle with lots of extras, you can even make an entry by clicking on **New** and then selecting your entry from the drop-down menu. It certainly makes classifying your calendar tasks, events, social gatherings and work projects nice and simple. You can change the priority, deadlines, which calendar it should appear on, add notes and delete any entry on your calendar simply by clicking on it and choosing the relevant option.

Compatible calendars

While Windows Live Calendar makes it easy to organize yourself, it's also very simple to bring others into the equation. You can share your calendars with friends, family and co-workers, making it easier to synchronize what you're doing.

The beauty of Windows Live Calendar is that it also provides support for other iCalendar programs (the standard for calendar information exchange), enabling you to use your operating system as your calendar, instead of using different types of software. You can export your previous calendars into Windows Live Calendar by simply exporting them via .ics file and you can subscribe to a wide range of different web-based services, too.

To import your file to Windows Live Calendar, click on **Subscribe ➜ Import**

Super Tip!
Easy invites

When creating a new appointment, you can easily add attendees from your contact list and then click **Invite** to send them an email with an attached ICS file of the appointment!

from an ics file. Alternatively, if you want to subscribe to an online calendar, simply select the box that says **Subscribe to a public calendar**.

If you need any assistance with converting your .ics files or in finding the correct information to subscribe to a public file, click on **Get help with this** in Windows Live Calendar for a complete easy-to-follow walkthrough.

Windows Live Calendar enables you to have multiple calendars running consecutively, giving you ultimate control over your busy life. Once you've imported your social and work calendars, you can keep them on show or dismiss them by checking the boxes in the left pane.

GO ONLINE With a layout this clear, you should never forget another appointment...

Share your schedule with others
Publish your calendar for others to view in a number of ways...

1 SAVE You can share your calendars as RSS, HTML or ICS files and you can determine which aspects can be seen. To start with, click on **Share** and choose the calendar you want to share.

2 PUBLISH Select **Share this calendar ➜ Send friends a view-only link... ➜ Get your calendar links**. Windows Live Calendar will save that calendar to a private web space.

3 AUTO UPDATE Now select what aspects of your calendar you want to send and what format you prefer. If you send it as an ICS file, the recipients can import it into their own calendars.

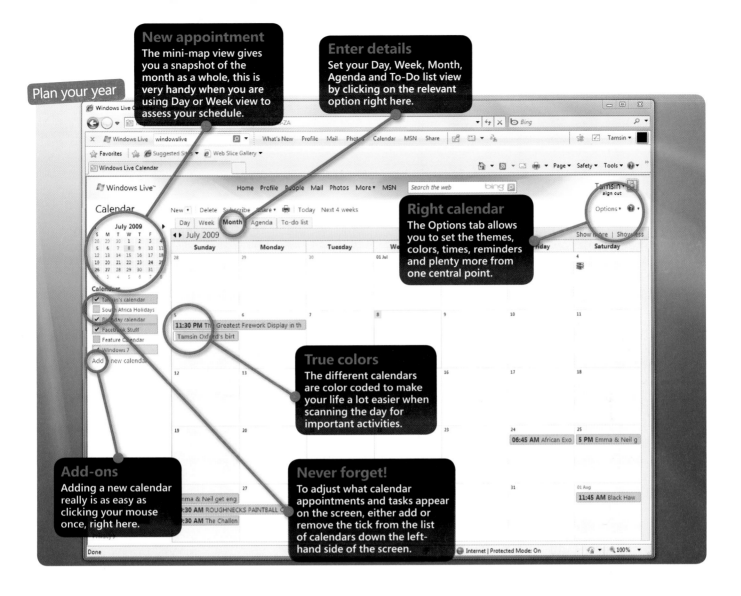

New appointment
The mini-map view gives you a snapshot of the month as a whole, this is very handy when you are using Day or Week view to assess your schedule.

Enter details
Set your Day, Week, Month, Agenda and To-Do list view by clicking on the relevant option right here.

Plan your year

Right calendar
The Options tab allows you to set the themes, colors, times, reminders and plenty more from one central point.

True colors
The different calendars are color coded to make your life a lot easier when scanning the day for important activities.

Add-ons
Adding a new calendar really is as easy as clicking your mouse once, right here.

Never forget!
To adjust what calendar appointments and tasks appear on the screen, either add or remove the tick from the list of calendars down the left-hand side of the screen.

Compare dates with friends or colleagues
Subscribe to a calendar to make arrangements easy

1 SUBSCRIBE If you want someone else's calendar to appear, click the **Subscribe** button. If they have sent you a web address, enter that into the Calendar URL bar along with their name.

2 ICS FILE Alternatively, your friends or colleagues can export their calendar to an ICS file. They can then email you the file and you can upload it using the **Import from an ICS file** option.

3 UPDATES Select **Import into a new calendar**, browse for the file, name it, then select **Import Calendar**. Windows Live Calendar will automatically update your calendar with the relevant info.

Getting the most from Windows Contacts

Keep all your important numbers and email addresses stored in this easy-to-access folder

Contact management is an increasingly important part of modern life. With email messages and mobile phone calls as primary forms of communication, it's essential to keep up to date with work and social contacts. Windows 7 makes life so much easier in terms of how it allows you to use and access your contact information. Like Windows Vista, Windows 7 no longer includes Windows Address Book but continues to use Windows Contacts, an accessible folder on your PC that makes storing details truly simple.

You access Windows Contacts from the Start Menu (**Start ➜ Search ➜**

Windows Contacts); if you've downloaded Windows Live Mail (http://download.live.com), access contacts in Windows Live Mail by clicking on the **Contacts** icon in the left-hand panel.

The new look and way of accessing Windows Contacts makes for a far more logical experience and one that, thanks to the new Internet Explorer design, can be accessed at any point.

As with Windows Vista, the Windows Contacts facility in Windows 7 is firmly integrated, and you can easily import and export contacts using a variety of programs in a variety of formats – useful if you need to hold contact data in a number of different places.

Of course, when it comes to finding contacts, you simply tap in the name of the person you're after and let Windows 7 Search do the work for you.

EASY EXPORT You can share contact details, even if your friends don't have Windows 7

Manage your contacts with ease

Import, organize and communicate with those all-important people

1 NO ONE HOME Once you've opened Windows Contacts for the first time, you'll find a blank slate to fill with all your friends, family and colleagues. It is simple to set up and you can easily import from other mail programs, too.

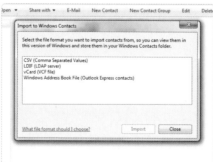

2 EASY IMPORT If you've got contact data stored in another program, Windows Contacts enables you to import it quickly and easily. Just click on the **Import** button in the toolbar and choose the appropriate option.

3 QUICK ADD There are no contacts to import in this example, so they'll need to be entered manually instead. To add a new contact, just click on **New Contact** in the toolbar and you'll see the tabbed dialog box shown here.

4 ENTER THE INFO If you've got a picture of the contact, you can add it to their entry by clicking on the arrow underneath their picture. There are a number of fields here, but if you don't know all the details, it's not a problem.

5 ALTERNATIVE EMAIL More than one email address? No problem, just add the email addresses to your contact's details and then click the **Set Preferred** button (bottom right of the dialog box) to choose the one you'll use most often.

6 MORE DETAILS Use the tabs to add any additional information, such as your contact's home or work address, notes, birthdays and so on, then click **OK** to return to Windows Contacts. Your new contact should appear in the list.

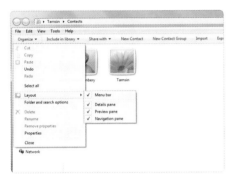

7 EASY ACCESS To view your contacts, go to **Organize → Layout** and select all options. When you select a contact they will appear in the preview pane. If you have Windows Live Mail, click on an email address to launch a blank email.

8 ORGANIZE YOUR INFO Windows Contacts can also manage groups. This comes in handy if you need to send the same information to several people. It's also useful for reminding you who certain people are!

9 COME TOGETHER Click on **New Contact Group**, then **Add to Contact Group**. Highlight the contacts you want to add to your group by holding down the **Ctrl** key and clicking on the contacts. Click **Add t**o continue.

10 EVERYONE'S ADDED The names of your chosen contacts should now appear in the middle of the dialog box. Give your group a meaningful name (for example, a work-based name or a sports club name), then click on **OK**.

11 SEE THE RESULTS Your new group should appear in your contacts list, and as you can see it has a different icon for easy identification. If you want to email everyone in a group, just right-click and select **Action → Send Email**.

12 CHANGE THE LOOK As with other folders in Windows 7, you can use the **Views** button to change the way contacts are displayed. This screen shows large icons, but you can see contacts as a list, a details view or as small tiles.

Enjoy better browsing with Windows 7

Equipped with Internet Explorer 8 and its suite of applications, Windows 7 provides a fast and safe online experience

When Windows 95 first appeared, nobody knew how important the internet would become. It had been around for a few years but expensive call charges, slow modem access and complicated software meant it was hardly a 'readily available' service. The 2001 launch of Windows XP improved the software side of things with easier networking and a better web browser, but the internet itself was still slow and expensive. Then broadband came along, absolutely slashing the cost of getting online and boosting connection speeds.

Broadband changed everything. While downloading songs had taken the best part of an hour, broadband could download entire albums in a

matter of minutes. Before, online video had struggled to offer anything bigger than a postage stamp; with broadband we could suddenly enjoy crystal-clear, decent-sized movie clips. And, while previously we'd only stayed connected for a few minutes at a time, we could stay constantly connected – which unfortunately meant that virus writers, malware creators and malicious hackers could attack our PCs 24 hours a day...

The internet became a dangerous place and, by 2006, if you connected your PC to the internet without first stuffing it with security software you could expect it to become infected within minutes. It's no longer enough

for your web browser to be useful – it needs to be as secure as Fort Knox, too. Luckily, with Windows 7, it is.

Feel secure

Windows 7 comes with a brand new browser, Windows Internet Explorer 8. In addition to its characteristic bright, fresh look and excellent features, it's also the safest version of Internet Explorer that Microsoft has ever created. That's partly because of Windows 7 itself, which is considerably more secure than any Windows platform in the past, but it's also because Internet Explorer 8 continues to see security as its priority. Now you can browse with confidence. ⊞

FIX IT Internet Explorer 8 now includes the new Compatibility View for older sites

Explore the web with Internet Explorer 8

Windows 7 packs the latest in browser technology

1 ACCELERATE Another great invention brought to you by Internet Explorer 8 is Accelerators. These handy 'highlighting' tools make your browsing life a lot easier to find the things you want without having to navigate to other websites.

2 MANAGE To set up and manage your Accelerators, simply click on **Page** in the top right-hand corner and select **All Accelerators → Manage Accelerators**. If you want to add more, simply click on **Find More Accelerators**.

3 ADD TO IE After you've selected **Find More Accelerators**, you'll be taken to a page with an extensive list from which to choose. To install an Accelerator, select **Add to Internet Explorer** and it will automatically join the list.

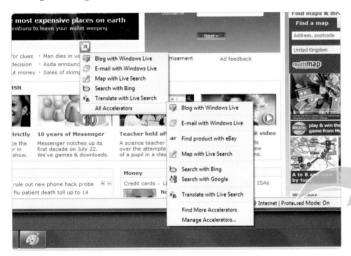

To use your Accelerators, you only need to highlight text on screen, then click on the blue Accelerator icon that appears

4 BLUE ICON To use your Accelerators, you only need to highlight text on screen – in this example, the word 'chocolate' is highlighted – then click on the blue **Accelerator** icon that appears. A list of your Accelerators will now appear in a drop-down menu and you can choose which one to click on.

Internet Explorer 8

This latest version of Internet Explorer is ultra secure and includes the new SmartScreen filter and other built-in security features that protect your privacy, identity and data.

5 NEW WINDOW Click on the Accelerator you want – for example, asking for a Map with Live Search – and a new tabbed window will open with the information you were looking for. Here, Live Search has shown that there is a place called Chocolate in Mexico!

Tailor your internet connection

There are further options available in Internet Explorer's tab system

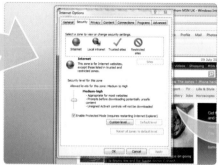

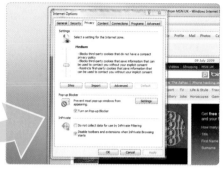

1 GENERAL KNOWLEDGE In the **General** tab, you can set not just one home page but multiple ones by adding several addresses in the Home Page box. When you launch Windows Internet Explorer these sites will open in tabs.

2 SOLID SECURITY The **Security** settings are stricter than previous versions of Internet Explorer, and there's a tick box for Protected Mode. Add trusted sites to the Trusted Sites list, which reduces the security level only for those sites.

3 PROTECTING PRIVACY By default, the **Privacy** tab blocks cookies from sites other than the one you're visiting. Internet Explorer 8 also introduces InPrivate Browsing and Filtering options for even more personal security.

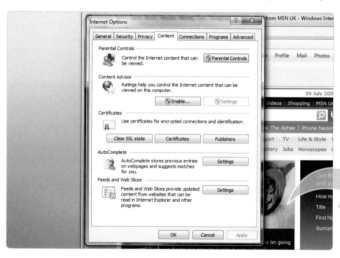

By default, the Privacy tab blocks cookies from sites other than the one you're currently visiting

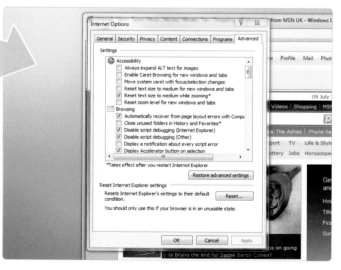

4 CONTROL CONTENT The **Content** tab enables you to set Parental Controls to stop your children from seeing unsuitable sites, and you can also enable the Content Advisor to block sites that don't have specific age ratings or which contain particular kinds of content.

Getting tooled up

Enhance your browsing experience even further by downloading the Microsoft Live Toolbar from http://download.live.com/toolbar/overview, providing shortcuts to your favorite search, news and more!

5 ADVANCED OPTIONS In the **Advanced** tab you can disable or enable pretty much any element, from text size to the way Internet Explorer deals with secure websites. This section is very much for power users; for most of us, the general, security, privacy and content tabs suffice.

Get internet feeds delivered

Don't waste time trawling internet news sites, you can get all the top stories to come to you

When the internet first came to mainstream attention, it was quickly monickered the 'information superhighway'. Well, now that superhighway can deliver its cargo of information to your door in handy streamlined form.

If you want to keep on top of news stories and new products, but don't have the time to trawl the internet for every latest bit of information published, web feeds are the answer. Originally named (and still often referred to as) RSS feeds, these news services are now more often called web feeds or news feeds. Web feeds enable you to take headlines from hundreds of sites and collect them in one handy place, so you can browse through your favorite news or information sources in a matter of minutes. Instead of wasting time trawling through a number of news websites at different times of the day, you simply choose the providers you want, set them up, and then receive an alert whenever a new story is posted.

Your feeds can be integrated into Internet Explorer 8, Microsoft Office Outlook 2007 and Live.com, collating your news in one place. A huge number of sites are offering feed options, such as www.cnn.com, YouTube and, of course, www.officialwindowsmagazine.com.

The explosion of user-based blog content has revolutionized the way we get our news, and has triggered an abundance of community sites, such as Digg.com. Initially, this explosion actually made things more difficult for people to keep abreast of breaking news, as even the major news organizations played second fiddle to the blogs. But now more people are using feeds to their advantage, by taking news straight from blogs and niche sites rather than traditional sources. This is great for 'news addicts' who love to be the first to know any juicy gossip or kept informed of the latest headlines.

Feed me now

There are hundreds of web-based feed readers on the internet, but Internet Explorer 8 enables you to integrate your favorite feeds with your day-to-day activity, so there's no time wasting. ➜

Set up your web feeds in five minutes

Get your news reports on Internet Explorer 8

1 GETTING STARTED Check that your chosen site (eg, www.msnbc.msn.com) publishes a feed. If it does there will be an orange icon in the toolbar. Click this to add it to your feeds.

2 SUBSCRIBE When you click the icon a screen will appear with the stories listed, so you can check it's the right feed. Click **Subscribe to this feed** and it will be added to the Favorites list.

3 VIEW Click the **Favorites** icon, represented by a star. A submenu called Feeds will show a list of services you've subscribed to. Each set of headlines can be viewed easily.

In real life...
The RSS advantage

Alun Rogers, Technical Director at Risual, specialist in security, management and infrastructure solutions
While RSS means easy ways of subscribing to content, there is the possibility for viruses and spyware to spread. Windows 7 and Internet Explorer 8 defend against this on two counts:
■ Malicious code embedded in a RSS news item is disabled by sanitizing all scripts in the feed, and all feeds are handled in the restricted internet zone – the most secure setting for Internet Explorer. So anything dangerous doesn't get a chance to install itself.
■ Potentially dangerous attachment types, such as programs or scripts, are blocked. The only way to install is if you allow it – make sure you know what it is before clicking **Allow**.

Adding feeds is simplicity itself. When you visit a site, check that the feed symbol in the toolbar of Internet Explorer is orange (if it's gray there is no feed option). If it is orange, click on the icon to add that particular feed to your Favorites list, which now includes a dedicated web feed section. The feeds will also be automatically updated in Outlook 2007.

then beamed straight to your desktop.
You can also download gadgets for specific news sites. These enable you to get all the news that is really important to you. You will also find that all the major news services offer gadgets that will deliver breaking news direct to your sidebar, meaning you'll never miss an important story.
Finally, thanks to the wealth of

The benefit of using your email program to view feeds is that it gives you the unique ability to treat stories like emails

The benefit of using your email program to view feeds is that it gives you the unique ability to treat individual stories like emails. You can sort feeds day by day, so you can see how old a story is. There are many options; you can also group reports together, save them to your inbox and send them on to other people.
Windows 7 has desktop gadgets that enable you to find feeds that you've subscribed to in Internet Explorer or Outlook. Go to the Options menu for the gadget and choose from the list of feeds; the top stories and headlines are

features in the Live family of applications, you can integrate feeds directly on to the page. This means, when you log on to your home page – usually the first venture of the day – all your feeds will be listed in front of you. How's that for convenience?
Feeds are often centered on news, but loads of other organizations are successfully using feeds as an effortless way of reaching and informing people, such as parcel delivery services or real estate agents. Set up a few different feeds today and see how much time you could save.

Get the news you want to read
Stay up to date by getting yourself some Web Slices

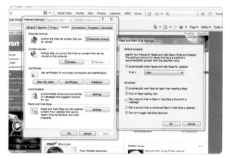

1 SLICE & EASY Web Slices are portions of web pages that you can subscribe to, which will notify you when updated. They make keeping up to date with the latest information really easy.

2 GO GREEN When a Web Slice is available, the button turns green. Click this, then **Add to Favorites**. When the Web Slice is updated the link turns bold in your Favorites bar.

3 ALERT To enable sounds for Web Slices, go to **Tools → Internet Options → Content → Feeds and Web Slices → Settings**, so you get a sound when a feed or Slice is found or updated.

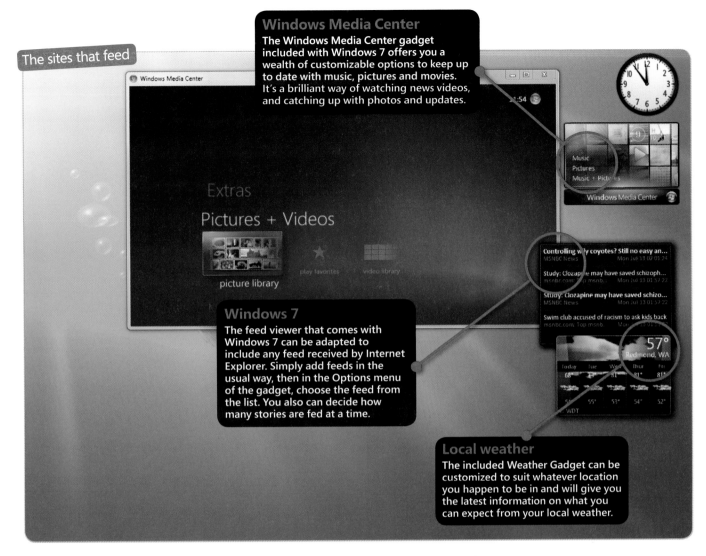

Windows Media Center

The Windows Media Center gadget included with Windows 7 offers you a wealth of customizable options to keep up to date with music, pictures and movies. It's a brilliant way of watching news videos, and catching up with photos and updates.

Windows 7

The feed viewer that comes with Windows 7 can be adapted to include any feed received by Internet Explorer. Simply add feeds in the usual way, then in the Options menu of the gadget, choose the feed from the list. You also can decide how many stories are fed at a time.

Local weather

The included Weather Gadget can be customized to suit whatever location you happen to be in and will give you the latest information on what you can expect from your local weather.

View feeds in Windows Media Center

Get news alongside your music, video, picture and television content

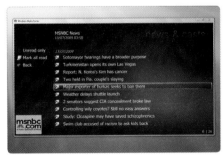

1 INSTALL Visit http://vistamcrssreader. oabsoftware.nl, install the Windows 7 RSS Reader; this will be added to Extras in Windows Media Center. Sign up for the activation code and enter it.

2 FEED ME NEWS All the feeds you've added in Internet Explorer will be listed in Media Center. Choose a feed and, from the headlines, choose a story. The synopsis will show in your viewer.

3 READ IN FULL To view a story's full text, click **Show page**. Media Center will say the content is Not Designed for Windows Media Center; click **View Now** and you'll see the page in all its glory.

Protect your ID with Windows CardSpace

With identity theft and credit card fraud increasingly common, Microsoft has come up with a safe way to work online

It's a pain in the neck entering the same data again and again in websites, but these days it's a necessary evil. If you've stored your personal details on your computer, it's possible that someone else could intercept it and abuse it.

However, Windows CardSpace may have the answer. That's because it stores the sort of information you'll use again and again in a way that combines ease of use with rock-solid security.

In some ways, Windows CardSpace works in a similar way to Internet Explorer's AutoFill, which you can use to automatically add your details to online forms, but the big difference between AutoFill and Windows

CardSpace is that the former doesn't do anything to protect your details while the latter wraps your personal profile in secure devices. As you'll see, creating cards in Windows CardSpace is easy, and the cards themselves are well protected. But how do you actually go about using them?

When you visit a CardSpace-enabled site you'll see the option to log in via Windows CardSpace, and if you choose that option, CardSpace will launch in a safe environment – the rest of your Windows 7 desktop will be faded out – and tell you about the site you're visiting. You'll then be able to choose which card you want to use to log into the site, and you can be confident that the whole process is safe and secure.

Windows CardSpace is included with Windows 7, so you only have to type Card into the Search function in the Start menu and the application will magically appear. Then just click on the application

ID PROTECTION Click on **Start ➜ Control Panel ➜ User Accounts and Family Safety ➜ Windows CardSpace**

Storing details in Windows CardSpace

Join today and beat identity criminals by protecting yourself while online

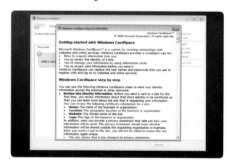

1 **SAFE AND SOUND** Windows CardSpace essentially halts the rest of your PC. The rest of Windows 7 fades into the background, so there's no risk of your activities being intercepted.

2 **ADD A CARD** Click **OK** on the welcome and you'll see the main screen, as shown here. To create a new card, click on **Add a Card** then click **Add** at the bottom of the dialog box.

3 **PICK A CARD** You have a choice – create a personal card with basic info or install a Managed Card you've been given. This example is for the personal option – click **Create a Personal Card**.

and you'll be taken to the screen where you can then fill in all of your details and create your first Card.

While CardSpace may not be in widespread use as yet, it is extremely useful to have your information so easily accessible and to hand. Windows CardSpace is a clever system that makes filling out online forms so much easier while also keeping your personal details safe, so it won't be long before we see it becoming more and more popular. It's well worth investing some time and effort into creating your own cards, you never know, you may find life just that little bit less frustrating...

In real life...
Validation technology

 Simon Arblaster, Disc editor, Windows: The Official Magazine

Much like the real world, the internet is full of good and bad people. Most are law-abiding 'netizens' who are happy enough discovering the wonders of the online world. However, some less well minded folk aren't. And, just as you wouldn't go waving your credit card details around for all and sundry to see, the same goes while you're online.

The problem with the internet is that it's this huge collection of computers all working together to pass information around the world. Very clever, but it means at any stage one of those computers could decide to take a look at the information passing by and that could be your debit or credit card details.

Thankfully, some very clever people have solved the problem. It's called Extended Validation SSL and it's a technology embedded inside Windows 7. This advanced technology guarantees that information being passed between your computer and the legitimate destination computer can only be read by that destination computer. If a system somewhere in-between tries to read the data, all it will get is a bundle of garbled rubbish.

If you're planning on sending information to a website, look for the padlock symbol at the end of the address bar. This means that the site is using encryption to protect your data. If the symbol is not there, then don't send the information.

PADLOCK If you're about to hand over your details online, make sure this icon is visible

4 ENTER THE INFO Enter the data you want stored. You can add as much or as little information to your card as you like, and you can replace the default image with a picture from your hard disk.

5 MULTI CARDS Once the info's in, you return to the main screen. You can create multiple cards, and when available you'll be able to get Managed Cards from firms such as credit card companies.

6 EXTRA To see the contents of your card, click **Preview**; in the top right of the dialog box you'll see an option to lock your card. This adds extra protection by asking you to enter a PIN.

Taking your PC out and about

The whole world's going mobile – and Windows 7 is the way to get the best out of your laptop

There was a time when if you wanted sheer power you'd buy a desktop, and if you wanted portability – and had a great deal of money to spare – you'd buy a laptop. However, in recent years that has all changed. Laptop prices have plummeted while at the same time their power has increased so, as a result, many people are now buying laptops as desktop replacements. In fact, in the last few years, laptops have been outselling desktops by a significant margin.

Performance v portability

These days, there are two main kinds of laptop buyer. Those who want a laptop solely for home or office use don't need to worry about battery life as their machines will generally be plugged into a wall socket. To these guys, it's performance that matters. Mobile users, on the other hand, need to squeeze as much life out of their batteries as they possibly can – a tough challenge when they too need their PCs to perform at a high standard, often while using power-draining wireless networking.

Super Windows 7

With Windows 7, Microsoft needed to provide features for both kinds of laptop user. But that's not all. Home and office users occasionally take their laptops out and about, while mobile users often use their laptops at home or in the office, so Windows 7 needs to be flexible enough to deliver maximum performance when a laptop's plugged in and still provide maximum portability when it's on the move. As if that wasn't challenging enough, tablet PCs complicate things even further. Twist a tablet's screen this way and it's a standard laptop; twist it that way and it's a touch-sensitive screen that uses handwriting recognition instead of a keyboard, and a stylus instead of a mouse. Turn to page 122 for more on tablet PCs. Then there's the Pocket PC, which ditches the keyboard altogether, shrinks a tablet PC to the size of a hardback book and is as likely to be used on a sofa as in a roadside café.

Windows 7 has to satisfy all of these demands – and here you'll discover that it does so very well indeed.

Introducing the Windows Mobility Center

Memorize this shortcut, because it's your new best friend...

1 INSTANT INFO Press the **Windows** key and **X** and the Windows Mobility Center pops up. It's a dashboard for various mobile system settings. Here, the battery's charging and Wi-Fi is on.

2 QUICK CHANGE The Battery section enables you to switch between power management schemes – handy if you've been running in power-saving mode but need a quick burst of power.

3 MISSION CONTROL Click specific icons to go to the appropriate Control Panel section. Here the battery icon has been selected: **Control Panel ➜ Hardware and Sound ➜ Power Options**.

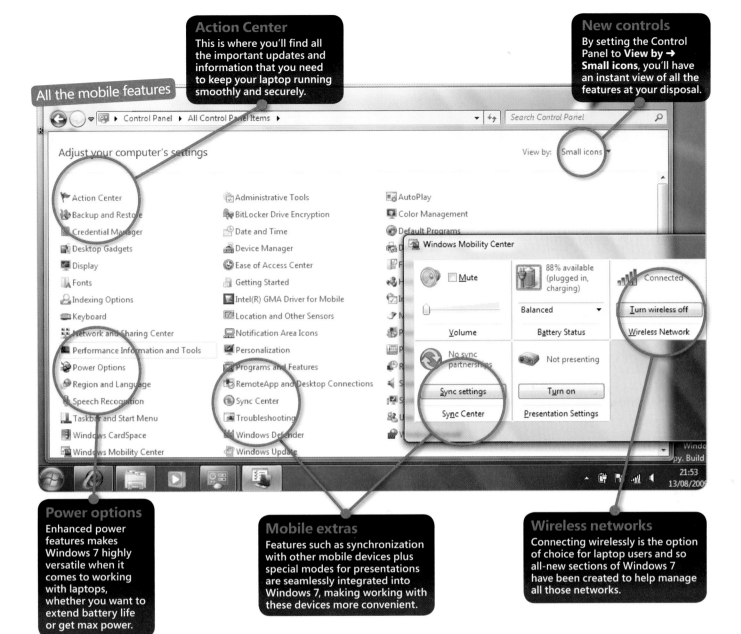

Action Center
This is where you'll find all the important updates and information that you need to keep your laptop running smoothly and securely.

New controls
By setting the Control Panel to **View by → Small icons**, you'll have an instant view of all the features at your disposal.

All the mobile features

Control Panel ▸ All Control Panel Items ▸

Search Control Panel

Adjust your computer's settings

View by: Small icons ▼

Action Center
Backup and Restore
Credential Manager
Desktop Gadgets
Display
Fonts
Indexing Options
Keyboard
Network and Sharing Center
Performance Information and Tools
Power Options
Region and Language
Speech Recognition
Taskbar and Start Menu
Windows CardSpace
Windows Mobility Center

Administrative Tools
BitLocker Drive Encryption
Date and Time
Device Manager
Ease of Access Center
Getting Started
Intel(R) GMA Driver for Mobile
Location and Other Sensors
Notification Area Icons
Personalization
Programs and Features
RemoteApp and Desktop Connections
Sync Center
Troubleshooting
Windows Defender
Windows Update

AutoPlay
Color Management
Default Programs

Windows Mobility Center

Mute

88% available (plugged in, charging)

Balanced

Connected

Turn wireless off

Volume

Battery Status

Wireless Network

No sync partnerships

Not presenting

Sync settings

Turn on

Sync Center

Presentation Settings

21:53
13/08/2009

Power options
Enhanced power features makes Windows 7 highly versatile when it comes to working with laptops, whether you want to extend battery life or get max power.

Mobile extras
Features such as synchronization with other mobile devices plus special modes for presentations are seamlessly integrated into Windows 7, making working with these devices more convenient.

Wireless networks
Connecting wirelessly is the option of choice for laptop users and so all-new sections of Windows 7 have been created to help manage all those networks.

4 WHICH WIRELESS? Clicking on the wireless network icon opens the Connect to a Network dialog box, which displays any wireless networks nearby that you could connect to.

5 MONITOR MONITORS The display icon launches the Display dialog box, which enables you to control the appearance of any external displays that you have connected to your computer.

6 PERFECT PRESENTATION Presentation Settings gives you options such as turning off the screen saver so it won't cut in mid-slide, and turning the volume down or off.

Battery power to the people

Improving your battery life will help you work for longer while on the move

Windows 7 has three pre-set power management modes: High Performance, Power Saver and Balanced. The first option delivers speed but eats battery power. The second squeezes out every drop of juice but can slow down your system. And the third tries to strike a balance between power and battery life. Here you can discover how to tweak these modes and take advantage of some clever power management features. While some are laptop and tablet PC-specific, many of the power management features are available on desktop PCs, too.

The biggest factor in battery life is the way you use your PC. As well as optimizing Windows 7 for battery power, if you want to prolong battery life you'll need to use your laptop slightly differently than when it's plugged into the wall. With mobile PCs, less is more: the less you expect your PC to do, the more life you'll get from its battery.

Power savers

So what do you need to think about? Accessing CDs or DVDs drains your battery more quickly than accessing your hard drive; processor-intensive tasks, such as gaming, drain your battery more quickly than word processing, and wireless communications, such as Wi-Fi or Bluetooth, have a bigger impact on battery life than wired connections.

Turn down the brightness of your screen – the brighter your display, the more power it's using – and unplug any external devices, such as USB mice, keyboards or lava lamps.

What you do in Windows 7 makes a difference, too. If you want to get the longest possible battery life, it's a good idea to make sure you're not running any programs or eye candy that you don't need. For example, while animated backgrounds look great, they use up processing power. Similarly, if you're not connected to the internet or to a network, temporarily disable security software such as anti-virus scanners (remembering to switch them back on again before you connect to anything) as they tend to churn away in the background, increasing the demands on your PC's processor. ⊞

Super Tip!

Power modes

Windows 7 has been designed to conserve power by not using background services, like Bluetooth, unless needed. It's also not as memory hungry as Windows Vista so overall performance is better.

In real life...
Look after your battery and it'll look after you

**Neil Mohr,
Contributor
*Windows: The
Official Magazine***

It may surprise you to know that the battery inside your laptop makes up a significant chunk of the computer's total cost. Look up replacement ones online and you'll see that they are quite expensive. So doesn't it make sense to look after them?

Almost all laptops come with a type of battery called Lithium Ion (Li-ion). This is a very high-capacity rechargeable battery. As with all rechargeable batteries it has a limited lifespan, typically lasting for around 1,000 charge cycles. However, certain conditions can reduce its lifespan, so they're worth knowing about – and avoiding. Firstly, Li-ion batteries do not like being stored fully charged. If you plan on not using your laptop for a long while, the general advice is to discharge the battery to around 40 per cent of its full charge. Secondly, if you're using a laptop that stays plugged into the mains for a long time it's an idea to remove the battery – it won't need it while it's plugged in.

LIFESAVER Treat your battery well and it will reward you by lasting a lot longer

Finally, laptop batteries don't like high temperatures; if you're storing your laptop, make sure it's in a cool place away from direct sunlight.

Energy management in Windows 7
How to get maximum performance for minimum power

1 **POWER UP** You can access the power management features by clicking on the battery in Mobility Center, or click **Start ➔ Control Panel ➔ Windows Mobility Center ➔ Battery Status.**

2 **PLAN IT** There are three standard power plan modes; high performance doesn't appear by default. The left side gives the option to **Choose what the power buttons do** – click on this.

3 **BUTTON IT** Here you can change the behavior of the power buttons and what happens when you close the lid. You can use different settings for either battery or plug-in power supply.

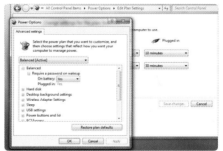

4 **MORE SETTINGS** Alongside each power plan you'll see a link that says **Change plan settings**. Here you can adjust the plans, and again have different settings for battery and mains power.

5 **MORE POWER** If you click on **Change advanced power settings** you can tweak all kinds of things. Next to each device you'll see a plus sign; click on it to see the available options for that device.

6 **WHACK THE WI-FI** Here are the settings for wireless. It makes sense to go for **Maximum Performance** on mains power but **Power Saving** with batteries: Wi-Fi can be a power hog.

7 **NO SHOW** Animations or slide shows impact on performance/battery life. Use the **Desktop background settings** to set slide shows to **Paused** on battery but **Available** on plugged in.

8 **DISPLAY DECISIONS** If you're often called away while working it's a good idea to set your display settings to rest after a certain amount of time. Go to the **Display** listing to set this up.

9 **SAFE SHARING** The Multimedia Settings enable you to change the way Windows 7 handles media sharing. **Away** mode enables your PC to share files while appearing to be off.

Discover the secrets of the tablet PC

Designed to allow PC interaction without a mouse or keyboard, tablet models are incredibly versatile

FLEXIBLE FRIEND Most tablets are convertible, so they can be used as normal laptops, too

If you twist a tablet PC's screen one way, it's a normal laptop – but twist it the other way to use its touch-sensitive screen and you can enter text via handwriting recognition. The Control Panel's Hardware and Sound options have a dedicated section for tablet PC users, which should please everyone that likes to make use of their stylus and expensive touchscreen.

Introduced back in 2002, Windows XP Tablet PC Edition brought the ease of use of tablet PCs to all users, while in Windows Vista the technology matured. Now with Windows 7, touch is an integral part of the interface; Home

Premium and Ultimate editions can take advantage of its useful features, which hinge around natural input based on both handwriting and voice recognition.

Strike the right note

Tablet PCs come into their own with note taking, as you can treat the folded-back screen as a giant pad of paper; make handwritten notes, doodle, scrawl diagrams and flip page after page. When you're back in the office after a meeting or note-taking exercise, you're able to review the notes, convert written words to text, save images as diagrams and generally reorganize your rampant scrawling into a useful form.

While the 'slate' style design makes a lightweight choice for those who only need to rely on handwriting recognition, most tablet PCs take the 'convertible' approach, so you can use it as a traditional laptop or rotate and fold back the screen on itself for slate work. The versatility is very useful – while straightforward data entry via the keyboard is the fastest way of working, at other times an electronic notepad is the most convenient.

Tweaking your tablet

Make life with a tablet more fun with these handy adjustments

1 TWEAK YOUR TABLET If you're using a tablet PC, you'll already have spotted the **Tablet PC Settings** link in the Control Panel's Hardware and Sound section. Click on the link now to find out all about the various options.

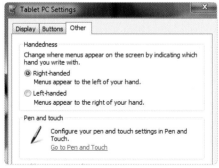

2 PICK A HAND The **Other** tab enables you to specify whether you're left- or right-handed. With this information, Windows 7 will display on-screen menus accordingly (to the left if you're right-handed, and vice versa).

3 GET IT WRITE In the **Pen and Touch** link, Handwriting enables you to turn the Automatic Learning feature on or off (only available on genuine tablet PCs). This constantly analyzes your handwriting to improve recognition.

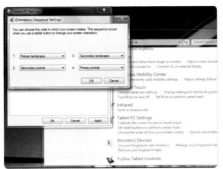

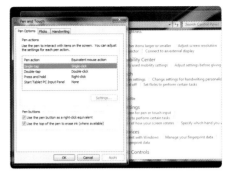

4 ORIENT EXPRESS The Display settings enable you to change your display's orientation – so you can make your tablet default to Landscape or Portrait. Use the **Orientation** link under Tablet PC Settings to change the screen rotation.

5 ORDER ORDER Click **Orientation** to see the order in which the **Rotate Screen** button changes the display. By default it's primary landscape, secondary portrait, secondary landscape, primary portrait – rotating 90 degrees each time.

6 PEN AND TELL-ER Close the Tablet PC settings dialog box and you return to Hardware and Sound in the Control Panel. Click on **Pen and Touch** to configure the way Windows 7 handles your tablet PC's pen input.

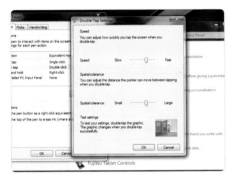

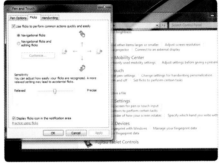

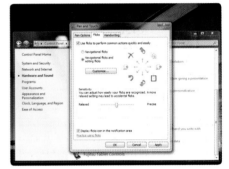

7 FIX MOVEMENT Windows 7 lets you adjust each pen action to ensure that it understands what you are doing. Select an option and click the **Settings** button to configure options such as speed and spatial tolerance.

8 SEE A FLICK Flicks are gestures that make Windows 7 do something. By default, you can navigate by flicking the pen across the screen, but click on **Navigational flicks and editing flicks** to make them even more useful.

9 CHANGE THE FLICKS Clicking the button changes the picture on the tab; in addition to standard navigation Flicks, you get four editing Flicks. You can stick with the default if you like, but to change them click on **Customize**.

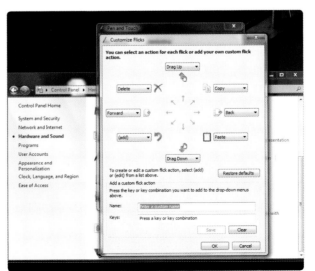

10 NEW TRICKS The Customize Flicks dialog appears, with a drop-down list next to each available Flick showing the default options. You can change them by clicking on the arrow at the end of the appropriate drop-down.

11 EASY ADDITION Adding your own Flicks is easy as pie. For example, if you wanted the vertical upwards Flick to launch Windows Mobility Center you'd click on its drop-down arrow, choose **Add**, give it a name and then click on the **Keys** field. Press the **Windows** key and X (the shortcut for Mobility Center), then click on **Save** and your new Flick will be available.

Save time on the move

Windows Mobile Device Center can help organize your life and save you valuable time. We show you how to make it happen

Today our lives are jam-packed with work, family and social commitments. Everyone's looking for ways to speed up mundane tasks, and a great way to do this is with a Windows Mobile device, keeping information and files to hand while away from your computer. However, so much time can be wasted trying to synchronize the information held on your PC with a mobile device, that the chore of doing that can often outweigh the benefits.

The whole point of Windows 7 is to make life easier, and the Windows Mobile Device Center has been included in the package so that you can update your mobile device in less time than it takes to make a cup of coffee.

To get started, simply plug your Windows Mobile device into your PC's USB port – or if you've got a Bluetooth connection for your PC, you can synchronize your devices wirelessly.

Once connected, Windows Mobile Device Center will automatically appear and show a picture of your device; you'll then be presented with two options.

If you're connecting to a computer that you want to be synchronizing files with on a daily basis, select **Set up your device** as this will make a permanent

The whole point of Windows 7 is to make life easier

pairing between your PC and that specific device. However, if this is a one-off pairing, click **Connect without setting up your device**.

You'll then be given a list of the types of data that can be automatically synchronized with your device. If you use Windows Live Mail, you can set it to automatically synchronize your inbox,

contacts, appointments and calendar, so wherever you are, you'll never be without that vital information.

Tweak to fit

These synchronization settings can be changed at any time by plugging in your device as usual and going to **Mobile Device Settings → Change content sync setting**. Check or uncheck each type of information to control whether it will be updated when the sync is complete. Most options also have a **Sync Settings** menu where elements can be tweaked.

With Windows 7, your devices don't have to be about work. Windows Mobile Device Center seamlessly links into Windows Media Player where it's easy to add music, pictures and videos to devices. Just drag and drop files into the sync pane on the right, click **Start Sync** and let Windows 7 do the rest. All that's left now is to enjoy that coffee – and your extra bit of free time. ⊞

Device management

Working with mobile devices just got a lot easier...

Windows 7 has made working with your mobile devices so much easier with the introduction of two new features. The first of these is known as Device Stage and this provides a single place for you to go to check all of your connected devices.

You can see the status of your device, along with information like battery life, photos, texts, available space, and so on. Each device you connect to your computer will have its own Device Stage, offering different options that match their

functions and features. You can manage your cell phones, printers, digital cameras and a wealth of other similar compatible devices from this central point. It's so well tailored you'll even have a picture of your phone sitting on your screen.

The second feature is the Devices and Printers folder on the Control Panel that takes Device Stage a step further. Here you can instantly check and see what's connected to your PC and you can access the properties and settings directly.

DEVICE SQUAD Windows 7 keeps you and your connected devices in perfect harmony

Setting up your mobile device
How to create the perfect partnership

1 CONNECT Plug in your device via USB (or use Bluetooth to connect wirelessly) and Windows Mobile Device Center should recognize it and start up automatically. If it doesn't load, search for it in **Start Search** and open it manually.

2 PAIR UP When you first plug in your device you can choose whether or not to start a permanent partnership. If this is your main PC, choose **Set up your device** to save effort next time. You can delete the partnership later if you wish.

3 START SYNCING You will see a list of media types to synchronize. The items you choose will be updated each time you sync. If you want to use email, contacts and calendar synchronization you'll need Windows Live Mail.

4 EXPLORE You can use Windows Mobile Device Center to peruse all the data on your phone. This allows you to add files manually to the device, or copy data from the phone to your hard drive using Windows Explorer.

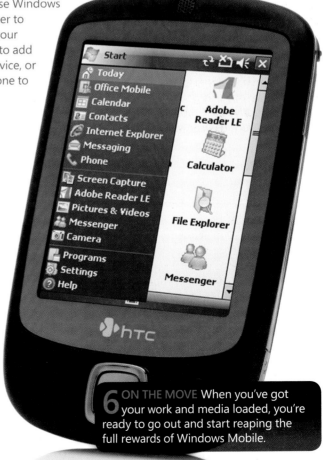

5 MULTIMEDIA Setting up your mobile device doesn't have to be about emails and appointments. Mobile Device Center lets you set up pictures, music and video clips to export. Go to **Pictures, Music and Video → Add media to your device from Windows Media Player**.

6 ON THE MOVE When you've got your work and media loaded, you're ready to go out and start reaping the full rewards of Windows Mobile.

Ensure a smoother, faster PC system

Keeping your system in tip-top condition has never been so simple – with help from Windows 7

A healthy system is a happy system, and a happy system is a fast system. Maintenance and performance go hand in hand, which is why you'll find tools for both in the System and Security section of the Control Panel. In addition to the features you'd expect – cleaning up unnecessary files, tweaking your PC's display, adjusting the power management options, and so on – you'll find some key new tools, too. There's the Windows Experience Index, which makes it easy to see how well your PC is performing, identify bottlenecks and decide whether your kit is powerful enough for particular programs; the Problem Reports and Solutions tool, which can identify and, where

appropriate, fix software and drive problems; and the Action Center, which reports any issues your PC is having and suggests ways to deal with them.

Two other key features are ReadyBoost and ReadyDrive. The former enables you to use cheap USB drives or memory cards to speed up your system, and the latter gets the best from next-generation hybrid hard drives.

Get experienced

There is a huge range of hardware on the market, such as memory, graphics cards, hard disks and processors. Obviously, the choice is great, but with so many different possible combinations you can never be entirely sure how a particular program will perform on your

system – whether it'll have a positive effect on your PC's overall performance or a negative one. With previous versions of Windows, the answer was 'buy the program and hope for the best', but with Windows 7 you can see exactly what your PC is made of and where any bottlenecks might be.

The new Windows Experience Index can analyze your hardware to see what's speedy and what's slow. It calculates an overall score that tells you just how quick your PC is, and also calculates individual scores for components. This feature has two benefits – you can immediately see which components might be worth upgrading and, in future, when you're buying software, you can tell how it will perform on your PC.

Experience in action

Updating your Windows Experience Index score is easy

1 INDEXING Go to **Control Panel ➜ System and Security ➜ Check the Windows Experience** to open the WEI. If anything has been changed recently, click **Update my score**.

2 BIG BASE You'll see a giant button with a number in it. This number is the overall score for your system. The bigger the number the faster your kit. The highest possible score is 7.9.

3 SUBSCORES Your base score is calculated from five crucial parts: processor, memory, graphics card, gaming graphics and hard disk. Click **View and Print details** for full details.

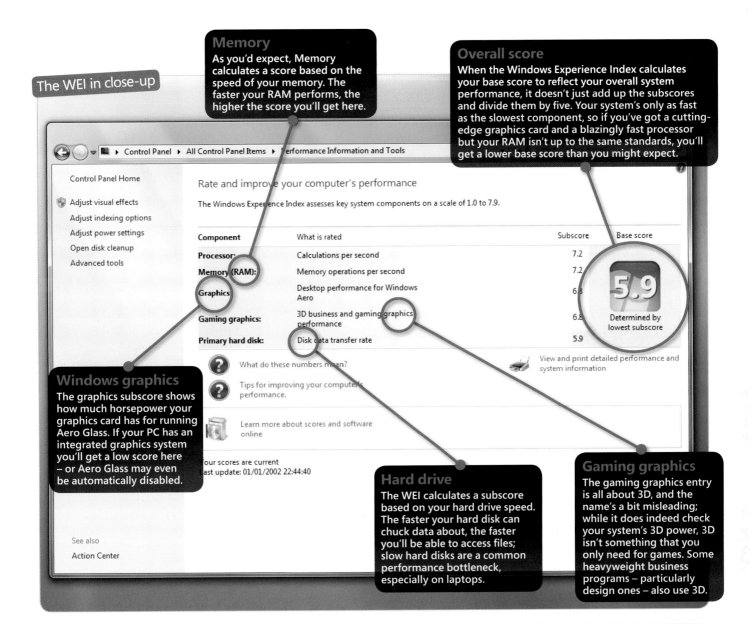

The WEI in close-up

Memory
As you'd expect, Memory calculates a score based on the speed of your memory. The faster your RAM performs, the higher the score you'll get here.

Overall score
When the Windows Experience Index calculates your base score to reflect your overall system performance, it doesn't just add up the subscores and divide them by five. Your system's only as fast as the slowest component, so if you've got a cutting-edge graphics card and a blazingly fast processor but your RAM isn't up to the same standards, you'll get a lower base score than you might expect.

Windows graphics
The graphics subscore shows how much horsepower your graphics card has for running Aero Glass. If your PC has an integrated graphics system you'll get a low score here – or Aero Glass may even be automatically disabled.

Hard drive
The WEI calculates a subscore based on your hard drive speed. The faster your hard disk can chuck data about, the faster you'll be able to access files; slow hard disks are a common performance bottleneck, especially on laptops.

Gaming graphics
The gaming graphics entry is all about 3D, and the name's a bit misleading; while it does indeed check your system's 3D power, 3D isn't something that you only need for games. Some heavyweight business programs – particularly design ones – also use 3D.

In real life...
Pick your upgrades with the Windows Experience Index

**James Stables,
Deputy Editor,
Windows: The
Official Magazine**

My cheap laptop was running slowly, so I used the Windows Experience Index to identify potential upgrades. The base score was 2.0, but the processor wasn't the problem as that got a subscore of 4.1. The hard disk was good, at 4.6, but things started to fall down with the integrated

graphics card, which scored 3.1 for gaming and just 2.4 for Aero Glass. I considered upgrading the graphics, but then noticed that the RAM was reporting a subscore of 2.0 – ah, so that's why the base score was so bad. A single upgrade would boost the Windows Experience Index score to 2.4, because then the graphics card would be the weakest link.

Basically, a subscore of around 2.0 means upgrading's a good idea.

If that's impractical, it's worth considering alternatives, such as disabling Aero Glass or, in the case of memory, using Windows ReadyBoost.

A subscore of 3.0 is OK, and an upgrade might not be worth the money. The exception is when the component in question is having an obvious effect on your system. For example, a graphics subscore of 3.0 is adequate for everyday PC use but might not be enough for gamers.

Fast and flash

The latest fad is flash, not the web animation tool, but solid state memory. It helps Windows 7 to run faster and smoother than ever

Buy a new PC, boot into Windows for the first time and, with no background applications, you'll find you barely have time to put your hand on the keyboard before the desktop is ready and waiting. A couple of months later, you can make breakfast in the time it takes to go from power-on to a usable desktop...

The key to faster boot times lies in improving hard drive speed, but even with a fast multi-core processor and lots of memory it can still take applications minutes rather than seconds to load.

The culprit is the magnetic hard drive. It's not all bad. This kind of drive can store lots of information for not a lot of money, and shift lots of consecutive data around quickly. Unfortunately, your hard drive often moves small bits of info around, not big chunks in one go.

As well as having to electronically process a request for data, there's the time it takes the read head to move across the platter. This seek time is what slows hard drives down.

The latest trend in hard drives is solid state memory. Using the same flash technology used to store information on camera memory cards and USB sticks, hard drive manufacturers are building discs up to 256GB in capacity which have no moving parts.

Mix and match

There are several advantages to Solid State Drives (SSD). The key one is that, because there's no mechanical interface, it's much quicker to locate and read data from an SSD, especially when you're looking for lots of small files all at once – as you are during the Windows boot process or when loading a program. They're also far less fragile than spinning platters, so are perfect for laptops which tend to take a few knocks.

The disadvantages of SSDs are that they're slightly slower at burning large files to memory – although that's

improving – and they're very expensive compared to similarly sized traditional disks. What system builders are tending to do is install an SSD as a system drive to install Windows on, and using a large magnetic disk for everything else. That speeds up the boot time, makes Windows more responsive, and still leaves plenty of room for data that's not so time dependent.

Windows 7 has many improvements over Windows Vista for utilizing SSDs, and several optimizations which are suited to the technology. For a start, it turns off defragmenting on flash drives, because they simply don't need it. It also has a feature called 'trim', which reduces the number of writes and re-writes it will perform compared to a hard drive, because SSDs have a finite lifespan before they start producing errors. Most importantly, though, Windows 7 is designed to speed up the way data is written on to an SSD, overcoming their traditional weakness. ⊞

Inside a solid state drive

Why flash is fast. Now here's the science bit...

Data on a traditional drive is stored as magnetic marks on a smooth platter; in an SSD, data is registered as a charged or uncharged transistor. Instead of sending out a tiny read head to find a sector, an SSD can poll the state of a transistor almost at the speed of light, just by sending out electrons along the right path.

On one level, the construction of an SSD is similar to a magnetic drive. There are two parts: the largest is the chips that store data. Unlike system

RAM chips, information is not lost when the power is turned off, which makes them 'non-volatile' but slower.

The second part, the controller, has a RAM-based cache which stores data waiting to be written and prefetches information it thinks will be needed next. It also has circuitry which lists where data is located on the main drive, and spreads files around to prevent any one area being overwritten too many times.

SOLID STATE The absence of moving parts in an SSD makes for a more robust device

Speed up with Windows ReadyBoost

Use flash memory to give your PC instant zip

Lack of memory can be a big problem because hard disks are so much slower than memory chips. When you've filled your memory, your PC starts using the hard drive instead, slowing things down. Adding RAM can be expensive, and there's only so much room. With ReadyBoost you can solve this problem by using flash memory, such as USB drives or memory cards, to add extra memory quickly, easily, and cheaply.

ReadyBoost is very clever, but before you start you need to make sure your USB drive or memory card is up to the job of serving as an additional memory cache. You'll need a minimum of 256MB storage and a maximum of 4GB, and it needs to be capable of specific speeds: 2.5MB per second for random reads and 1.75MB per second for random writes. ReadyBoost will test your memory when you first plug it in and, if it's not up to scratch, ReadyBoost will refuse to use it.

The good news is that provided your memory card or USB drive meets the specs, ReadyBoost is simple to set up and makes a massive difference to your kit.

Q Isn't using flash memory slower than a hard disk?

A In terms of data transfer speeds, yes – but finding things on a flash memory device is much quicker than most hard disks, and it's the seek time rather than the data transfer speed that really matters here.

Q If I remove the memory card or USB drive, will it crash my PC?

A No. Everything ReadyBoost does is mirrored on your hard disk for that very eventuality, but as long as your memory is connected ReadyBoost will use it. If you unplug it, ReadyBoost just uses your hard disk instead. And you don't need to worry about privacy, either; ReadyBoost scrambles every bit of data that's stored on your memory card or USB drive.

Q How much memory do I need to have available my flash drives?

A Microsoft recommends a ratio of one to three times the amount of memory installed in your system. So,

for example, if you've got 512MB of installed RAM then you should consider a ReadyBoost drive of between 512MB and 1.5GB. There's little point in exceeding the recommended amount, as you'll get little noticeable benefit.

ReadyBoost really makes sense when your PC's suffering from inadequate memory – it's the perfect solution.

Q What's the difference between ReadyBoost and ReadyDrive?

A The same technology that powers ReadyBoost powers another performance feature in Windows 7: ReadyDrive. Unlike ReadyBoost, chances are you can't take advantage yet. That's because ReadyDrive is designed for hybrid drives, which combine traditional hard disks with flash memory and deliver faster performance, better reliability and, in laptops, longer battery life. While ReadyDrive means Windows 7 supports such devices, hybrid hard disks are only just beginning to appear, although they're sure to become more common in the near future.

Ready, steady, boost

Provided you have the right specs, ReadyBoost is simple to set up

1 NO GO Make sure to check the specs before buying; when you plug it in and choose ReadyBoost, Windows 7 checks it's up to scratch. If it's not, ReadyBoost will refuse to use it.

2 RIGHT SPECS Try again with a memory card at the required speed. When you plug it in you'll see the AutoPlay dialog shown here. Click **Speed Up My System** to enable ReadyBoost.

3 TURN IT ON Here's the ReadyBoost tab of the Removable Disk Properties dialog. Windows 7 works out the best amount of space for ReadyBoost, then click **Use This Device → OK**.

Top 10 speed boosts

Knowing what affects performance can help speed up
an older system, or get even more from a box-fresh PC

An easy way to make your computer run more quickly is to remove unnecessary eye candy, and you can do this from the Performance Information and Tools dialog box.

You can make your PC quicker by disabling visual effects. For example, if you click the **Adjust for Best Performance** button, Windows 7 will disable Aero Glass. That's probably a bit dramatic, though, and you'll find that

LESS IS MORE It's easy to get more display performance by turning off fancy features

disabling the following display options will make your system seem speedier:

■ Animate controls and elements inside windows
■ Animate windows when minimizing and maximizing
■ Fade or slide menus into view
■ Fade or slide tooltips into view
■ Fade out menu items after clicking
■ Slide open combo boxes
■ Slide taskbar buttons

Search and destroy

The search system in Windows 7 is very handy, but the more files it's keeping an eye on, the more of an effect it's going to have on performance. If things are a little sluggish, use the **Adjust Indexing Options** link. Use the **Modify** button to change the locations the Index keeps an eye on, and use the **Advanced** button to limit the list of files – for example, if you use your PC mainly for work, you could disable the indexing of non-work files such as images, media files, document templates, and so on.

The power management feature is another handy tool. Many desktops default to the Balanced power plan, and switching to High Performance results in a noticeable speed boost when running processor-intensive applications. But if even the High Performance mode isn't delivering as much speed as you'd like, click on **Change plan settings → Change advanced power settings**. You can now change settings such as maximum and minimum processor performance, whether indexing should favour energy efficiency or sheer speed, and so on.

The last link provides you with some additional performance tools... Task Manager, which shows you what programs and processes are running on your PC, and Disk Defragmenter, which automatically reorganizes the contents of your hard disk at scheduled times to speed up file access. There's also a range of information tools including System Information, Event Log (which tracks any problems with your hardware or software), the Reliability and Performance Monitor, which tracks your

Manage your startup programs

Check your software and get rid of unnecessary programs

If you're logged on as an Administrator and type 'msconfig' into the search bar in the Start menu, you'll be taken to Windows 7's advanced set-up panels, which change the behavior of Windows during start-up.

If you find your PC is taking a long time to boot up it may well be because it's trying to load too many programs and services in the

background. Some of these will be essential, like the Family Safety applications, but others, such as games, are not – and will have launchers that set themselves up to constantly run in the background.

You can stop them from doing so by either uninstalling them or going to 'msconfig' and clicking on the **Startup** tab. Simply uncheck the tick box next to their name.

THE NEED FOR SPEED Change the startup programs to increase startup speed

The PC trend is for processors – the bit that runs your programs – to have more cores. The good news is, Windows 7 is set to take full advantage of that power.

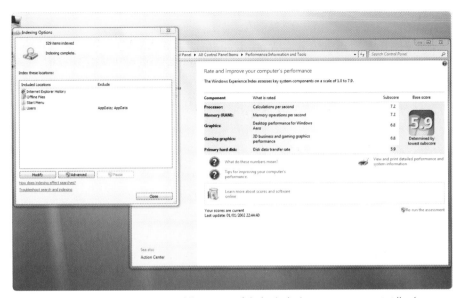

PC's robustness and shows the results in reports and graphs, and System Health Report, which provides a detailed insight into the state of your system. This takes 60 seconds to get data and reports on everything from whether your PC has anti-virus software to how active your network adaptor is.

Upgrade your memory

Memory is an essential part of your PC – programs including Windows 7 itself are loaded into random access memory (RAM) because it's the quickest way of accessing them. Windows 7 requires a minimum of 1GB of RAM to run, but if you want to enjoy its advanced features, you'll need at least 2GB (2,048MB). If your budget will run to it,

LOCATION, LOCATION, LOCATION While very useful, the indexing system can actually slow down your computer, so it's a good idea to change the locations your PC keeps an eye on

a memory upgrade is one of the most effective ways of speeding up your PC.

If the idea of opening up your computer to fit more memory doesn't appeal, or you want even more performance, take advantage of Windows 7 ReadyBoost. If you have a USB flash drive that is compatible you can speed up your PC by inviting Windows 7 to use some or all of the drive to store information it needs to access. Just plug your flash drive into a spare USB port, and when the Autoplay menu pops up, select **Speed up my**

system using Window ReadyBoost to enjoy a faster computer.

As you add, edit and delete files on your hard drive, they become all jumbled up – or fragmented – across the disk. As a result, your computer takes longer to access each file. Windows 7 has a tool called Disk Defragmenter that runs at set times to keep your files in order. You can alter this schedule to a more convenient time, or run the utility manually by clicking **Start ➜ All Programs ➜ Accessories ➜ System Tools ➜ Disk Defragmenter**.

Give your PC a spring clean

Maintain a good level of hard drive space by clearing out clutter

A computer can accumulate a huge amount of unwanted files and it can be a real chore to track these down to reclaim hard drive space.

The good news is that Windows 7 comes with a handy program called Disk Cleanup, which can help get rid of unnecessary files. This scans your hard drive for anything you might not need – log files, downloaded programs, files created when your

system was hibernating, and so on – and it enables you to get rid of some or all of them.

When Disk Cleanup has finished, click on **More Options**. Here you'll find two options – the first enables you to get rid of programs or components you no longer need, the second enables you to get rid of old restore points (keep the most recent one), backups and other safeguards.

SPRING CLEAN Use Disk Cleanup to remove temporary or unnecessary files

Cut down on crashes and solve PC problems

Does your PC crash or hang up? Windows 7 contains tools that can help you discover why, and make your system more reliable

Anyone who uses a PC soon gets used to error messages; applications that hang up, and others that simply die. After a while, you see it all as an occupational hazard. But with Windows 7, it doesn't have to be that way. The new system includes a rewritten crash-handling facility that does a far better job than previous versions of Windows in recording what errors have occurred. And it's packed with useful tools to help diagnose crashes, and hopefully prevent them from happening again. There's no need to live with an unstable PC – Windows 7 can help get your system working again.

Easy to use

The traditional path to fixing PC crashes involved trying to decipher cryptic error messages, or browsing incomprehensible log files. Fortunately, Windows 7 offers a different route. It maintains a database holding the details of all your program crashes (for up to a year), and can go online to look for possible fixes.

To give this a try, connect to the internet, then open the Action Center by clicking on the flag in the bottom right-hand corner and select **Change the Action Center settings**. Now choose **Problem reporting settings.** Windows 7 will send information about your crashes to a Microsoft server and will then display solutions. These aren't always helpful – sometimes it will just say your application isn't compatible. But usually they offer practical help, telling you that you need to download a new driver or

else has reported the same crashes, you might just find a solution to the problem without having to rely on anything else.

The Problem Reports and Solutions applet is a welcome addition to Windows, but unfortunately it won't won't solve everything. But there are other tools around...

The Reliability Monitor provides in-depth coverage of your crash history. It also details software you've added and removed, making it easy to tell if your problems began right after you installed

Windows 7 includes a completely rewritten crash-handling system

Windows patch, and even providing a link to where you can find it. Sometimes the program won't find any solutions, but Microsoft is adding new fixes all the time, so you can always try again in a week. And there are a few tricks you can try for yourself, too.

Help yourself

Of course, you don't have to rely entirely on the Windows 7 reporting options. If you're experiencing regular problems with system crashes that Windows 7 doesn't seem able to sort out by itself, you can find repetitive error messages by clicking on **Select view archived messages**. Double-click on the one that's causing you difficulty for more information on it, and make a note of the Problem Event Name and Application Name. Use these as keywords in a search engine – if anyone

a particular application. Device Manager now has its own Control Panel applet. Open this and you'll see faulty devices highlighted with a yellow exclamation mark. Double-click to read more advice, and click the **Check for solutions** button.

One of the most welcome and useful additions to Windows 7 has to be the new Memory Diagnostics Tool. Faulty RAM can cause all kinds of problems, but now there's an easy way to detect it. Click **Start**, enter 'Memory' in the search box to launch the program, then allow your computer to be restarted. Press **F1** to choose Extended tests, select **0** as the Pass Count to keep them running, and let the tests repeat overnight. If faulty RAM is behind your problems, a few hours with the Memory Diagnostics Tool should be enough to reveal the source and set you on the road to restoring your computer's health.

MEMORY PROBLEMS Use the new Memory Diagnostics Tool to check for faulty RAM

Find out what's causing crashes

Use Windows 7 to chase down and fix problems

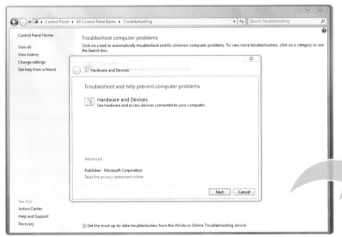

1 GET HELP It's frustrating when your applications crash, but Windows 7 may be able to help. Go online, then click **Control Panel → System and Security → Action Center** for an alternative way to open up the Action Center.

2 CHECK ONLINE Windows 7 will check with Microsoft to find out if there are known solutions to your crashes. This might take a moment, particularly if there's a lot to report or you've a slow internet connection.

3 FIXING PROBLEMS Windows 7 comes with a handy troubleshooter that you can open up from the Action Center. Find the topic heading that sounds closest to the problem you're having and Windows will run a diagnostic check.

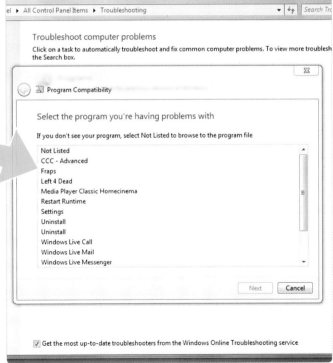

4 KIT WORRIES If you've installed a new piece of hardware or plugged in a mobile device that isn't working, for example, the Hardware and Device troubleshooter will scan for driver updates or suggest other fixes for you. There's a similar help section solely for audio problems.

Often you'll find solutions; for example, you may need to update a driver, and you'll be provided with the links

5 OLD PROGRAMS If the problem is that you're trying to get a program designed for an older version of Windows to run, try the Compatibility troubleshooter. This detects what the best settings are for the application in question and configures it.

Making the most of System Restore

If your PC becomes unstable, Windows 7 boasts a number of features to help restore to its former status

Each time a critical change is made to Windows 7, the System Restore software creates what it calls a Restore Point. This stores a back-up copy of all the system files that are about to change, so if it turns out the new software or hardware driver causes your PC to become unstable, for whatever reason, you're able to restore your PC to its previous status, before the changes were made, and – typically – remove any associated problems.

And, in true Windows 7 user-friendly style, System Restore works entirely invisibly in the background, creating restore points automatically as new software and drivers are installed.

It is possible to create these manually through the Backup and Restore Center but for the vast majority of people this is unnecessary. Take a look at the opposite page to get a better idea of how to access and use System Restore.

Roll back

A spin-off of the System Restore feature is that each driver on a PC can be Rolled Back. This means that if you're having problems with a new driver, it's possible to use the Device Manager – found within the System Control Panel – to revert Windows 7 back to an earlier, problem-free driver.

The easiest way to access this is to open the Start Menu, type 'Device Manager' and press **Enter**. If you open one of the device-type categories, double-click a specific device and click the **Driver** tab. Here you'll find information about the current device's driver and a selection of options. It's best not to make any changes here, but if you were having problems with the current device it is possible to disable it, remove it or, most helpfully, roll its driver to the previous version.

System Restore and the Roll Back option combine to offer powerful yet simple problem solving, enabling you to easily remove troublesome software, drivers or even problems of unknown origins with just a few clicks of the mouse button. ⊞

Discover hidden PC alerts

How to find the problems that don't cause a full-blown crash

The typical PC crash is almost impossible to miss. An application displays a big error message, locks up or disappears completely. But it's not the same with every problem. Some errors may be raised as events, and while Windows logs these, it doesn't display them. So if your PC seems unstable and you don't know why, it's a good idea to check recent events for clues.

Click **Start**, type 'eventvwr' in the Search box, and press **Enter** to see what the Event Viewer reports. Expand the Custom Views section in

EVENTFUL The Event Viewer is packed with information on your computer's problems that you won't find elsewhere on your system

the tree on the left-hand side of the screen, then click **Administrative Events** to see a list of issues that have cropped up on your system.

Not all these events are important. If you find one that looks trivial, just move on. You'll often find more serious registry issues, application errors, even reports of imminent hard drive failure, none of which may have been reported elsewhere. The contents of your Event Log could well point you to the application, device or Windows component that's behind most of your current crashes.

Troubleshoot computer drivers

How to pinpoint your PC's driver problems

Faulty drivers are one of the major causes of PC crashes, but could they be responsible for the issues on your system? There's one way you can try to find out, but be careful – this method of enquiry is not for beginners! If you're not familiar with, for instance, booting into Safe Mode to recover a faulty PC, you'll probably want to give this a miss.

Otherwise, if you do feel confident, confirm that you want to start in Safe Mode – reboot your PC and keep tapping the **F8** key until you see the

Startup Menu. Use the cursor keys to choose **Safe Mode** from the list and press the **Return** key. If that works, boot Windows 7 normally again, then launch Verifier.exe. Select **Create standard settings → Next**, choose **Automatically select all drivers installed on this computer** and **Finish**.

Reboot your PC and Verifier will begin testing your drivers. If it reports a problem, then make a note of the driver name – this is the one you'll need to replace. Unfortunately, that problem will also crash the PC, so reboot back into Safe Mode, launch Verifier and select **Delete Existing Settings**.

If Verifier doesn't spot a problem, you'll see no messages. Give it five minutes, then try the process again. If there's still no response listing problems, use the **Delete Existing Settings** option to remove Verifier, as it looks like your drivers may not be faulty, after all.

DRIVE-BY Detect driver problems with this useful, if technical, Windows 7 tool

Quick questions

Solving your crashes

Q My applications are crashing frequently. What can I do?
A Click **Control Panel → System and Security → Troubleshoot common computer problems** and let Windows 7 check for fixes.

Q That helped, but there are some problems left...
A Click **View Problem History**, make sure all your problems have been reported, and you've installed recommended solutions.

Q I'm still crashing occasionally. Any other ideas?
A Double-click on any unsolved errors. Use Live Search to search for the error name, and you may find some answers.

Q How can I fix my one or two remaining problems?
A Use tools like Device Manager, the Reliability Monitor and Memory Checker.

How System Restore works

Rolling back your Windows 7 installation is easy as 1, 2, 3!

1 START RESTORE System Restore can be accessed via **System and Security → System → System protection**, or open the Start Menu, type 'System Restore' and press **Enter**.

2 CHOOSE A POINT Click **Next** to view the restore points. These are listed with a time and date and an explanation of why it was created, usually listing a program or driver installation.

3 RESTORE AWAY If you spot a likely restore point, select it by clicking on it with the mouse and clicking **Next**, and **Next** again. You're given a warning; click **Yes** to proceed.

Reliability and Performance Monitor

If you're still concerned about the status of your system, Windows 7 measures the performance of your PC

As part of the Windows 7 remit to provide a secure system, the Reliability and Performance Monitor is on hand to provide you with advanced performance analysis. If your system goes wrong, this is where you'll find details of what happened. Although the Task Manager gives you some of the same information and options, the Reliability and Performance Monitor gives you that little bit more.

You can use it to determine how the programs you run affect the overall performance of your system. There are a number of features built into it that you can use to create logs, measure the state of your system and monitor activity.

To launch the Reliability and Performance Monitor, click **Start**, type 'perfmon.exe' and press **Enter**. Click **Reliability Monitor** and in the right pane you'll see a detailed chart. Each column represents a particular day and you'll see the corresponding date beneath. The five rows indicate potential problem areas, including hardware, software and Windows itself. If you see a cross against anything, that means an error's occurred.

To see information about an error, click a date. Look at the System Stability Report under the graph, and check for dates that carry a symbol. Either a cross, or information or exclamation mark notes something worthy of inspection. As well as complete applications, this category covers updates for individual programs; updates for Windows Defender are also recorded here. System problems often result from the installation of a particular program, and you can follow a program's progress under Application Failures. The exact name of the application is listed here, along with a reason for the failure.

If your system does crash, the information provided here will help pinpoint the reason. Errors under Windows Failures are rare, but if one does occur, look under Failure Detail for specific error codes. Carry out a search on this code using either Windows Live Search or the Microsoft Knowledge base – you'll usually find a solution.

What is the Stability Index?

Understanding your stability rating in Windows 7

Under the date drop-down box in the Reliability and Performance Monitor, you'll notice an Index score. This refers to the rating your system has been given for a particular date. The System Stability Index uses a number between 1 and 10. The lower your rating, the poorer your PC is performing. The rating that's given is based on data gathered since you first started using your system. The number of errors and failures you've encountered in the course of use affect the measurement.

For example, uninstall a problem

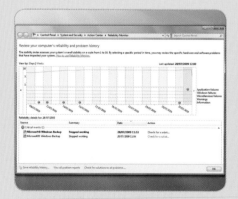

PC LIFELINE If you've been experiencing problems, check the System Stability Index to see how your PC is performing

application and keep an eye on the Performance and Reliability graphs – you should see your score improve. Your rating is calculated by taking into account a number of different factors. For example, greater significance is placed on the most recent errors. To avoid inaccurate readings, any days when your system is powered off aren't included. Don't confuse the System Stability Index with the Windows Experience Index. The latter measures the performance capability of your PC's hardware and software configuration.

How stable is your PC?

View the charts, graphs and stats to see where any problems are

 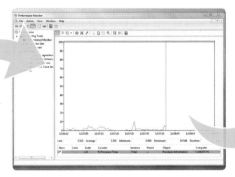 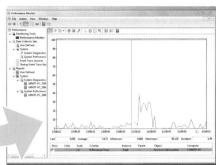

1 RELIABILITY MONITOR Your PC seems to be getting more unstable. But is that really true? Click **Start**, type 'perfmon' into the Search box and press **Enter** to launch the Reliability and Performance monitor.

2 DETAILED GRAPH The System Stability chart shows just how reliable your computer has been. Scroll back, and you might even see where problems began. Did you install a program at that time? Maybe that's the cause of your issues.

3 CHECKUP Click **Performance Monitor** to see how things are running. Click the green '+' sign and choose something to watch (eg, **Memory → Available MBytes**). Now run programs as normal and watch as your free memory changes.

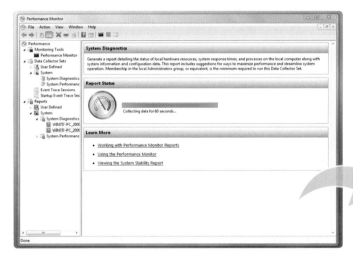

The System Stability chart shows just how reliable your computer has been; you might see where problems began

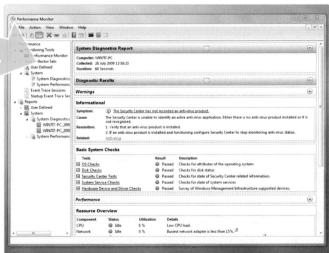

4 COLLECT DATA The program can also run system diagnostics reports – a handy way to identify PC problems. Click **Data Collector Sets**, then double-click **System** to see everything it checks. Now click on **System Diagnostics** to see everything it tests, then **Action → Start** to begin the report.

Report feedback

Many people are guarded about reporting problems back to Microsoft. However, each report is useful to Microsoft for reporting back to hardware and software partners, along with tracking general errors.

5 DIAGNOSTIC REPORTS It can take a moment for the report to be generated, so be patient. When it's complete you'll find there's lots of information here, but anything particularly significant will appear in the first Warnings section so you don't actually have to read every word.

Do More

Windows 7 can help in the office and at home. Benefit from improved organization and efficiency – and have fun!

Watch recorded TV on your cell phone

Want to watch the latest episode of your favorite TV series on the subway? It's easy to play it on your phone...

Super Tip!

More formats

Windows 7 is geared up for high definition entertainment, so it supports more file formats than ever before. That means movies and home videos in HD will play in Windows Media Player.

RECORD YOUR PROGRAMME
The easiest option is to use Windows Media Center, although any TV tuner card and video-recording software should work fine.

With all the continuing enthusiasm for video-capable music players, it's easy to forget that you're probably already carrying around a multimedia device in the form of your cell phone. Most handsets boast headphone connections and color screens ideal for music, photos and even recorded TV – and Windows 7 makes it very easy to fill them with footage.

How you transfer material depends on the phone you've got. It's easiest with phones running Windows Mobile, as these come with pocket versions of assorted PC programs including

Windows Media Player – so you don't have to worry about different file types or having to master a new interface. If you've got a different sort of phone, then it's still fairly straightforward to copy files over but you'll need a decent-sized screen and a memory card slot; very few cell phones come with the hefty amounts of storage space required to store video. You may also need to install a separate bit of software – usually this comes on CD in the box your phone came in, but you can also download it from the manufacturer's website.

The final crucial component is a way to copy the files over. The simplest option is

a good old-fashioned bit of cable – most Windows Mobile phones just use mini-USB connections, so you can usually pinch the cable from your digital camera if required. Other models might require a specific cable that you should be able to buy from a mobile phone shop or the manufacturer's website.

Smaller phones might only have wireless connections, such as Bluetooth or infra-red (IR). Check your phone's details in the manual or on the manufacturer's website. Infra-red connections aren't much good for copying anything bigger than text or photos; Bluetooth is faster and easier. ⊞

COPY First, find your video and open up the folder it's in. TV recorded in Windows 7 Media Center will be in Recorded TV in the Favorites list in Windows Explorer; other formats will be where you saved them.

CONVERT THE FILES
If the clip you want can't be converted by Windows Media Player, use a conversion program such as MyTV ToGo. If you have an ATi graphics card, you can use Avivo.

CONNECT YOUR PHONE Hook up your phone using the supplied cable, and Windows Mobile Device Center starts automatically. Click the **Pictures, Music and Video** button and Windows Media Player opens.

Click **Sync** and Windows Media Player converts and copies your video over automatically

WINDOWS MEDIA PLAYER The Sync window is already open; all you have to do is drag your video file from its folder into the left-hand Sync pane. You can see how much space you've got using the graph at the top.

MEDIA FRIENDLY If you're using Windows Media Center, you don't even need to use Media Player. Just connect your phone, and go to the Sync tab (top right) to select what video or music you'd like to copy.

SYNC ACROSS Click **Sync** and Windows Media Player automatically converts your video (if required) and copies it over. This can be a long process, particularly with large video files, so be patient as it completes.

KING OF QUALITY If your phone has a lot of memory and a big screen, you might want to use higher-quality video; increase it by going to **Sync → More Options → Properties → Quality**.

WATCH ON THE GO And that's it. Open Media Player on your phone, go to **Menu → Library** and select your footage from My Videos.

Use your PC to control your TV

With Windows Media Center you can record and watch your favorite shows when you want

There are just too many television channels out there today; while much content is of debatable quality, many shows are truly unmissable. Fortunately, viewers are no longer at the mercy of station controllers... Bring your PC into the picture, and you can ditch the TV listings. Record what you want and watch it when you want.

If you own the Windows 7 Home Premium, Professional or Ultimate edition, you've got Windows Media Center. It offers quick, no-fuss access to the multimedia content stored on your PC, and the effortlessly navigable menu is designed to be easy to view on a TV.

You'll need a TV tuner or cable card in your PC to use the television features in Windows Media Center, but if you haven't already got one, it's a simple business to add a USB TV tuner.

Making life easier

The first time you run Media Center, you'll need to go through a brief set-up (see opposite). Once you've got it working, press one of the cursor buttons on the keyboard or remote control (if you've got one) and a mini guide will pop up at the bottom of the screen. From here you can check what's on or, alternatively, hit **Pause** to freeze live TV as if it were a tape or DVD; the signal is recorded to the hard drive, so when you come back you can click **Play** and it will start where you left off.

That's the answer to those irritating phone calls that come through just as your main character is about to do

something heroic, but the really good stuff comes from planning ahead. Delve into the integrated Guide, take a look at what's coming up over the next couple of weeks and tag the shows you want to watch. When they roll around, Media Center will record them automatically.

You can even record a whole series with just one click, thanks to Record Series. However, it's worth noting that older stuff does get deleted to make room, so if you plan on building up an archive, go to **TV + Movies** on the main menu and choose **Recorded TV ➜ View Scheduled ➜ Series**, select the series and click **Series Settings ➜ Keep**. The

You can record a whole series with just one click – and then burn to DVD

number of episodes you can keep depends on the size of your hard drive. If you run out of space, consider boosting it with an external hard drive. Plug it in and tell Media Center to record to it under **Tasks ➜ Settings ➜ TV ➜ Recorder ➜ Recorder Storage**. Not that you have to leave everything on the computer... You can easily burn to a DVD, or even sync to an external device such as a portable video player.

Again, both of these processes can be handled straight from the Media Center menu, under **Burn DVD** and **Sync to Portable Device** respectively.

On the subject of DVDs, Windows Media Center offers basic playback controls, and a handy extra: Parental Controls. Go into **Tasks ➜ Settings ➜ General Parental Controls**, set up a four-digit code and you'll be able to set limits based on a movie's rating.

The last great advantage of using your PC for your viewing pleasure is that you can junk the airwaves and download shows direct. Keep an eye on the Online Spotlight section of the main menu for the ability to get the latest shows whenever you want them.

In real life...
Time-saving series

Adam Ifans, Editor, Windows: The Official Magazine
Windows Media Center is well known by those who've used it, but many Windows users didn't know how to add it or even if they had it at all. As it's now part of Windows 7 Home Premium, Professional and Ultimate Editions it's far more available. It's worth persevering with the set-up as, once it's up and running, features such as TV guide and Record a Series make enjoying your favorite shows much easier. For many, though, watching on a PC monitor isn't great and this is where Media Extenders, such as the Xbox 360, come into their own.

Windows 7 PC turns TV

Setting up the ultimate remote control is so easy

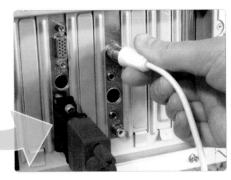

1 TUNING UP The first thing you need is a TV tuner or cable card – a device that can take a signal from an aerial or cable source. If your PC lacks one, you'll need to get one. Naturally, ensure that it's compatible with Windows 7.

2 SETTING UP Setting up Windows Media Center requires a number of steps (see page 86); needless to say, you will need to select the correct type of TV tuner card that you have and allow it to detect available stations.

3 ANTENNA-SHUN! Now it's time to plug an aerial or cable connector into your tuner card. For the best analog signal, a rooftop antenna is the ideal option. For the best results, buy a wideband one with a signal booster.

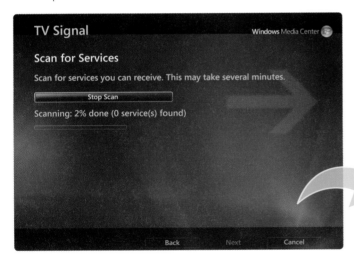

For maximum comfort, you'll need to connect the PC to your TV – using an Xbox 360 is the flashiest route

4 SETTING UP TIME Fire up Windows Media Center and in the menu select **Tasks**, then **Settings**. Enter the TV sub-menu and choose **Set Up TV Signal**. The computer will take you step by step through the tuning process, seeking out and storing channels. Now you're ready to start watching.

Media Center extenders

Media Center Extenders are handy devices that can connect to a Windows 7 PC via a wired or wireless network and make it easy to share your media, and stream movies, music and photos through to your TV.

5 VEG OUT For maximum comfort, you'll need to connect the PC to your TV. Using an Xbox 360 as a Media Center Extender is the flashiest route, but a cable will do. See which ports you have on your TV and PC and ask at an electronics store or check a web forum to see which one you need.

Go high-definition with Windows 7

Your guide to getting hi-def video from your PC to your TV – with Windows 7 it couldn't be simpler

So, you've invested in a high-definition LCD TV? Then you're about to watch TV and movies with significantly sharper, clearer picture quality than anything you've goggled at in the comfort of your own living room before. Congratulations!

And now you can use your PC as a gateway to a massive hi-def archive – either on Blu-ray or HD DVD disc or downloaded from a website.

There are two ways to get movies and TV shows from the PC to the TV; through a Media Center Extender or by connecting your PC or laptop directly. Only video files on your hard disc that are downloaded or created will work with an extender – if you're looking to use your PC to play HD movies from disc, directly connecting to your TV is the only way.

Xbox 360

The most popular Media Center Extender is the Xbox 360. When Windows 7 spots an Xbox 360 on the same network it will automatically configure the connection between the two for media sharing. It's as simple as turning on your console, switching to the video blade and just selecting a file to play.

Except that it *isn't* quite as simple as that... There are two standards for hi-def video, described by the number of vertical lines in the picture – 720p and 1,080p. Even the basic 720p resolution requires between 15-20Mbps of continuous bandwidth for smooth playback. So trying to stream an HD feed over a Wi-Fi connection is almost impossible – especially as the Xbox 360 wireless adaptor uses the older 802.11g standard rather than the newer, faster 802.11n. If you're trying to run HD video from your PC to the Xbox 360, make sure that both have a cabled connection to your router.

Want to keep your PC in a separate room? Try powerline networking. A 200Mbps kit plugs into a socket and creates a connection between either PC and router or Xbox 360 and router.

Build your own media empire

Five things to include if you're making your own media PC

1 GRAPHICS CARD If you go for an Nvidia or AMD graphics card, their latest chips support HDCP and are capable of decoding HD video without any trouble. AMD cards natively support HDMI too, for the best TV connection.

2 A GOOD CASE There are plenty of well designed Windows Media Center cases on the market, and many have displays to let you know which channel you're tuned to. The majority come in mini or slimline cases.

3 REMOTE CONTROL Get a wireless keyboard and mouse – you don't want cables lying around. Ideally, get a Windows Media Center remote – this has all the controls you need for using your PC as a set-top box.

If you don't own an Xbox 360, or want to play HD DVDs from PC to TV, you'll need to connect your PC directly to your TV. This isn't as tricky as it sounds. Most modern TVs offer a variety of signal inputs that should work with your PC. The first is the VGA port. Despite its age, and the connection being analog, you should get a good picture by setting the desktop resolution to 1,280x768. If you accidentally change the resolution to one your TV can't display, reboot the PC and press **F8** as it starts up. This will take you to Advanced Boot Options, where you can select **Enable low-resolution video** to take you back to a TV-friendly display.

HDMI ports

All you need to connect in this way is the DVI to VGA adaptor that came with your graphics card and an appropriate cable – but, because VGA can't carry an audio signal, you'll need a separate cable to connect your sound card to the TV or speakers. There is one big limitation to VGA cable, though. Encrypted content – like that on HD DVD or Blu-ray – requires a digital HDCP connection between player and TV; VGA on its own isn't going to cut it.

QUALITY ENTERTAINMENT Enjoy hi-def TV with the help of Windows Media Center

The only digital input most TVs use is the HDMI socket – many new graphics cards now offer these either directly or via an adaptor. Some of them will also send the sound signal through the HDMI port, so you only need one cable for movie playback. One of the benefits of using HDMI to connect to your TV is that your graphics card should adjust itself to the correct resolution – either 1,920x1,200 or 1,280x768. It's important to use a 1:1 ratio for desktop to screen resolution – an attempt by the screen to guess at missing pixels will result in messy text. So why are the resolutions quoted slightly higher than the HDTV resolutions of 1,920x1,080 and 1,280x 720? Because there are often unused lines in the panel which your PC display will try to fill. If they don't work, try the HDTV standards.

Now use your TV controls to raise the brightness and lower the contrast and sharpness until the text on your desktop is readable. Right-click on your desktop and go to graphics options for extra settings.

Now you have two ways of interacting with your PC. The easiest is Windows Media Center. If you're feeling more ambitious, and want to surf the web or answer Windows Live Messenger while watching video, try these two tricks.
1 Click anywhere in the desktop area and hold down **Ctrl** while scrolling the mouse wheel – this will adjust the size of the desktop icons to make them easier to see.
2 Right-click on the desktop and choose **Personalize**. In the left-hand bar you'll see an option for **Adjust font size (DPI)**. This will allow you to smoothly scale the system fonts to a size that's easy to read on a large screen in high resolution.

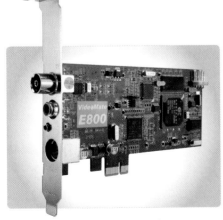

4 TV TUNER Make sure you're not reliant on pre-recorded media. Digital TV cards now come with one, two or four tuners on board so you can record several feeds at once, and use your PC's hard drive for pausing live TV.

5 MOTHERBOARD If your case doesn't ship with a motherboard, there are a host to choose from. Pick one that's correct for your type of processor and potentially save money by picking one with on-board HDMI video output.

Your hi-def questions

High-definition? It's all too confusing... Well, here are answers
to your most burning questions about the successors to DVD

1 What is high-definition?
High-definition is a
new way of recording and
watching TV, video and
console games. The picture
is made up of a larger number of parts,
which makes for greater detail and clarity.
In technical terms, high-definition (hi-def
or HD) is an increase in the resolution; in
practical terms, pictures seem clearer,
sharper – more vivid.

2 What is HD DVD?
HD DVD is a disc format based on
standard DVD technology. A single-sided
HD DVD disc can hold 30GB of data (15GB
in two layers) – equivalent to 7,500 music
files – more than six times the capacity of
standard DVD. The HD DVD standard also
incorporates features such as interactive
content. You can buy an external HD DVD
drive for your Xbox 360. (Although in
February 2008, Toshiba – principle
designer of the format – announced it
would no longer continue to develop
or manufacture the drives.)

3 What is Blu-ray?
Blu-ray Discs (BD) work in a slightly
different way, offering higher capacities
than HD DVD but higher production costs.
The Sony PlayStation 3 plays Blu-ray as
standard. The Blu-ray format can hold
25GB per layer; with the demise of HD
DVD, Blu-ray is now first-choice for the
high-definition optical disc format.

4 Do I need a hi-def TV to play
high-definition discs properly?
Yes, your TV needs to be HD ready –
fortunately, most new TVs are. When
choosing a new TV, make sure that you get
one with the 'HD ready' logo. This means
the TV meets the hardware requirements
to play high-definition videos and games.

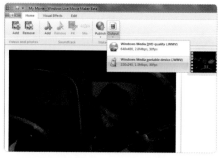

MOVIE MAKER Windows Movie Maker
can publish to various formats and sizes

5 Will my PC and monitor be capable
of high-definition content?
Unless you bought your PC with specific
hi-def hardware in mind, chances are
you'll need to upgrade. Your monitor,
for example, needs to be 24-inch
widescreen to cope with HD videos at
1,080p. You'll also need an HDMI and
possibly HDCP support, and if you want
to watch discs as well as downloaded clips,
you'll need a suitable HD DVD or BD drive.
You'll also need a capable graphics card
and modern processor with a good chunk
of memory. Happily, Windows 7 was
developed with HD in mind.

6 Can I make HD videos?
Yes you can – but it needs to be filmed
in HD for the true hi-def experience, which
means you need an HD camcorder. You'll
also need editing software for your
Windows 7 PC – see question 8.

7 Does Windows Media Player
play Blu-Ray/HD DVD discs?
The way HD films are stored requires
additional software so you'll need a third-
party program; ideally, try to get one that
supports both formats. Bear in mind,
though, that if you buy an HD DVD or
Blu-ray drive it may very well come with
the appropriate software anyway.

8 What hi-def stuff can I edit with
Windows Live Movie Maker?
You can edit and publish all your high-
definition videos in a variety of different
formats using Windows Live Movie Maker.
The output profiles are called Windows
Media HD and are available from the
Windows Live Essentials pack.

9 Are the discs just for videos?
No – though it will be the most
common use. Both types can be used
to store data, in much the same way as
a USB flash drive, external hard drive, or
a standard CD or DVD. The difference is
that both formats can store much more.
A Blu-ray disc, for example, has potentially
more than enough space on it for a full
system backup.

10 What do I need to stream
hi-def from my Windows 7
PC to my Xbox 360?
This can be done wirelessly, but it's
advisable to do it via an Ethernet cable
– a wired network connection. So you'll
need a Home Premium or Ultimate
Windows 7 PC, appropriate software, an
Xbox 360, an HDTV and an HD DVD
or Blu-ray disc drive.

11 What about drives to make and
record my own hi-def discs?
You'll need a drive capable of reading and
writing whichever format you want to use.
That means buying either a Blu-ray or HD
DVD recorder, with appropriate software.
Once you do this, you'll not only be able
to watch your HD videos on your HDTV
but also be able to make data discs.

12 What are HDMI and HDCP
connections?
HDMI (High-Definition Multimedia
Interface) is a connector that enables the

hi-def audio and video signals to travel from, for example, an HD DVD player to an HDTV, in a similar way to an S-video lead and socket. Your monitor and graphics card or motherboard will need to have HDMI ports or an adaptor to convert the more common DVI connection.

HDCP (High-bandwidth Digital Content Protection) makes an encrypted connection between the source and the destination display hardware before a video can be played. It's intended as a form of copy protection designed to protect the video during transmission, and all the hardware involved needs to support this standard to correctly play the video.

13 Where can I download high-definition content from?
You can download hi-def television programmes and movies through your Xbox LIVE service. You can also download sample clips from www.microsoft.com/windows/windowsmedia/musicandvideo/hdvideo/contentshowcase.aspx.

What to watch...

OK, so you've gone HD, but where do you get the programs to watch?

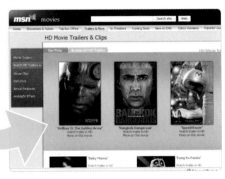

1 OPTICAL ILLUSION Now you've got your PC up and running, what on earth are you going to watch? The largest selection of HD media is still on optical disc, but you'll need a Blu-ray or HD DVD drive for that.

2 MOVIE DOWNLOADS Head to http://movies.msn.com for all the latest high-definition movie trailers and for links to download sites, such as www.cinemanow.com, which are becoming increasingly popular.

3 ONLINE MEDIA You'll find a number of premium content digital download channels in the Online Media section of Windows Media Center. Just fire it up from the Start menu and navigate to **TV + Movies ➜ More TV**.

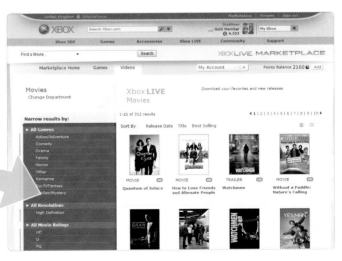

4 STANDARD DEF If it's standard definition TV you want, the MSN TV portal offers clips and full episodes to stream alongside features and news. Head over to http://tv.msn.com/tv to browse the all the latest TV programs.

5 XBOX LIVE Microsoft is already offering the best new movies in HD format as downloads via the Xbox Live Marketplace, and it won't be long before other PC providers catch up. Make sure your PC and TV are ready.

Make your own cell phone ringtones

Don't waste money on downloads – you have all the music you could ever want sitting there in your CD collection

Even if you ignore half the features in your cell phone, the ringtone is one thing that's always worth changing. At the very least, you want to avoid being one of those people patting their pockets when the default ringtone is heard in a crowd. At best, you want a tune that makes you glad to receive a call. While the tones that come with your phone won't necessarily fit the bill, it's easy to create something that does by turning one of your CD tracks into a ringtone.

The process is more straightforward than you might think. Finding a track is simply a matter of copying it from a CD and saving it as an MP3 file – the format that nearly all polyphonic phones support. You don't need to download specialist software to do this – Windows Media Player is fine. You only need extra software if you want to edit your clip first (see the example for using Audacity editing software opposite).

It's worth spending a bit of time picking a suitable tune. Choose something distinctive but tolerable; rich sounds aren't going to sound very impressive on a phone's tinny speakers. Also, try to pick a few bars that won't

sound too 'cut off' when you answer. It's a small thing, but it can be wearing to keep cutting off a track mid-melody every time you pick up the phone.

The only practical consideration then is how to transfer your MP3 from your

phone to your PC. There are a number of ways to do this. Most phones come with a USB cable that connects the handset to your PC. Alternatively, you can use an infra-red or a Bluetooth connection, but to use either of these methods your laptop or PC will require the correct adaptor or built-in hardware – consult your computer manual for more details. To show just how easy this is to do with different phones and connections, the following pages look at editing software and common ways in which various cell phones connect to and work with Windows 7...

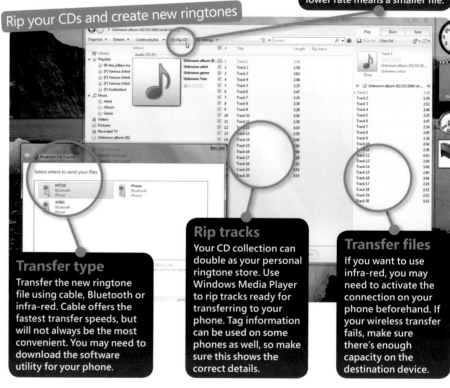

Rip your CDs and create new ringtones

Set bit rate
There's no point using the highest audio quality for a phone's tiny speakers – and a lower rate means a smaller file.

Transfer type
Transfer the new ringtone file using cable, Bluetooth or infra-red. Cable offers the fastest transfer speeds, but will not always be the most convenient. You may need to download the software utility for your phone.

Rip tracks
Your CD collection can double as your personal ringtone store. Use Windows Media Player to rip tracks ready for transferring to your phone. Tag information can be used on some phones as well, so make sure this shows the correct details.

Transfer files
If you want to use infra-red, you may need to activate the connection on your phone beforehand. If your wireless transfer fails, make sure there's enough capacity on the destination device.

Edit down your audio files

If you want to edit tracks before uploading them to your phone, you can download software from the internet. You'll find that some music

editing software is free, and you'll be able to trim songs to just the best sections, and reduce the bit rate to take up less space.

Editing your ringtone
Use free sound editing software to set the tone

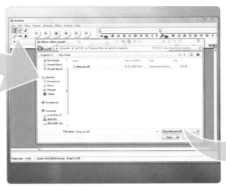

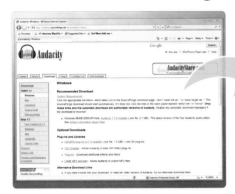

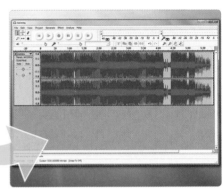

1 INSTALL Go to http://audacity. sourceforge.net/, click **Download Audacity 1.2.6**. Click **Audacity 1.2.6 installer** to install it. You also need to download and install the LAME MP3 encoder (on the same page). This enables you to save your edited file as an MP3.

2 NAVIGATE Open Audacity, go to **Edit → Preferences**. Click **File Formats**, then **Find Library**. Click **Yes** at the next dialog box and navigate to the installed LAME MP3 encoder (by default this is C:\Program Files\Lame for Audacity). Click **lame_enc.dll**, select **Open**, then **OK**.

3 SELECT Next, click **File → Open** and select the song you want to turn into a ringtone. The MP3 is saved by default in your Music folder. Audacity then imports your ringtone and you can see a graphical representation of your song alongside the various Audacity tools.

With Audacity software the MP3 is saved by default in your Music folder

5 STORE Ringtones and music files are one and the same on many phones, so stored tracks can be set as tones.

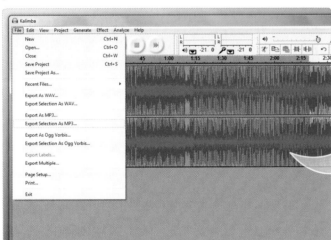

4 EFFECT Highlight the section of the song you want to turn into a ringtone and press the spacebar on your keyboard to preview it. You can add effects from the Effect menu. From the menu, select **Fade In and Fade Out**. Once you are happy with your ringtone, make sure the section is still highlighted and go to **File → Export Selection As MP3...** and choose a name.

Windows Mobile phones

The most Windows-friendly option for ringtones

1 SHARE DATA Use Windows Mobile Device Center to synchronize PC files with your device. Outlook contacts, calendar and email can all be kept up to date. The easiest way to get files on to most phones is to open **Computer** in Windows 7 then drag and drop.

2 SPACE RACE You can use MP3 files if you like, but the WMA format does have the advantage of taking up less space in your phone's memory. If you rip from a CD using Windows Media Player you can switch between WMA and MP3; go to the **Rip Music** tab in Options.

3 SYNC OR SWIM Sync your phone automatically to keep information up to date. Alternatively, just open **Computer** and take a look. Connect your phone to your PC with a USB cable and you'll be able to browse its contents as if you were using another drive.

5 LISTENING Click **Start**, browse to Settings, select **Sounds**. Under Ringtone scroll though the list of sounds, select your track to hear a preview of it. If you want to be able to listen to your ringtone as an audio track, copy it to the My Music folder. MP3 or WMA will be OK.

The Windows Mobile Device Center makes synching easy – just drag and drop your files

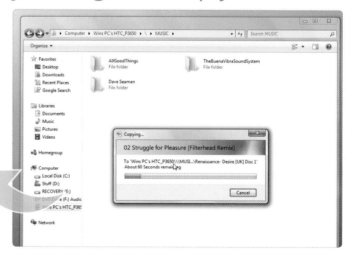

4 SOUND FILES Although your ringtones can be in MP3, WMA, MIDI or WAVE audio formats, for notifications or reminders you are restricted to WAVE (.wav) and MIDI (.mid) files. Many cell phones allow you to simply drag and drop or copy and paste files into the Music folder.

Using a Bluetooth connection
Wireless transfers can make life a lot easier

1 GET CONNECTED If your PC doesn't have Bluetooth built in, you can purchase an inexpensive USB adaptor. You can also use Bluetooth across a home network to share files and devices.

2 SEND FILE The Bluetooth icon is placed in the hidden icons menu, accessible by clicking the small arrow next to the clock. Right-click and choose **Send File**. Check the Use authentication box.

3 ATTACH Your PC will look for devices in range, and then ask you to locate the file on your PC. Simply find the MP3 file that you've ripped or edited and select it for your PC to send.

Bluetooth is another easy way to transfer files from your PC to your mobile device

5 SEND Once the pairing codes are matched, you can send your file, and it will appear as a new message on your phone, where it can then be saved to the relevant folder for music or data.

4 PIN READY For security your PC will ask you to set a pairing code, in order for the transfer to take place. You'll find the code either displayed on the device or on literature that came with it at purchase. This code simply has to be typed in again on the mobile phone for the transfer to be enabled.

Get fit using your PC

Getting fit used to be about blood, sweat and tears, but now your computer can take some of the strain

James Stables, Deputy Editor of *Windows: The Official Magazine* wanted to see whether his PC – and some techno gadgets – could help to improve his fitness levels...

My feet would barely lift off the ground, my legs ached and my heart felt as though it was about to burst out of my rib cage. That was the last time I took up running in a bid to get fit. As you can imagine, my new regime didn't last long.

If, like me, you feel guilty about the amount of exercise you don't do but lack the motivation to do anything about it,

there's good news. A mass of new technologies can make battling the bulge more enjoyable, and get even the most inactive of us off the sofa. To prove this, I set a mission to use my PC as a training aid to get fit in six weeks. I was scientifically assessed before and after the six-week period with the aim that, by sticking to my training schedule, the second round of tests would show some improvement in my overall health.

I chose three products that link with the PC to help me change my slothful ways. The first was the humble dance mat – already a champion with eight-year-olds everywhere, but anyone who has used

one knows it to be a demanding activity. The second, a product called the PCGamerBike – a USB exercise bike that doubles as a games controller. The third was the Nike + iPod, which links your trainers to your iPod nano and maps your runs online. In addition, I used a Polar Heart Rate Monitor to see what impact each device had on my heart rate levels.

Plan of attack

My personal training plan was as follows: running using the Nike+ iPod on Mondays, Wednesdays and Fridays; 45-minute dance mat and pedal game sessions on Tuesdays and Thursdays; rest

TESTING On the treadmill, and connected to a machine that will tell it like it really is!

Fit favorites

Work up a sweat with these...

LCD Soundsystem 45:33
As the title suggests, this is a 45-minute mix by one of the most respected producers around – James Murphy. The ups and downs are designed to keep you motivated, with a peak around 25 minutes to give an extra boost.

The Crystal Method Drive
The first 45-minute mix made specifically for running, designed to transfer the energy of the dance floor into your exercise.

Rage Against the Machine Self-titled
If steady beats aren't your cup of isotonic liquid, the renegades of funk can provide an alternative. Angry lyrics, blistering guitars and anti-establishment rants will get you pumped.

Queen Greatest Hits
With songs such as *We are the Champions*, *Another One Bites the Dust*, and *Bicycle Race*, Queen are the undisputed kings of music to work out to.

and recovery at weekends. If I was going to complete the mission, I would need some serious help. I met up with Gavin Reynoldson, a fitness and personal training tutor from a local university which specializes in health and fitness.

Gavin agreed to assess my health before and after my computer-aided fitness regime, so I could see if my new lifestyle was doing me good. He also checked over the merits of my equipment. The verdict on the dance mat was that it would improve the efficiency of the heart and lungs, in turn delivering more oxygen to the tissue; it should also improve flexibility in the muscles.

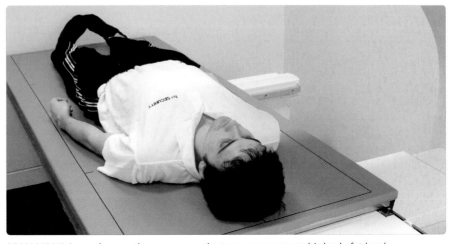

SCAN ME UP James lays on the scanner so the team can measure his body fat levels

Gavin seemed impressed with the Nike + iPod; running provides a great aerobic workout, and the high impact training helps prevent osteoporosis.

In order to test how effective this exercise regime could be, it was essential to check my overall fitness, so I was checked over for blood pressure, body weight, standing heart rate, body fat and

blood oxygen levels before and after the six-week period. Most of these tests are quite easy to perform at home. You can buy blood pressure monitors on the high street, and some pharmacies even check it for free. My blood pressure was 130/81 – a little high – 120/80 is normal and anything over 140 means medical advice may be needed.

To test your resting heart rate, it's important to be sitting comfortably for about five minutes to make sure the test is as accurate as possible. Locate the artery on the thumb side, underneath your wrist, and count the beats for one minute. Gavin took three readings of my pulse, which averaged 70. Any reading between 60 to 80 beats is normal; anything over may indicate a medical problem or a need to embark on a tentative exercise regime.

Next I was subjected to a VO2 test – this involves a body scan to determine body fat and a run on a treadmill to assess my body's ability to deliver oxygen to my

SOUND & STATS With the Nike + iPod you can play music and record your stats

My aim was a reduction in body fat and an increase in oxygen uptake

blood. The result showed my body was 25 per cent fat, over what it should be, while my oxygen uptake was 38.8ml/kg/min, well below average for someone of my age. My aim was a reduction of body fat and an increase in oxygen uptake.

How to set up Nike + iPod
Put your best foot forward with this nifty device

1 CREATE ACCOUNT Sign up to Nike+ on the website at http://nikerunning. nike.com and create an account. After a workout, connect your iPod nano to your PC; Nike+ will store and display your data through its dynamic interface.

2 SET SOME GOALS Have an idea of what you want to achieve and use Nike+ to set some realistic goals. Aim to do a certain amount of runs per week; you can also access your own personal trainer with Nike+ Coach.

3 JOIN THE COMMUNITY Nike+ is community based... You can join in with forums and chat to other runners, purchase Powersongs to motivate or share routes with Map It. You can even pair up with others and set challenges.

Primed and ready for action, I headed out on my first run with the Nike + iPod. I set it for a 20-minute workout, which Gavin recommended as an introduction, and started running at a gentle pace. However, I'd already had to stop to catch my breath when the merciless woman who encourages you from your iPod informed me that I had been running for five minutes – it felt like days!

However, the Nike + iPod does make the experience a lot less painful. I had chosen my playlist, and the iPod enables you to select a power song for moments of weakness, which drives you on for that extra mile. I hadn't yet travelled one mile, and I'm not sure the power song is designed to be used so early in the workout, but I needed it.

Back at home, plugging the iPod into my PC made the device come alive. It displayed the distance travelled, calories burned and a graph of my journey, showing every downturn in my

Keep fit kit

Everything you need to keep yourself in peak physical condition

Nike + iPod
A sensor in your trainer links to your iPod nano, recording time, distance, and calories burned.
Price $29 for the Nike+ sensor
Web http://nikerunning.nike.com

Polar Heart Rate Monitor
This wrist watch/chest strap combo monitors your heart rate, enabling you to plot fitness charts.
Price $300 (models/prices vary)
Web www.polar.fi/polar/channels/uk

Logic 3 Dance Mat
The humble dance mat makes for a mean exercise machine. Sustained use is good for muscle flexibility.
Price $40
Web www.spectravideo.com

PCGamerBike Mini
This device replaces a button on your keyboard, allowing it to be the input device for most games.
Price $179
Web www.gamecycles.com

4 ADD YOUR RUNS When you plug in your iPod nano, your data will be automatically updated on the Nike+ website. It plots a line graph of your run showing your pace, distance, time and calories burned.

5 TRACK YOUR PROGRESS All your runs are listed together, and can be viewed by week or month. The chart shows how far you have run each time and the improvement achieved in your fitness levels.

Desk stretches

Avoid injury before exercise...

Before exercise it's important to warm up to steer clear of nasty injuries. Here are five stretches you can do at your computer desk

Calf stretch
Put one foot in front of the other. Put your hands on the desk and lean forward, bending your front knee so you feel tension in your back leg. Reverse and repeat.

Hamstring stretch
Stand up and put one foot on the desk, so it's perpendicular to your body. Point your toes back and try to touch them, holding the tension for 10 seconds.

Quads
Hold on to the corner of the desk and pull your feet back to touch your buttocks, keeping your knees together. Hold the stretch, swap and repeat.

Groin
Sit up straight in your chair, and bring your feet together between your legs by tucking your knees up to your chest. Push your knees apart, hold the stretch for 10 seconds, relax and repeat.

Elbow press
Sit up straight and pull your arm up and back over your shoulder, stretching it down between your shoulder blades. Put your hand on the point of your elbow and hold it here for 10 seconds, then repeat with your other arm.

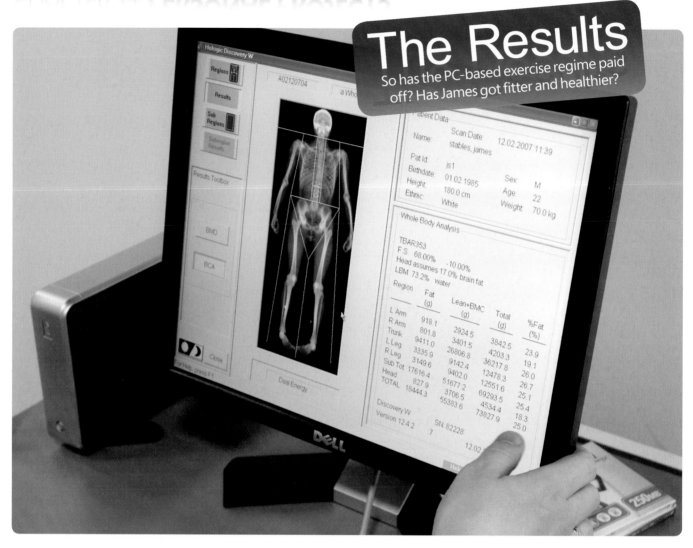

The Results

So has the PC-based exercise regime paid off? Has James got fitter and healthier?

performance like the crash of a stock market. Having a visual representation of my efforts made the aftermath seem a lot less painful, and it really does drive you to get out there and do it again. On my repeated outings to pound the pavements, I could see real improvement and, after four runs, the voices of Paula Radcliffe and Lance Armstrong congratulated me on my progress. I felt proud of my efforts.

While the assisted running was a high-effort activity, taking plenty of motivation to get out into the cold night air, the dance mat was one that could be done with relative ease. And it really is fun to use – in fact, it is really addictive.

Aerobically, it's OK; while it may not compare to a full run, a 20-minute session left me sweating and tired, and I can really see what Gavin meant about it helping a variety of muscle groups.

Rather helpfully, the Logic 3 Dance Mat also records your statistics, and tells you

Almost two per cent of the fat was lost, and my muscle mass increased

how many calories you have burned on each dance. My 20-minute session burned 110 calories, which sounded like a fair bit to me but turned out to count for little more than the packet of low-fat

chips I had eaten 10 minutes before I started dancing.

The PCGamerBike is a novel idea, guaranteed to have your mates crowded around you, begging for a go. You can use it to play any game that usually uses the keyboard, by assigning forwards and backwards to specific keys. However, the degree of success you achieve depends on the style of game.

The best games are racing ones, where one key command dominates your movement. You can then use the keyboard, which is quite awkward, or a joypad to control lateral movement.

The bike enables you to change the resistance and therefore vary your workout and, like the dance mat, does leave you pretty exhausted. An on-board

What you can achieve
The benefits of training with technology

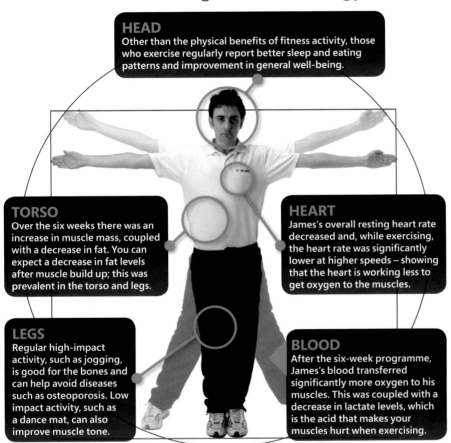

HEAD
Other than the physical benefits of fitness activity, those who exercise regularly report better sleep and eating patterns and improvement in general well-being.

TORSO
Over the six weeks there was an increase in muscle mass, coupled with a decrease in fat. You can expect a decrease in fat levels after muscle build up; this was prevalent in the torso and legs.

HEART
James's overall resting heart rate decreased and, while exercising, the heart rate was significantly lower at higher speeds – showing that the heart is working less to get oxygen to the muscles.

LEGS
Regular high-impact activity, such as jogging, is good for the bones and can help avoid diseases such as osteoporosis. Low impact activity, such as a dance mat, can also improve muscle tone.

BLOOD
After the six-week programme, James's blood transferred significantly more oxygen to his muscles. This was coupled with a decrease in lactate levels, which is the acid that makes your muscles hurt when exercising.

computer also records the distance pedalled, time spent and calories burned – and all this effort, while playing your favorite PC games.

And after six weeks...
Six weeks later and the fitness program has definitely improved my well-being. I've only lost one per cent in terms of body fat but that's actually equivalent to about half a kilogram, and my oxygen levels are up, too.

The PC peripherals may not transform me into a marathon runner but they are a fun way of exercising without the 'slog'. Getting fit will always require effort, but involving the computer means you can work out indoors or track your results. Every little bit helps...

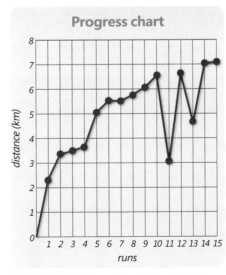

Progress chart

distance (km) vs *runs*

FRIDAY NIGHTS James found the odd Friday night out seriously affected his performance

The verdict
Do exercise gadgets work?

Nike + iPod
Having some way of tracking your performance and setting goals helps you improve, and makes the experience more enjoyable.
Rating ★★★★★

Logic 3 Dance Mat
A fun back-up exercise tool. The dance mat provides an opportunity for indoor exercise.
Rating ★★☆☆☆

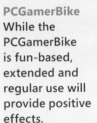

PCGamerBike
While the PCGamerBike is fun-based, extended and regular use will provide positive effects.
Rating ★★★☆☆

Polar Heart Rate Monitor
Serious equipment for athletes, or for those who are focusing their fitness for specific events.
Rating ★★★★☆

Create your perfect patch

Yes, your computer can turn your fingers green and help you make the most of your backyard!

The prospect of transforming your backyard can seem daunting. You have to know what to plant, when to plant, how long your seedlings will take to grow, and so on. Fortunately, there's a veritable orchard of sites on the internet, where you'll find no end of fruitful information.

A rich resource is the easily customizable and handy Windows gadgets, where you can install a web feed to suit your exact requirements and levels of expertise; some gardening sites offer users a constantly updated live feed with reminders for bulb planting.

There's also an abundance of software that will help you to design, organize and understand your garden. One such example is Garden Organizer Deluxe (http://www.primasoft.com/deluxeprg/goodx_try.htm), and this gives you all the elements you need to start and maintain your garden in a freely downloadable demo (see the walkthrough opposite).

Manage your garden

Once you've figured out how it all works, you're going to need to start planting. The calendar in Windows 7 makes it easy to organize and manage your horticultural chores; helping to ensure that you don't overuse one patch of soil from year to year, and that you vary your colors if you have a more floral garden.

If you want new seeds or bulbs, or need to replace that dodgy trowel, you'll find many websites offering everything you need, from plants to pitchforks, only one mouse click away. Alternatively, you can chat with, be inspired by, or even just watch the daily lives of other gardeners as they muddle on through, by reading their gardening blogs. A great place to start is Windows Live Groups, where you can set up a network of like-minded people. Your group has its own unique web address, and members can share photos, files and chat on Windows Live Messenger, so your garden will benefit from years of combined experience. ⊞

PLANNING AHEAD There are iCal calendars online that can remind you to do regular tasks or you can create your own

ONLINE FRIENDS Online communities can provide you with invaluable help, support and ideas for your new garden

Tips and tools from Garden Organizer Deluxe

Plan, budget and maintain your garden

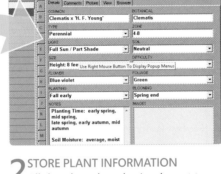

1 ACCESS WEB RESOURCES Using Garden Organizer Deluxe, you can make a list of, and then access, all of the various web resources you think you might need. You can also customize the layout to suit your requirements.

2 STORE PLANT INFORMATION All the plant data that's relevant to your planning is stored in the cleverly laid-out spreadsheet, which covers everything from plant type to weather and soil condition to eventual size.

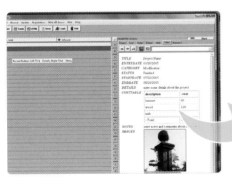

3 PLAN AND BUDGET YOUR IDEAS The Project Data section helps you to list not only the scope but all of the costs of any garden project. It also enables you to look at before and after shots of your projects.

4 PLAN ACCORDING TO THEME The Idea Data section helps you to plan and allot a themed garden of your choice, such as a water garden, alongside all the relevant web applications you might need to access for the project.

Home & garden

Windows 7 and a suitable download can help you get so much more from your garden – but you needn't stop here. All aspects of your home life can be enhanced by using Windows 7 and Microsoft software, learn more at www.microsoft.com/athome.

Five tips for great greenery

And there's more you can do to landscape to your liking

1 **PC-savvy packets** Look at the downloads listed on some seed packets to populate your electronic calendar instantly. You'll also get access to plant photos and links to more detailed instructions and pre-formatted, printable plant labels.

2 **Shoot a shoot** Whenever you take a trip to a garden center or show, make sure you take a camera or camera phone along with you, so you can photograph the various plants and – as importantly – their labels to make sure you can remember what you need to do at home.

3 **Time lapse** By either setting up a spare webcam or taking photographs from the same vantage point, you can not only build up a fascinating timelapse of your garden as it grows over the year but you can use the footage to track how well your displays are working, enabling you to reposition plants over the winter.

4 **Seed pod to podcast** Listen to gardening podcasts on your MP3 player – type in 'gardening podcast' into Bing and it will list the latest ones that various gardening organizations have on offer.

5 **Search for inspiration** If you're short of inspiration, make full use of all that Bing has to offer. Use the Image link to track beautiful shots of all sorts of gardens and displays.

Find your family history

Fancy finding out a bit about your past and tracing your family tree? Here's how to do it

Super Tip!

Pedigree pool

Head on over to the unattractive but useful Worldwide Topsites (www.worldwidetopsites.com/sites/genealogy.html) for a list of over 200 free genealogy sites and tools.

Creating a family tree has become an incredibly popular pastime, with thousands of online services to help your project.

The best place to start is close to home. After you've written down your own details, gather information from the birth and marriage certificates of as many relatives as you can. Get in touch with every aunt, uncle, brother, sister and cousin, and ask them to send you details. This will give you a wealth of information to start inputting into your family tree.

Next, go to the Office of Vital Statistics website for your state (or the state your relatives lived in); most support genealogy enquiries. Alternatively, try www.freesurnamesearch.com. Soon, though, you're going to discover some gaps, which is where the investigation truly begins... You'll need to access more archived information, such as census records, to hunt down elusive family members. www.ancestry.com and its sister site, rootsweb.com, offer access to the census (from 1790 through to the 1930s) for a monthly fee. Sites such as Findmypast.com and FamilySearch (www.familysearch.org) also provide census information.

Church records are are an excellent source for births, deaths and marriages before statutory registration was implemented. FamilySearch has the superb International Genealogical Index (free). It's worth pointing out that many genealogy sites are contributed to by volunteers so you'll need to cross-reference a lot of the initial returns.

Finally, you should consult voting lists, immigration/emigration archives and military records. You'll find the national archives at www.archives.gov; alternatively, www.interment.net provides a free database of records from 5,000 cemeteries across the world.

There are lots of free sites you can use to create your family tree and many of these include interactive content. Findmypast.com (www.findmypast.com) has over 650 million records and is easy to use, or there's www.genealogy.com. Geni (www.geni.com) is a Facebook-style site where you can add photos, get birthday reminders, send gifts, have discussions and share your tree.

Create your own family tree book

Set up an online family tree and compile a book to treasure

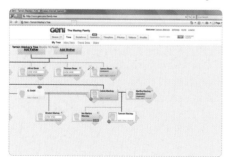

1 FAMILY FILES Build your family tree using a website that offers you the option of storing it as a GEDCOM file. Sites such as Geni and paid-for software such as Family Tree Maker offer this.

2 SAVE THE TREES Once you've made your tree, save it as a GEDCOM file. Now you need to go to FamilySearch (www.familysearch.org) and look for the Personal Ancestral File.

3 PERSONAL The Personal Ancestral File is a free program that helps you collate data. You can use this to create your family tree but you don't get many of the extras that sites such as Geni offer.

GENERATION GAME Old family photographs are a great place to start – who are all those faces? Can you sit down with a relative and try to name everyone?

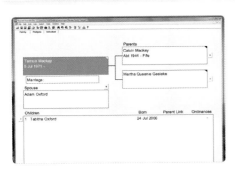

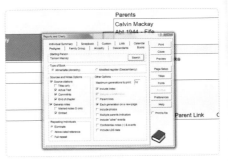

4 FILE Download the software. On the opening screen, select **New PAF file**, then save it. With the file open, select **Open**, change **File Type** in the dialog to GEDCOM, select your file and **Open**.

5 PRINT The GEDCOM file updates your PAF file once opened. Add extras or changes, go to **Print Reports → Books**. Choose layout and style, then Preview it and, when happy, press **Print**.

Create a paperless home with Windows 7

Households throw out masses of paper every week – most of that could be saved by using your Windows 7 PC to its full potential

Is a paperless existence really still a distant pipe-dream? Or can we clear the clutter and save the rainforests at the same time?

Opt for online billing

Getting up to a pile of bills at breakfast is never fun. Increasingly, though, credit card and utility companies allow you to switch to online bills or statements. Many companies even discount your bill if you go for this option.

Bank online

With so many payments now made by card rather than in cash, money is more virtual than ever. That's why online banking is so important. It's a secure, accessible way to keep an eye on your cash and, with daily

updates, you can budget more effectively. You may never get another warning letter from your bank again – saving both paper and money.

Scan your documents

With some companies your only choice is a paper bill. Our advice? Once paid, scan bills and important letters. Save the scanned image as a PNG file, giving the document an apt name. You now have an electronic copy of your bill or letter that's easy to find. With Windows Live Photo Gallery, you can even add tags to the image. As for the paper original, put it in storage or shred it.

Email everything

Almost any correspondence can be sent by email; letters to friends and relatives, queries to your bank, complaints to the local government. Just occasionally,

READ ALL ABOUT IT It's quicker and easier to get your news online – and less messy, too

you may get asked to fax a form or photocopied document to someone. Ask them if they have an email address – you can scan in any document and send it as an attachment using Windows Live Mail (available from http://getlive.com). And why not send greetings cards by email? Great for the environment, cheaper for you and far more personal for the recipient. Add text to your own photos to turn them into electronic postcards.

Transferable text

Printing off a word-processed document for a friend? Give them an electronic copy instead. Rather than saving in your word processor's format, save as an RTF. Standing for Rich Text Format, this Microsoft file type is readable on almost any computer – and maintains your formatting and text styles.

Ditch the address book

Windows 7 features Windows Contacts integrated directly into Windows Explorer. The quickest way to get to

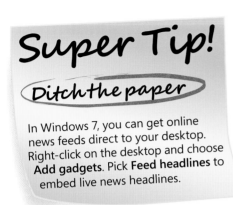

ADDRESS BOOK Windows Contacts enables you to export contacts from your old PC

Contacts is to go to your user folder and open the **Contacts** subfolder. Add a new contact by right-clicking and choosing **New ➜ Contact**. You can export contacts to transferable formats in Windows Contacts, too.

Read papers online

With expert content and in-depth features, magazines and books give tangible value that the web can't compete with, but when it comes to news the net is far faster and will save you from the scourge of inky fingers. All the major newspapers have their own websites now, and you'll find a plethora of gossip-based pages, too.

Create PDFs

Adobe PDF (Portable Document Format) files are the best cross-platform format for moving digital documents. They preserve formatting, text styles and fonts and can even include embedded

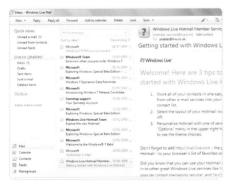

FIRST POST Windows Live Mail is the replacement for Windows Mail – download it and use it to send scanned in documents

images – and the reader is free so everyone you send them to should be able to view them. If you use Microsoft Office, you can download a PDF converter as a free add-in. Go to www.microsoft.com/downloads and search for 'Save as PDF', then download and install Save as PDF or XPS.

Digitize your notes

Stop scribbling on envelopes and scraps of paper – take notes on your computer instead. Windows Notepad is ideal for quickly jotting down the odd telephone number, shopping list or appointment. If you use Windows Live Hotmail or Windows Live Mail, you can add this information at your leisure, or transfer lists to your cell phone. Need to insert today's date into Notepad? Just hit **F5**.

Opt out of junk mail

From your letterbox straight to the bin... junk mail accounts for a large percentage of paper waste, and the plastic address windows in those envelopes mean they're difficult to recycle. Opt out instead, by visiting an online mail preference service;

register your postal address at one of these service sites and you should see a substantial reduction in the number of unsolicited advertisements landing on your mat.

Share photos

Don't print out your digital pictures – share them online instead. Sign up with Windows Live Spaces (spaces.live.com) and click **Share photos** to add digital images quickly and easily to online albums your friends can access. You could splash out on a smart new digital photo frame, too...

Shred and recycle

Windows 7 helps you protect user accounts with passwords and secure your data using advanced encryption. And yet many of us still throw paper documents containing personal information straight in the bin. Bank letters with our account numbers, new PINs, invoices and receipts – they all contain data that identity thieves can use. Invest in a shredder and make sure you destroy all personal information before putting it in the Recycle Bin.

Make your own must-see movie

Turn a fun day out into a film you can share, using Windows Live Movie Maker

Super Tip!

Output for DVD

Windows 7 offers one-click access to Windows DVD Maker from within Windows Live Movie Maker. Simply open the Tasks pane and click **Publish to DVD**.

Not only are digital camcorders more affordable than ever, making a recording can be a simple case of pointing and shooting. The difficult part is turning the results into a professional-looking movie. Fortunately, Windows Live Movie Maker is an easy to use video editing suite that can help you create your own home movies. It doesn't come included with Windows 7, so download it from http://download.live.com.

Editing is more than just assembling clips into sequence. Turning a collection of events into a coherently told story is both an art and a craft. Turn to page 82 for some ideas on footage. Then, when you've got some material to play with, you'll need to get it on to your PC.

With digital video, it's a painless process transferring footage to your PC. You can use Firewire and USB to import your files with the Windows Live Wizard that automatically pops up when you connect your device.

Start editing

Windows Live Movie Maker detects transitions in your footage and creates clips from your video. One of the reasons Windows Live Movie Maker is simpler to use than its predecessor is the fact that both the timeline and collection functions have disappeared. You only work with a storyboard view of your project and all the files you upload appear in your project. Once

you've built up your selection, simply drag and drop them into your project window in the order you want. You can chop and change by selecting the relevant image and clicking on **Remove**. In the Edit window, you can also adjust the length of your movies using the **Trim** function.

You'll find that you cut a lot, and you won't even need all the material in every clip that you do keep. Getting

With digital video, it's a painless process transferring footage to your PC

Import video to your computer

Use Windows Live Movie Maker's video import wizard to transfer clips

1 DOWNLOAD Open Movie Maker; go to **File → Import from device** to download movie files from your cell phone. You may have to install software to sync your device with Windows 7.

2 SELECTOR A dialog box will open showing all the devices available to download from. Select the device and **Import**. Windows Live Movie Maker will ask you want you want to import.

3 FILM FILING You can choose **Import all new items now** or **Review, organize and group items to import**. It's an idea to choose the Review option, as you can organize your files.

How to shoot great footage

Top tips that will make your footage good enough for the silver screen

Look for movement

This isn't photography, so outside of the odd establishing shot you want to have change in every frame. Take video footage of things that are moving (people, animals, water) or pan the camera across the scene.

No great shakes

Don't worry too much about keeping steady; a little movement adds energy and reality to a shot. Many modern cameras have built-in sensors that reduce shake anyway.

Don't zoom

When you're watching TV, how often do you see zoom shots? If you need to get a close-up, move closer. And bear in mind that camera shake increases as you zoom in.

Keep shooting

Shoot more than you need. You may have to video for a minute to get the four or five seconds you want.

Look for the light

You can't always control the lighting in the real world – but you can make sure you don't shoot directly into it. Ideally, you should have a light source behind you, not your subject.

4 TAG & LIST If you select **Review...** you will be taken to a dialog box that allows you to customize file names and and tags. Take some time to create easy to remember names and listings.

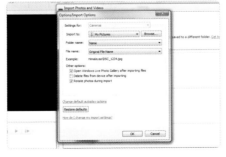

5 OPTIONS Hit **More Options** to open Import Options. Here you can determine settings for future downloads; what your file name conventions will be and where you want the files saved.

Three to try

A range of camcorders fill the market, all with different abilities

High-end hard drive based camcorders offer hours of recording time, high-def resolutions and are perfect for people who want semi-pro results from their home videos.

For ease of use, many people still enjoy camcorders that can record directly to optical discs in one of the many DVD or CD formats. These are convenient to use but can be limited on the record time.

The latest generation of digital camcorders are compact and lightweight. These use flash memory cards to record video and, while this can limit the overall record time, these are generally a lot more affordable.

rid of this 'fat' is the first stage of editing. Use the **Trim** tool again to pare down your clips even further.

Now to business... click on **Add videos and photos** in the bar at the top of Windows Live Movie Maker. A dialog box will open and ask you to choose the location of your files. If you followed the walkthrough on the previous pages, simply choose the location you saved them in or select **Pictures** (the default location provided by Windows Live Movie Maker).

Once inside Pictures, choose the first clip that you want to edit by either double-clicking on it with your mouse or pressing **Enter**. Your movie clip will now appear inside Windows Live Movie Maker with the editable footage on the right and the movie viewing screen on the left. Watch your movie through to assess what you want to cut and what you want to keep.

To split your clip, right-click on the part of the movie you want to cut and select **Split**. You can then drag and drop the cut footage to the position you want it to fill or you can simply delete it if you're not happy with it. Once you've got a rough cut you can tweak your movie using the **Trim** tool.

In real life...
Making better movies

Nick Odantzis, Section editor, Windows: The Official Magazine
1 Have fun! Editing will be as much fun as you want to make it. Either edit raw footage into a great home movie or try to film a movie from scratch following your own script.
2 Less is more People have a tendency to leave every second of footage in... Don't. Long shots are usually dull and unnecessary, cut back to what gets the message across.

3 Keep it simple While a good transition or effect can help lift a shot or smoothly cut between two, stick to one type and don't throw every available option at your movie as it will end up looking messy.
4 Use narrative Even in a holiday movie you're telling a story – make sure you have a beginning, middle and end, told out through your shots.
5 Try everything Remember this is digital media, you can experiment as much as you like and still start again from scratch if you're not satisfied.

Play around
Play back your rough cut. Some sections will seem too long and others won't follow on well from the footage that precedes them. Click on **Edit ➜ Trim** and then enter in the number of seconds you want to cut to create a new start point and then enter the seconds for the end point and **Save your Trim**. You can then play around with your footage, swapping it around as you see

fit until you're completely happy with it.

When you think you've reached picture perfection, select **Add music** to include a soundtrack that will flow beautifully with your film. You can add a title, caption and credits with a single click – these are all easily customizable so you can do anything from making a silent movie with flippant text comments to a more serious family memoir to treasure.

Transitions and effects
Some finishing touches to give your movie a professional feel

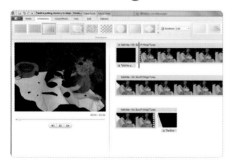

1 DON'T GO OVERBOARD Don't make the mistake of throwing every effect you have at your clips: not every edit needs transitions or effects. Use them sparingly when context demands.

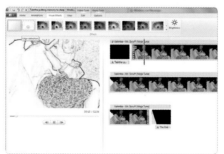

2 VISUAL EFFECTS In this example, the scene has been colored in using Edge Detection. Go to **Visual Effects** and hover your mouse over each effect to see how it will affect your movie.

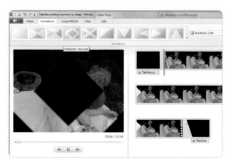

3 APPLYING EFFECTS Just double-click on an effect to add it to your movie. If you want to insert an animation or transition, just split the scene and insert it by clicking on it and pressing **Enter**.

Create a slide show or publish online

So now you've created a masterpiece, what are the options for your directiorial debut?

With Windows Live Movie Maker, you can upload and manage your images as well as create stunning slide shows in minutes. To start with, upload your photos directly from your mobile phone, your camcorder or your digital camera; Windows 7 is equipped to recognize all types of devices. Follow the walkthrough on page 164 to find out about storing your images and how to tag them.

Open Windows Live Movie Maker and select **Add videos and photos**, click on the folders you want to include in your slide show. You can use as many images as you want and delete those you aren't happy with. To insert more than one photo at a time, press **Ctrl** and **A** then **Enter**. Play around, create your slide show and use features like AutoMovie to do all the hard work for you.

Now that's a wrap, why not publish online? You automatically have access to YouTube but if you want to publish your movies to your Facebook page or through providers like SmugMug or Pixelpipe to your website and blog, you're going to need some plug-ins. Fortunately, this is easy. Click on the small arrows

AUTO MOVIE Use AutoMovie to do the hard work for you, inserting transitions and effects and making a title and credits sequence in under 10 seconds (depending on PC/movie size)

to the right of the DVD image under **Sharing**. This will open a dialog that offers a link to **Add a plug-in**. Click on the link and it will take you through to a page that lists the different plug-ins available for Windows Live Movie Maker. Choose your plug-in and follow the on-screen instructions to install it. You may have to restart Windows Live Movie Maker.

Before you upload your final product to the internet make sure your file sizes aren't too weighty and are right for the media you've chosen. Windows Live Movie Maker includes several instant resizing options for you – go to **Sharing**, click on the arrow and select **Other settings** to save a movie on your computer. Voila, you're done.

4 MASS EFFECT If you don't want your backgrounds to stay black and would like to experiment with color, go to **Video Tools ➜ Edit Background color** and choose one that you like.

5 SMOOTH PASSAGE Transitions are placed between the end of one clip and the beginning of the next. These are useful to smooth jarring changes, where a normal jump cut would be too harsh.

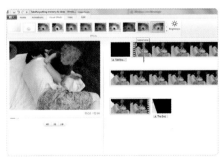

6 PLAY AROUND While too many transitions and effects can be overwhelming, it doesn't mean you can't experiment. Play around with brightness, mono and even mirror images, too.

Shoot and share

Unleash the creative power of your digital camera
and Windows 7 to capture great memories

There's no more rewarding time to take photographs than during a vacation. With children constantly excited and adults in high spirits, it's a magical time for the whole family, no matter if it's summer or fall. During winter, the crisp mornings and the possibility of snow make the most perfect picture-postcard landscapes – irresistible to anyone with a digital camera. While during the summer, blue skies and lush scenery make a stunning backdrop.

If you've invested in a new digital camera or Windows 7 PC and you're itching to test them – whether you're a long-standing photographer or just opening the box and plugging in for the first time – creative help and finishing touches aren't far from your fingertips.

You've been framed

Every great image begins with the incentive to press the shutter and take the picture. The golden rule is to keep your camera with you at all times, with batteries fully charged and space on your memory card, as photo opportunities constantly appear in front of your eyes.

Spontaneity may be key, but it doesn't hurt to think ahead. Think of all the great occasions when the entire family gets together – events like Halloween, Thanksgiving and Christmas make for perfect photo opportunities.

Take Christmas morning when the kids open their presents... Frame them in the LCD and press the shutter halfway to focus. Wait till they gasp in delight – or

HELP YOURSELF If you have Microsoft Word 2007 you have access to a library of templates

have a tantrum in disappointment – then fully press the shutter to capture that critical moment. Keep shooting, too. Switch your camera to a continuous shooting mode and take a few; you can always use Windows Live Photo Gallery (http://live.microsoft.com) to whittle out the bad ones later.

Turn the lights on and open the curtains to let more light in the room, as using your flash will kill any festive atmosphere, counteracting any subtle lighting. Give your zoom finger a workout and fill the frame with their faces to really capture those expressions of happiness on Christmas morning.

During quieter periods, why not grab a sneaky shot of grandpa sleeping off his dinner in front of the TV, or children

"I've trashed my photos!"

What to do when it all goes badly wrong...

There are few things more precious than those special moments caught on camera. Losing or ruining them doesn't bear thinking about. However, it can happen, and you'll need to know what to do if it does.

A major benefit of fixing your photos in Windows Live Photo Gallery is that you can crop and adjust images in the knowledge you can revert back to the original file at any time – even years later! Simply

open your photo in Fix and click the **Revert** button to go back.

Pictures that have disappeared from your PC or memory card take longer to fix, but it's not impossible. The usual culprit is accidentally formatting a memory card or hitting delete by accident. Don't worry, there are programs that can usually find and recover data from memory cards and hard drives even if it's corrupt, been deleted or formatted.

SAVE ME Changes made through Windows Live Photo Gallery can be reverted

GREAT SNAPPER Take a few shots in succession to be sure of at least one winning pic

frowning in concentration as they get to grips with their new toys? What about posing the whole family around the Christmas tree? Pull a comfy chair in front of it and get older family members to sit in the chair, keep the taller adults behind

When the kids open their presents, capture the delight or disappointment!

and get the kids on the floor. Don't forget yourself, either. Use a tripod or place the camera on a table and use the self-timer.

And why not try for a creative macro shot you can use to make thank you cards? Switch your camera's Macro mode

on (indicated by a flower symbol) and close in tight on some colorful tree decorations or festive food. Focus on a bright area of interest in the frame, such as a fairy light, hold the shutter halfway, recompose the shot so it's off centre and fire off the shutter.

Get out!

Remember that macro photos aren't just for indoors, either. Think of all that sparkling winter frost covering fallen leaves and branches, just waiting to be turned into stunning photographs and creative images. Zoom in a little and try to get as close as possible to pick out the frozen detail. Alternatively, if there's snow around, make sure you make the most of it and head out to the country to capture some winter wonderland scenery. If your camera has a snow scene mode then use ➡

1 For a cosy family winter shot get the clan huddled together. Use a tripod and timer to make sure you're in the photo, too!

2 Be ready – keep your batteries fully charged and memory cards empty.

3 Give your landscapes a more dramatic feel – take them when the light is at its best in the early morning or at sunset.

4 Avoid dark, underexposed landscapes by switching your camera to Scene mode and choosing the Landscape setting.

5 When out and about, concentrate on details such as leaves and flowers by using your camera's Macro mode.

6 For party pics packed with energy, switch the flash on and select the Night Portrait mode.

7 Capture dusky evening cityscapes by setting your camera on a tripod, using the self-timer and shooting as the sun sets.

8 At Christmas, shoot a 'fairy-light portrait' of a loved one by positioning them near the tree and turning the camera flash off.

9 Switch your camera to Macro mode and take lots of close-ups of seasonal decorations – great for decorating cards.

10 Capture the delight on kids' faces as they open presents by switching to Continuous shoot mode and taking lots of pictures.

DIGITAL FREEDOM The latest digital cameras offer amazing levels of details and features

it to capture bright white snow rather than dull gray slush. Compose with a frozen puddle or frosty bench in the foreground for maximum impact.

Easy editing

When you're back from your walk, get the camera's batteries on charge as you'll definitely want it ready for action at all those festive parties. Remember to switch your camera into a night party mode. Any low-light mode will get you great pictures, but to be sure of the best results – with plenty of color and movement – turn the flash on and select the night portrait setting.

Don't worry too much if things don't go to plan on the night – Windows Live Photo Gallery can help. Download Windows Live Photo Gallery from download.live.com to get the latest editing tools and the most from your shots. Use the Fix tool to sharpen blurry images; create amazing panoramas, and increase the color saturation and contrast with precision for max impact. Remember to use the full power of the program to organize your images, too. Use star ratings to identify all your favorites, and be sure to tag your shots with relevant keywords so you're able to dig out all of those wonderful memories for many years to come.

Share photos on Windows Live Spaces
Show off your holiday snaps with friends online

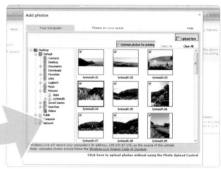

1 GET SPACE To share photos online, try putting them on Windows Live Spaces – it's free and easy. Go to spaces. live.com. If you have a Windows Live ID, sign in with this, otherwise you'll need to create a new account.

2 SET LIMITS Once signed in, click **Share Photo**, click **Add Album** on the next page. Before adding images, click **Permission** to restrict who can view the images – everyone, selected contacts, Spaces friends or just you.

3 UPLOAD Click **Add Photos**. You'll need to accept the security prompt to install an ActiveX control before this will work. Browse to your photos and click the top-left tick box in each image you'd like to upload, then click **Upload**.

4 SHARE The uploading will take a few minutes depending on how many photos you're uploading and how fast your connection is. Once done, give the album a name and click **Save**. Depending on your permission settings, friends and family will now be able to view and enjoy your photos.

You can restrict who can view the images from everyone, select contacts or friends, or just you

Photo opportunity

Forget filling an album with prints, you can do so much more with your snaps

1 Download a favorite photo to your mobile phone and send it out with a personalized message.

2 Use an editing tool to caption photos and send by email.

3 Use your website to send out holiday greetings by uploading your best pictures to your blog.

4 For an extravagant gift, why not send a loved one some of your best photos on a digital photo frame?

5 Use Windows Live DVD Maker to put your pics on DVD and spice them up by adding music and text.

6 Upload your best holiday photos to an online gallery.

7 Print your best shot and use your home printer to make a bespoke and traditional style Christmas card.

8 Use Windows Live Photo Gallery to publish your images directly to a Windows Live Spaces blog.

9 Create a calendar with pictures from relevant times of the year.

Use your photos to create stunning cards

A home-made card implies lots of effort, but it's actually really easy!

1 WHERE TO START You can create your own cards by using an art package, a word processor or online template. For inspiration, office.microsoft.com has a range of projects to try.

2 WORD IT Here's how to make a card using Microsoft Office Word 2007. Create a new document, choose **Layout → Orientation → Landscape**. You may want to zoom out to see the whole page.

3 INSERT By selecting **Insert → Picture**, you can choose an image to add. Right-click this and choose **Text Wrapping → In Front of Text**, so you can resize and move the image at will.

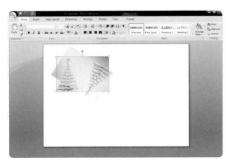

4 FLIP & MOVE Hover the mouse over the green handle to rotate the image 180 degrees. Size it and move it to the top-left corner; once the paper is folded into four this will be the front of the card.

5 ADD TEXT Select **Insert → Text box** to add a text message bottom right. You may want to do the same on the back, but flip this again to match the image. Add in any other images.

6 PRINT OUT Adjust the print options and check the alignment of the images on the page. Try a black and white draft print to check before the color version, and then your card is done.

Take the hard work out of homework

Windows 7 has an array of features to help your child with schoolwork – they might even enjoy their next project!

Windows 7 can help make studying a whole lot easier for your child; whether it's organizing work, researching, creating and listening to podcasts, or completing assignments, Windows 7 has the tools to help.

Writing an essay or compiling a project means pulling together information from a variety of sources and preparing it all to a set length. Thankfully, children no longer have to rely on textbooks from the local or school library. Instead they have access to millions of sources on the internet. But then there's almost too much information to tap into and digest!

By the time your child's finished researching, they may well have thousands of random snippets scattered randomly on your PC's hard drive, and won't know where to start to collate it all.

Fortunately Windows 7 provides some very useful tools, even for the very disorganized. At its simplest, the Instant Search function enables your child to find all references to a topic. Quotes can help narrow the search (for instance 'dinosaur' AND 'carnivorous') to weed out all the references to the herbivore kind. There are a whole series of other filters you can apply to narrow searches further, whether it's the size of the file, when it was created

or what program was used (see more on this in the Files and Folders chapter starting on p40). In Windows 7 you also get Natural Language Search – a flexible search that doesn't require brackets, inverted quotes or capital letters. To turn on Natural Language Search, click **Start**, then **Control Panel ➔ Appearance and Personalization**, and select **Folder Options**. Click the **Search** tab and select **Use natural language search**.

Having found the files they want, your child can keep them as a Saved Search by clicking the button on the Results toolbar. This is very useful when it comes to revision as it keeps all references to a

All their own work...

The thin line between research and plagiarism

Computers have made plagiarism much easier; it's just a matter of a quick cut and paste job. There are even websites selling essays, ready to be downloaded and passed off as a child's own work.

Of course, teachers aren't stupid. When the school truant suddenly turns in a well written assignment, somebody is going to smell a rat. And, be warned, the technology that makes it easier to steal work can also help to catch the cheats.

So how can your child avoid plagiarism? Journalists often say: "Stealing from one source is plagiarism; stealing from many is research." There's an element of truth in that – no piece of work is 100 per cent original. The best essays take ideas from a number of sources and say clearly where the information has come from; a process made easier using Office Word 2007's Source Manager. The student should then organize those arguments logically and reach a clear conclusion based on them. Most marks are awarded on the basis of how many specific points

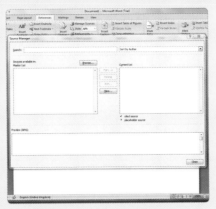

REMEMBER ME Never forget another source thanks to Microsoft Word 2007

relevant to the question are included in the essay. It's often useful to see how other students have answered similar questions. Some websites are dedicated to coursework, and you can search for and analyze existing work.

The internet is a valuable research tool and that's exactly how it should be used. Make sure your children source facts and information, but also that they reflect on what they've learned and inject their own individual 'spin' on their work.

particular topic in one handy place.

Another way of keeping track of files is by using tags. Your child may, for instance, use the tag 'geography project' to keep together all text documents, pictures, video clips and sound files that they need.

Word to the wise

For day-to-day work your child will doubtless use Microsoft Office Word 2007. Be sure they know about all its functions. There are research options available when you right-click on a word; synonyms, available in the same way, can help make an essay read better by reducing unnecessary repetition, and

the same goes for Office Word's invaluable grammar and spelling checks.

Microsoft Office 2007 is competitively priced; if you're not a business user, you can buy a copy of the Home and Student edition for about a third of the Standard edition price. Both suites include Office Word, Office Excel and Office PowerPoint.

The Home and Student edition has a copy of OneNote 2007, in place of Outlook 2007. OneNote offers a way to gather and organize information in a variety of formats – whether it's text, pictures, handwriting, audio or video recordings and more, into one place on your computer.

Seven ways to better grades

Philip Collie, managing director of Schoolzone (www.schoolzone.co.uk), one of Britain's largest educational resource websites, gives advice on how your child can achieve academic success

1 Use the Track Changes feature in Office Word when studying or using revision notes. They'll gain confidence from seeing how their understanding of a subject is changing. It allows for notes to be added and hidden from classmates and teachers.

2 Create revision aids in Office PowerPoint and share with friends.

3 Use Office Excel to keep a record of test or homework scores and track progress or identify areas of weakness.

4 Create audio files of revision notes as podcasts. Groups of study friends may want to divide up a set of notes and do a section each, then share online.

5 Use MSN, Bebo and Facebook social networking sites to share ideas and help each other with homework and school projects.

6 Find titled videos, for instance, 'chemistry experiment', 'photosynthesis' or 'Tudor England' on YouTube. They can then write a revision guide based on the clip to use in class.

7 Use Windows Live Calendar to create and share revision timetables, then they can log their success at meeting targets.

Projects and assignments

Windows 7 and the PC literate generation...

Using a computer to work on school projects is not just the domain of the pre-teen. Children starting at pre-school are soon trained in the art of mouse control, too...

Bob Phillips was keen to upgrade to Windows 7 for both business and personal use, and for the needs of his growing family. "My son Richard is 12," explains Bob, "so he's really relying on the PC for research, report compilation and even presentation. He finds Windows 7 a lot more intuitive – and cool – to use than Windows XP."

Bob's also invested in a Windows 7 laptop... "Richard's assignments involve Office Word, Publisher and PowerPoint, and I can access his files on the laptop to give them the once over before he hands them in. Just wish my work stuff looked so slick!"

Bob's daughter Rosie (9) loves using the webcam to keep in touch with relatives in New Zealand and is also using the PC for homework. "I've just made a collage in Office Publisher that's all about family holidays, so I've scanned in tickets and pictures I've drawn, and downloaded pics from the camera."

SAFETY FIRST Use the Parental Controls to restrict your child's access to websites

And Peter, who's just turned six is pretty PC savvy already. He loves playing games on his favorite children's TV websites.

"They all love playing games on the PC," says Bob. "So it's a huge relief that we don't have to worry about them trying to access or play anything that's not suitable, thanks to the Parental Controls and User Accounts." Richard agrees... "I know Mom and Dad are looking out for us and I can always discuss what I'd like to play. And I love the fact that I've got my own User Account so that when I log on, the PC is set up exactly how I want it – not with Dad's boring wallpaper!"

OneNote is a great feature for students. References and handouts can be copied or scanned and dragged into OneNote and organized in sections, pages and sub-pages. Then, as your child searches the web, useful information, links and pictures can also be dropped and stored in OneNote notebooks complete with personal annotations. Everything can, of course, be searched, shared online and is

You can download thousands of useful podcasts on various school topics

automatically backed up. The information can also be reorganized and restructured to fit the way the project is developing.

Then, because OneNote is part of Office 2007, it's easy to export the results into Word or PowerPoint. One of the many improvements in Microsoft Office 2007 is that it makes producing attractive documents a lot easier – it's easy to alter formats and access the huge number of templates that are available.

The only disappointment if you use OneNote with an ordinary desktop or notebook PC is that you miss out on one of its coolest features. Tablet PCs have a microphone and, if your child takes notes while a teacher is lecturing, it will tie the text to the audio so they can check to hear exactly what was said, rather than what they wrote at the time. Having said that,

WORD PERFECT The 2007 Microsoft Office system has many tools for perfect projects

some relatively inexpensive MP3 players now have a recording function, and you can save anything that's been recorded as a sound file to your computer.

Pod project

In an ideal world you'd then be able to convert that sound file to text using the voice recognition function in Windows 7. Unfortunately, the software still has to be trained to recognize an individual's voice using a process of reading and correcting the results. There is, however, a trick: stick one ear bud in your ear so you can hear the recorded speech, then speak the words into the mic attached to your PC and you'll change the spoken words into text without having to type. Simple.

Of course, you could think of the original lesson recording as a sort of podcast. In fact, if your child wants to create a useful revision tool he could make his own podcast using sound editing software, such as the free program Audacity, from audacity.sourceforge.net.

They would, however, need to use other software if they wanted to publish the podcasts online. A less powerful, but easier to use, free alternative is WildVoice (www.wildvoice.com). You can also publish direct from this software.

Online oracle

Get an online revision buddy

When it comes to research and revision, the internet can be of great assistance. Just type 'online revision tools' into Bing (www.bing.com) and you'll get endless results covering every subject imaginable. From Wikipedia, to WordPress blogs to student forums to educational supplements to TV sites.

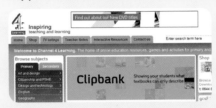

ENCYCLOPAEDIC KNOWLEDGE Whatever your subject, you'll find online help, and you can even download revision plans

There are thousands of useful podcasts available to download, usually for free, on all sorts of study topics. To find out what's available, go to your favorite search engine, such as Bing (www.bing.com), type in, say, 'podcast US & World History SAT' and see what comes up.

Many podcasts are created by teachers, but don't let that put you off! After all, they do know how to present a topic to make it easy to understand. It's surprising how hearing familiar topics discussed by different people can make them easier to digest and remember. Podcasts are great for when the dreaded revision time comes and they don't want to waste a moment – they can revise when walking to school or waiting at the bus stop.

Smart study aids
Gadgets that look good and help!

LAPTOP
With Windows 7-capable laptops now as affordable as budget desktop systems these make the perfect choice for your child's education.

DIGITAL AUDIO PLAYER
Not just handy for enjoying music, many models now offer microphones so they're perfect for recording and listening to lectures and podcasts.

POCKET PC
Have the best of all worlds in the palm of your hand. Many Pocket PCs offer phone, audio features and Microsoft Office support in a tiny package.

How to get the best grades

With help from Windows 7, getting a good result can be as easy as a click of the mouse...

Super Tip!

Space cadets

Need to work on a group project? Then link up to Office Live Workspace (http://workspace.officelive.com) where you can view, edit and share Word, Excel and PowerPoint documents.

Take charge of how well you or your children do in the next round of exams by using the technology that Windows 7 puts at your disposal. While there's no magic formula for studying, there are some sure-fire ways of getting into the top stream.

The first method is to schedule effectively. A good schedule helps you to allocate realistic units of study time. The Windows Live Calendar (http://live.microsoft.com) can alert you minutes, hours or days ahead – either on a one-off or recurring basis. Many universities offer the iCalendar format, with which Windows Live Calendar and Windows 7 are both compatible, listing exam times, podcasts and more.

Should you want to tailor your reminders, you'll find various examples of downloadable software on the internet that you can add to your Windows 7 desktop as gadgets. Some of these even offer a speech function so that your reminders are read out loud

and, if your concentration span is limited, you can set a number of prompts to beep at regular intervals during your study, just to keep you alert!

If you can, go to a café or a park when reading through material – a relaxed environment can help you absorb information. This is when a tablet PC can come in handy. And Windows Live Messenger (get.live.com/messenger/overview) is perfect for linking up with fellow students to test each other, or you can use a webcam for a video chat.

Many colleges offer free podcasts, enabling you to revisit lecture themes. These are a good way to revise

when your eyes are too tired to carry on reading. The Windows Vista Innovation Café also gives you online access to the British Library.

So you've scheduled, prepared and dug in when you realize that you are missing one of the most important study ingredients: pizza. You don't have to leave your study zone – make use of the fact that Windows 7 is an extremely secure system and order some thin and crispy inspiration online! Make sure the padlock icon is there when you enter your details, and don't start studying the menu instead of your homework.

ONLINE RESOURCES A host of online reference libraries make research easy

Keep to the agenda

Get on top of your revision schedule

1 GET STARTED If you haven't already, get yourself a Windows Live ID and your own Windows Live Calendar. Go to login.live.com, click on **More → Calendar** and you're in; if you don't have a Live ID, just follow the simple registration process.

2 ADD APPOINTMENT Find the date you want to highlight using the Month or Week view tabs at the top of your calendar, then select the relevant date and simply click **Add**. In the dialog box enter, say, 'Biology revision' and the time.

3 RECURRING EVENTS To specify particulars, click on **Add more details** at the bottom of the dialog box. Now you can set your revision allocation to recur daily, weekly, yearly, etc; how many times it repeats, and when it should end.

4 FINISH UP Keep adding your different revision slots, choosing how often they recur and whether you want reminders; Live Calendar can send you reminders via email or Live Messenger, just set up your preferences in the Options menu.

Get some new gadgets!

Take a study break – visit the gallery...

Tired of studying? Well, Windows 7 is just as good at giving you a break as it is at helping you study.

Go to http://gallery.live.com and immerse yourself in toys, gadgets and Sidebar fun. My Mood-Clock is a nifty little web gadget that you can load directly on to your Live Spaces site. No matter how happy or sad you feel, you can let everyone know by instantly expressing your mood to your visitors.

Five top tips

Improve your revision online

1 Make full use of all your study aids and not just the obvious ones. Your most precious resource is time – use online tools such as Windows Live Calendars to create study schedules and stick to them. As they're online you can access them anywhere – in the library or even your cell phone – and have them send you reminders via text message or email.

2 The simplest way to get the most from your lectures – if permission is granted – is to record them. This enables you to listen to them whenever required, catch that vital point you missed or relive them months later. Many MP3 players and cell phones now come with mics and enough storage for hours of audio.

3 Store research, papers and your own essays online with tools such as Microsoft Office Live Workspace. This will enable you to access them wherever you may be as long as you have an internet connection and web browser.

4 Use online research tools with intelligence. Resources such as Google and Wikipedia are great as a starting point but do not quote from one source alone, always research the original source of the information used and attribute these in your work.

5 Explore and use the rich and ever increasing number of academic journals that are supplying helpful RSS feeds and podcasts. They're out there to be used so it would be foolish not to take full advantage of them.

Never forget anything again

Our lives are getting more hectic, but there are ways to organize your life cheaply and simply

Everyone forgets things from time to time, and the busier you are, the more easily it can happen. There are lots of 'tried and tested' methods for reminding yourself of important events: bits of paper, knots tied in handkerchiefs, notes on your hand... The trouble is that a piece of paper can get blown off a desk, you wash your hands, and what was that knot for again? By using your Windows 7 PC you can make sure you never forget anything again. It's a bold claim, but there are some great free services out there, and they work.

The first step on your path to total recall is Windows Live Calendar. Go to www.windowslive.com/online/calendar, click on **Get Calendar** and you'll be

whisked into your own, customizable online Calendar. Windows Live Calendar takes organization to the next level.

Your Live Calendars are completely secure and can only be viewed when you grant specific people access. The best thing about Windows Live Calendar is that you can sync it with all of your other online calendars; create a calendar for every aspect of your life and merge with other calendar applications. If you want to use other online calendars, such as those for the Major League baseball season or release dates for upcoming PC games, then you have a huge range to choose from. Just head to www. icalshare.com to find locations of online calendars and merge those that capture your fancy – the sky's the limit! Because

Windows Live Calendar is 100 per cent web based you can import your existing calendars using .ics files and it really is easy to automatically link your content to other calendars.

Keep connected

Life is busy and usually you find that when you need your calendar the most, it isn't easily to hand. This is what makes Windows Live Calendar such a pleasure to use. Thanks to the fact that the application is web based, you can access your calendar whenever you want, from wherever you want, as long as you have an internet connection. Now no date stands a chance of escaping you!

Of course, as we all know, calendars have several major weaknesses. The main

> ### Super Tip!
> ### Perfect prompts
> Windows Desktop Gadgets are the perfect tools for putting reminders where you can't help but see them! Use the built-in Windows 7 Sticky Notes or a Calendar Gadget.

Keep your diary up to date
Subscribe to a sharing calendar to transfer important dates

1 SHARE Use Bing (www.bing.com) to search for an iCal calendar. Websites often have an **Add to Calendar** link. Web addresses of iCals look like webcal:// or end in .ics. Make a note of the address.

2 SUBSCRIBE Sign in to your Live Calendar with your Windows Live ID and select **Subscribe** from the toolbar. Then select **Subscribe to a public calendar** and enter the iCal web address.

3 REMEMBER In Windows Live Calendar you can set the color of each calendar so it's easy to tell which is which. They are also all listed on the left, so just click on one to get more details.

BREAKING POINT
Don't give in to chaos! Use your PC to get organized

Virtual PA

Remember The Milk services...

1 ONE-OFF **Remember yourself of that meeting: 03/14, 1-2pm**

2 EVERY WEEK **Remind yourself about the yoga class on Tuesdays, 8-9am @weekly**

3 ANNUAL DATES **Remind yourself Mom's birthday is January 13th @yearly**

4 TO DO LISTS **Prepare for an event using Lists**

5 SHARE **Share tasks with others for improved collaboration**

6 TOTAL RECALL **Choose how to receive your reminders**

BREAKING POINT Don't give in to chaos! Use your PC to get organized

---

problem is that you have to remember to write on them and if you're prone to forgetfulness, it's not going to work.

Thankfully, a brilliant internet service called Remember the Milk (www.rememberthemilk.com) has been created that makes managing your tasks fun and leaves you with loads of free time to focus on other stuff.

To get started with Remember The Milk, sign up with your own unique username and password and activate your account. Once you've got the admin out of the way you can start setting up your tasks and reminders. These are simple to set up – just click

on **Continue to Tasks** and here you can manage them, add them and see what Tasks are still outstanding. Not only that but you can create lists, set reminders and you get your own personal search engine to locate old tasks and smart lists that group specific tasks together.

One of the best parts of Remember The Milk is the fact that your reminders can be sent to you via different means including email, SMS and Instant Messenger. You can even enter new tasks via Twitter, get MilkSync for Windows Mobile and find locations for your appointments using the incredibly handy map service. ➲

ONLINE CALENDAR The Windows Live Calendar lets you take your life online

Using Microsoft Live Labs Listas

Five steps to keeping all your favorite URLs in order

  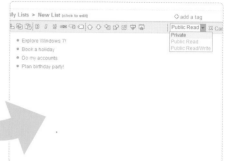

1 SIGN IN Head to http://listas.labs.live.com and sign in using your Windows Live ID. Download the Microsoft Listas toolbar, which will appear at the top of Internet Explorer 8. Normally toolbars are a pain, but this one makes your life easier.

2 FIND OUT MORE Now you can search lists to get a flavor of the kind of things the community are interested in. Use the community panel to start exploring the most active users, or the search tab to look for specific material.

3 ADD YOUR OWN Go to the My Lists tab and choose **New**. A blank page will be displayed, where you can give your list a title, tags and content. Choose to make it public or private, or whether the community can make amendments.

4 ADD CONTENT Writing endless lists can be tedious, so this is where the toolbar comes in handy. If you're researching a holiday, start a list called 'Holiday'. Then, when you come across useful websites, click **Add Link** on the toolbar and choose which list to add it to, and it will be instantly updated.

With Microsoft Listas you'll be able to create and share lists, view other lists and contribute to online communities

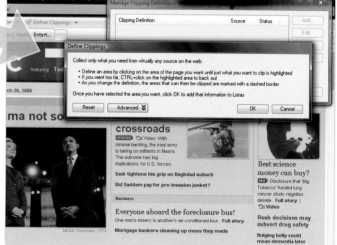

Microsoft labs

If you find Listas interesting you can learn more, and join in with other innovations from Microsoft, from its labs site at http://labs.live.com. Here you'll find the latest technologies being developed and tested.

5 CUTTINGS If you just want a snippet of information, the cuttings system can really help. Just click **Define Clippings**, and areas of the page will be broken up into sections. Click the article or paragraph you wish to clip, and click the **Add** button in the corner. The cutting will be pasted into your lists.

MAKE IT PERSONAL Windows Live Events lets you create a customizable invitation page

Links and Listas

While the Favorites Center in Internet Explorer 8 is very useful, it can become a bottomless pit of links that you simply save and forget. The information held is often tiny too, so if you do remember to retrieve a page, finding the relevant snippet is virtually impossible.

One impressive service from Microsoft really does offer a wealth of options that will genuinely revolutionize the way you browse the internet. The Microsoft Live Lab Listas application enables you to create and share lists, view other people's lists and contribute to online communities. It's very slick – and very Web 2.0 – but if you're not into the community aspect, there are features of real personal value, too.

If you're researching buying a new car, make a 'New Car List' and store a series of URLs on to it. When you're done researching, you can go to the list, which will now be complete with all your information. Microsoft Listas can even break web pages into 'cuttings' that you can save to your lists like an online scrapbook. This makes it easy to save small parts of information. Microsoft Listas is an online service, so all the lists

you create are available on the internet. While it's still in the relatively early stages of development, the improvements that could be made in terms of mobile access are endless.

Another great service from Microsoft is Windows Live Events. This is a similar service to the successful feature in Facebook, where you create an event and send invitations to your friends. Windows Live Events offers added versatility, as it doesn't rely on your contacts using Windows Live.

Simply go to the events tab and you can create an 'event' page with times, dates, venues and any comments you wish to make. Then you can start inviting people using your Windows Live contact list, or manually type in people's email addresses, who will then be sent an invitation. They can view the event and download .ics calendar entries so there's no way your event can be forgotten.

By making your PC work for you, rather than allowing information to stagnate in calendars, forgetting things becomes virtually impossible and, with so many products on the market that can sync with Microsoft Office Outlook, you'll always be organized.

Windows Live

Dave Law, Windows Live Product Manager on how to get the most from Windows Live

1 Use Windows Live Hotmail to not only send or receive mail from your family and friends, but also send or receive mail from your other accounts – Gmail, Yahoo, etc. You can go to www.windowslive-hotmail.com to find out more.

2 Keep large files organized with Windows Live SkyDrive, a free storage and sharing service on the web with 25GB capacity. Go to windowslive.com/online/skydrive to find out more.

3 With Microsoft Office Outlook Connector, you can check your Windows Live Hotmail account in Microsoft Outlook; in addition, any changes made to Hotmail from Outlook are synchronized to your Hotmail account.

4 Organize photos and videos with Windows Live Photo Gallery. Import photos from your camera and Windows Live Photo Gallery will organize them based on date and time. Create panoramic photos and use the editing tools to improve shots.

5 Finally, get quick and easy access to all your Windows Live services at http://login.live.com. Whether it's accessing your mail on Windows Live Hotmail, viewing your friends' Windows Live Spaces profile or instant messaging with Windows Live Messenger, the all-new home.live.com home page lets you access all your Windows Live services from one handy hub.

Host the ultimate party with a firework finalé

If you really want a party to end with a bang, you've got to put some preparation in before the big night

 Arguably, the greatest asset of Windows 7 is the ability to use it for fun, too! Yes, your home computer can help you to prepare for a great party. So why not go all-out with an impressive firework display?

First things first, before you even think about rockets, you want to make sure you have an audience for your show. Obviously, you could just text your friends, but there's a much easier way.

Put the date of your party in Windows Live Calendar (www.windowslive.com/online/calendar) or invite the world using Windows Live Events (http://events.live.com) using your Windows Live ID. If you don't have a Windows Live ID, don't worry, the site will take you through the simple registration process. Once you've registered and logged in to Windows Live Events, click on **Create your Own** in the right-hand corner. This will take you through to another page where you can

Check out your pyro purchases by watching videos before you buy

fill in all of the details you need, such as the date, the location, the time and even the theme (you could try using the Fourth of July theme to get some fabulous firework images all over your event page). Once you've filled it in to your satisfaction, click **Create**.

Now you'll be taken to your event's very own web page. Here you can customize the design, create an up-to-date blog of events leading up to the party and even have group discussions with your guests.

To start inviting people using Windows Live Events, simply click on **Invite Guests**, add in any extra info and press **Send**. You can also post photographs and add your event to your Windows Live Calendar with just one click.

If you've got 2007 Microsoft Office software you can also download some impressive invitation templates that are extremely customizable and fun. So why not design an invite and send it via email

Bang, flash, what a party!

If you've got a firework finish planned, capture the moment

1 FLASH
Don't use flash – it won't reach far enough to light the fireworks that you're launching skywards.

2 SHAKE
If you turn off your flash, your camera may try to compensate by slowing the shutter speed; consider using a tripod to keep your camera stable, and your pictures sharp.

3 EXPOSURE
If your camera allows for such an adjustment, increase the exposure to make pictures look brighter (although if you increase it too much, they will look blindingly bright). If your camera is a little more basic, flick the mode to night setting, and it will automatically increase the exposure for you.

4 BRIGHT LIGHT
Don't take shots next to a bright source of light because it will interfere with your pictures.

WHOOSH! If you put on a pyrotechnic display, make sure you record the moment

5 MULTIPLE SHOTS
When the fireworks display takes off, try to take as many pictures as you can; with something so unpredictable you'll find many shots don't come out too well. By taking as many shots as possible you will increase your chance of getting at least one really good shot. Make sure you have plenty of batteries and a spare memory card.

Wireless sound

Get music in your backyard

FAR OUT! Make sure your guests can enjoy your party mix in the backyard

So you want your music outside, too? Thankfully, there are many portable, weatherproof outdoor speakers ready to entertain you. There's a raft of basic, highly-portable systems that will work with an MP3 player; typically battery-powered these are easily carried around, though aren't usually too loud. For a more meaty sound, try something specifically designed for outdoor use. If you want something easier to install, try a wireless outdoor speaker – most will stream music direct from your wireless laptop!

---

as a follow-up to your Live Events invitation? You could even use Live Events to send out a Save the Date card while designing the official invite with Office. To send your invitations via email, open up Windows Live Mail, open a new message, select **Attach** in the menu bar and attach your sleekly designed invite.

Party poppers
If you do want to end your party with a firework display there are a number of things to take into consideration...

When it comes to purchasing fireworks, consumers have until fairly recently been subject to a bit of a lottery. Forgetting quality issues, you also have to choose from some pretty random – and boastful – firework names that don't

necessarily translate to the actual display at the point of ignition! Fortunately, there are now websites dedicated to all things pyrotechnic – you can even see examples in action, by watching the streaming videos before you buy.

You must also be confident that any fireworks you buy are safe to use. Go to a dedicated firework safety website to get details of the different sorts of fireworks to look for, and how to prepare your display safely. You will also be able to find information on making sure your family pets are looked after.

Ready? Not quite. No party – as visually impressive as it might be – is complete without a good selection of tunes. Fortunately, you can now get speakers that you can put in your back

garden to pump out the sounds. You'll need to couple these speakers with a media extender, such as an Xbox 360, to access all the songs stored on your PC. Obviously, if you're really clever you'll arrange the music to complement the display! Also, as you will be displaying such a visual feast, your friends will be taking photos of the evening; make sure you get all the shots downloaded to your computer, ready to share with everyone else over the internet – you can tag them in Windows Live Photo Gallery so that you know which party they're from, and who's taken them.

Until then, why not get in the mood by prepping your party tracks in Windows Media Player or downloading a 3D fireworks screensaver?

Create a killer résumé – and bag that dream job

In the market for a new job? Then make sure your résumé is looking its best – a polished introduction is essential

Employment is a buyers' market, so it pays to sell yourself with a high-quality résumé. There are various styles you can choose from, ranging from ultra-simple to stylized formats. The two most common types are chronological and functional. The former should start with details of your current or previous employment. Functional documents are geared towards the position you hope to attain and focus more on your skills and experience. These look better if you're hoping to change your type of employment, or if you're entering the market for the first time or after a break.

There are certain items that must be included, and some things that should be left out. The latter is particularly important, as your curriculum vitae should be no longer than two pages. The first things to include are your personal details. These should include your name, date of birth, postal address and phone number, and also your email address. Think about emailing your finished application as an attachment to a prospective company, as well as posting.

Making the grade
Further content should include a list of your qualifications, as well as when and where you attained them, starting with your most recent. If your grades aren't particularly notable then it's a good idea to simply list the subjects you passed. Another essential is a detailed list of your most impressive work achievements, especially where they have a bearing on the position you're applying for. If there are no formal achievements as such, you could give details of challenges you've faced and how you overcame them. It's also a good idea to include a brief list of any hobbies and pastimes, especially where they're relevant to the job. Finish off with the name and address of both a personal referee, and a reference that's a current or recent employer.

Simplicity works best, but that doesn't mean your résumé should look dull. Tables are easy to set up and format in Office Word 2007, so making use of them for education and employment history can give a clear, neat look to certain areas of your personal profile.

Organize your résumé with tables
Tables can help make areas of your curriculum vitae more legible

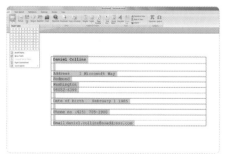

1 GET PERSONAL To make areas of your résumé clear, use tables. In Office Word, convert the text you want into a table by highlighting it, then click the **Insert Table** icon in the toolbar.

2 ADDING IN Here, the basic table has the right number of rows but only one column. To add extra columns, highlight the table and right-click, then select **Insert columns to the right**.

3 SPLIT AND MERGE You can give your table a neater look by merging and splitting cells as required, by right-clicking individual or groups of cells and using the relevant pop-up commands.

Create a great résumé

Use your PC to put together a profile that's easy to read, visually interesting and informative

Stand out
Use eye-catching fonts and styles, and be consistent throughout. Different colors will break up the page and make reading your boasts much easier. However, if it resembles a Picasso it will go straight in the bin.

Break it up
Use bullet points to break up long paragraphs. This will make your document easy to read and get the attention of even the busiest employer. White space is easy on the eye and looks good, too.

Things to avoid
Make sure you check the spelling throughout. With checkers built into most word processing software, there's no excuse for mistakes. Don't add flowery borders or a picture of yourself – make sure you keep it simple.

Be concise
Don't forget, the document is a summary of your experience, not a draft of your forthcoming autobiography. Two pages are OK, but one is better.

Details
Rather than simply listing your past jobs, tell the employer what you learnt there. If you worked in a burger joint then talk about people skills and customer service. It all counts. Employers are looking for skills so make sure to sell these.

Go get 'em champ
If you're struggling, 2007 Microsoft Office system has downloadable templates where you can edit generic résumés. However, a CV should be unique, so try to add your own edge to it.

Show a rounded person
Talk about your hobbies and outside interests, as well as employment. An employer wants an impression of you as a whole, not just your work.

Daniel Collins

Age 23, born 1 February 1985.
One Microsoft Way, Redmond
orson@widgets.msn.com

Education:
2006: Graduated from Maple University with a BA degree in Multimedia Journalism.

Areas Covered by BA Multimedia Journalism:
- News: I wrote many stories involving local news, and interviewed councillors a
- Features: I wrote a wide range of features, from an interview with a foreign
- Dissertation: I conducted a study into political spin and interviewed political
- I have passed Law and Ethics, Public Affairs, Newspaper Journalism and Newsp Handout exams and I am currently working towards 100wpm shorthand.
- Television: I filmed a 10-minute TV package about bovine TB. I interviewed, le farmers and welfare activists, which led to me being nominated for a journalis

Professional Experience:
I was the news editor of a full color newspaper with a readership of 15,000 students at Maple University. Under my editorship the news section uncovered poor conditions of accommodation.

I have completed three weeks' work experience at the Adventure Works.

In summer 2005 I worked for two weeks at School of Fine Art. I interviewed sen police officers and former football manager Noel Asuncion. I also made packages girl band and the top ten Christmas accidents countdown.

Work Experience:
I worked for two years at Fourth Coffee from 2001 until 2003 and took no sick days. I helped customers, and eventually ran the warehouse single-handed on weekends. The store would take in excess of $30,000 a day in peak season. From 2004 until 2006 I worked as a mentor at a scheme called Playing for Success, where I helped children with confidence, learning and behavioral difficulties with their literacy, math and computer skills. I organized the children to make their own newspaper as a literacy exercise.

Hobbies and Interests:
In my spare time I play baseball, and golf with a poor handicap.

Music is one of my passions, and I am always trying to discover new artists. I attended the Elm Festival in 2004 and 2005 and Maple 2002. I have been to countless gigs and shows, and regularly travel to club nights.

Take your office with you using Windows 7

With Windows 7 your office is no longer a place – your work can move with you. All you need is a PC and an internet connection

Where's your office? With Windows 7 it could be in a room at home, or at a local café using a latte-splashed PC, or absolutely anywhere with a wirelessly-connected laptop. The internet enables you to share files, access resources and use all the programs you use at work every day. You could be waiting for a train, sitting in a library or lying on the beach – no one need ever know you're not at work.

The first step in taking your office out on the move with you is to make sure you have the right tools at your disposal. Your office software – word processor, spreadsheet and task scheduler – should be available on whichever machine you choose to use. You could spend money on second copies of all your software. Having all the same programs (and same versions) you use at work is the only way to guarantee compatibility; this also works out as an expensive option.

Think alternative

Another route is to use an online, web-based office suite when you're away from work. The advantage here is that you can access the same programs on any computer – including machines you can't install software on. This has been a boom area lately, with a number of tools to choose from. Look for packages that work well with Microsoft Office – with spreadsheet and presentation applications, alongside word processing tools – preferably with the ability to import Word documents from your work machine. The best thing about these web suites is that they're absolutely free.

Make contact

With web mail services like Windows Live Hotmail (www.hotmail.com), you can access your email from any connection – even some mobile devices. (Some people are reluctant to use a free web mail service for their work address, as it can appear unprofessional, and it's probably not advisable to put a Hotmail address on your business cards.) However, there's a quick fix to make it look like you're accessing your mail from the office. Hotmail lets you change the 'Reply to' address so that replies appear to come from your office or any email ➡

Meeting in Windows Live Messenger

Need to have a meeting while you're out of the office? This can help

1 ONE-TO-ONE Why bother picking up the phone for that quick query when your colleague is just an instant message away? It's quick, free and easy to use – as long they haven't got you blocked!

2 GET TALKING Turn your one-to-one chat into a meeting by inviting other contacts to join in. Go to **Actions ➡ Invite a contact to this conversation**. You'll get a list of all your online contacts.

3 SHARE FILES Windows Live Messenger lets you share files. In a conversation window, click on **Files ➡ Send a file or photo**. A new window will then appear for you to add a file or a photograph.

I've just popped out for a coffee...

Seven ways to convince your colleagues that you're in the office when, in fact, you're not

1 **Be right back** Leave your jacket on the back of your chair.

2 **Sounds good** Record yourself typing. Leave it playing while you nip to the shops.

3 **Office supplies** Call your mate at work and ask to borrow a stapler. Then quickly call again to say: "It's OK, I've got one."

4 **On hold** Re-route your office phone direct to your mobile.

5 **Keeping cool** Cover yourself in factor 40 sunscreen as you sit by the pool for that office pallor.

6 **Colleague's birthday** Get the card early, sign your name and add the correct day's date.

7 **Time for a drink** Turn up at the end of the day, then head to the bar like you've been at the office all day long.

4 VOICE CONFERENCING To start a voice call in the current conversation, click **Call** and you can start speaking when the other person accepts the call. Don't forget the microphone...

5 GO MOBILE Go through **Options ➜ Phone ➜ Mobile Settings**, then on the website that pops up, register your number to start using Windows Live Messenger on your mobile.

6 VIDEO MEETINGS For face-to-face communication, you'll need a webcam connected to your computer. Then, just click the **Start or stop a video call** icon when you're in a conversation.

Pocket office

If you're not working from home but sipping a cocktail by the beach and need to be contactable, you could do with Windows Mobile 6.1

Windows Mobile 6.1 is Microsoft's operating system for PDAs, handheld computers and mobile devices. With mobile versions of Microsoft Office Word, Excel and PowerPoint it gives you an office in your pocket. Of course, these are scaled down versions of their bigger siblings, but they're still jam-packed with enough features to make sure you can create and edit documents on the move.

When you've finished working with a file, you can deliver it in a number of ways. Synchronize your PDA with a PC to transfer documents across or sync with another user's mobile device to send a file direct to them. You can also email files to any account using Office Outlook or Windows Live Hotmail.

Microsoft Outlook is the email and scheduling tool that comes as part of Microsoft Office. The Windows Mobile version will synchronize with

EMAIL MOVER If you plan to write emails on the move, the HTC Touch Pro offers a full integrated keyboard for rapid typing

Office Outlook on your main machine, importing and exporting contacts in a variety of ways. One recent innovation is Direct Push technology – which sends new emails, calendar and contact updates direct to your phone. You no longer have to specifically connect

OFFICE PHONE The HP iPAQ Voice Messenger lets you take your entire office on the move along with your Office applications

to the internet to check your mail.

Windows Live Messenger is included in Windows Mobile 6.1, too – so even when you're out and about, you can hold virtual meetings with work colleagues, exchanging instant messages, files and images.

---

you choose rather than Hotmail. In Hotmail you do this in **Options ➔ More Options ➔ Send and receive mail from other e-mail accounts**.

Of course, if you're on the move you'll need access to all your contacts, too. If you use Microsoft Office Outlook, there's a simple way to synchronize your online address book. You'll need a Windows Live Hotmail email account and an add-on for Microsoft Office Outlook called Outlook Connector. You can download the latter from http://office.microsoft.com/en-us/outlook/HA102225181033.aspx. Once this is installed on your main machine, you'll be prompted to create a connection to your Hotmail account. When you restart Outlook, you'll have access to the

Hotmail account – including your inbox and contacts – from Outlook. Now you can simply drag and drop your work contacts from Outlook to your Hotmail account, so you can access them anywhere.

SKYDRIVE Send files off to the file-store in the sky with Windows Live SkyDrive

So far, you can access office tools anywhere, keep track of your contacts and send email from your desk when you're not even there. What about all the important files that are already on your work machine? What you need is some storage – a place to keep those files so you can always get to them. There are several possible solutions to that particular problem – just take your pick.

Online storage

Online file storage and sharing services are an easy way to make your documents available on any internet-connected machine. Simply sign up for an account and upload the files you want to store. Then you can access your files and choose whether uploaded

TOUCH ME The HTC Touch Diamond interface makes it a compelling device; a phone call is possible in just a few taps and it offers full Wi-Fi and a 3.2MP camera

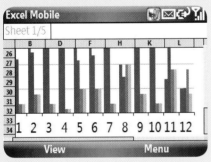

GRID TO GO You can even check your spreadsheets with the mobile Office Excel

means you'll never lose a file again. This much peace of mind costs though – so compare subscription rates before making your decision.

Microsoft offers the Live SkyDrive service, which not only enables you to access your own files online but enables you to make them available to other users, if you so choose. The great news is if you already have a Hotmail or Windows Live account then you already have access to 25GB of online storage via Live SkyDrive, just browse to http://skydrive.live.com and click the **Get Started** button or else create a fresh Windows Live account and get going.

The interface lets you easily upload documents, music, pictures and videos, along with making files available to specific Windows Live users or to all users. When sharing files it's possible to specify people as Editors or Readers – a helpful shorthand for those with full or just read-only access to the files that you upload to the new folders.

Online file storage is an easy way to make your work available on any PC

The easiest way to keep your files accessible everywhere is to just carry them around with you in your pocket. USB flash drives, or USB keys, used to be novelty devices. Now you can purchase drives that will store as much as 4GB of data – enough memory for a thousand songs in Windows Media Audio format or tens of thousands of text files. The beauty of these is that you can plug one into the USB port of any computer to instantly access your files – your PC will recognize it as another drive attached to your system. For extra peace of mind, keys can also be password protected for extra security.

Use a combination of the facilities mentioned here, and you'll be ready to take your office on the move.

Being there

How to access your work PC when you're away

TAKE CONTROL Remote Desktop allows you complete control of your work PC

Remote Desktop
Take control of your work PC from afar. Go to **Control Panel → System and Security → System → Remote settings** and click **Allow Remote Access** on your work PC and your own machine. To connect to the work PC, launch Remote Desktop, then enter its IP address.

MEETING UP Make sure you're all on the same page with Office Live Workspace

Office Live Workspace
Collaborate with colleagues using Office Live Workspace. The internet-based service allows you to give shared access to uploaded files – it'll even list any amendments, to make sure everyone's up to date. Go to http://workspace.officelive.com and sign up for a free space with 5GB of storage.

documents should be private or shared. With shared files, you can send a web link to anyone via email. They can download the file direct from the link you give them. Most of these sites also let you store pictures and you can post the links on message boards or in blog posts. While these services are good for the occasional picture or memo, what if you need access to all your files? In this case, you'll need to create an online back-up of all your files. An online back-up means you can access your files – using the relevant software – from your internet-connected PC as though it were another hard drive. These services are fast and easy to use, working in the background to save documents as you update and change them. This also

Childproof your home office

While working from home is convenient, it can be hazardous. Keep your kids, and your PC, safe

Super Tip!
Safety gear
When you're not working, don't forget that Windows 7 can help protect your children when using the PC. Go to **User Accounts** to find out more (or read more on p38).

For parents, working from home can be a blessing – but all your office paraphernalia can be hazardous to children, and children can certainly be hazardous to your precious work documents and computer hardware.

That's something Linda Jones had to learn the hard way. "I'm naturally an untidy person, but I had to be really organized while working from home.

I was concerned about the number of cables and switches for little hands to get hold of or trip over; when my daughters Emily and Melissa were toddlers, they were never allowed in my 'office' unattended," she recalls. Despite this, Linda originally let her daughters sit on her lap now and again as she worked – and her computer ended up the casualty.

"Every time an exasperated computer repair man came to see us, he'd say

'don't have drinks near the computer!' and we'd smile, nod and say "OK" before counting the days before something else ended up over the keyboard." After a year of crumbs and drink spillages, Linda's PC finally gave up the ghost entirely.

Eventually, Linda decided that working from home and children didn't mix, and she hired a separate office... Something Jake Ludington considered when his son Wyatt crumpled up a crucial contract he'd left on his desk. But instead of giving up, Jake decided that something should be done! He embarked on a quest to make his home office childproof – and he's helpfully

Identify dangers – explore your office from toddler level

published his advice online at www.jakeludington.com/child-safe-home-office. As Jake discovered, it is possible to make a childproof office – but it does take a bit of work first.

Home office hazards
One of the easiest ways to identify potential dangers in your work room is to 'do the crawl' and explore your office from toddler level. If something can be pulled, poked, prodded, bashed into or tripped over it probably will be, and doing your own personal crawl is a good way to spot the risks.

"Once you get past the obvious

Child-friendly Windows 7

Use Parental Controls to protect kids from net nasties

The most obvious concern about mixing computer equipment and young children are the physical risks but, of course, there are other risks, too. It's all too easy to encounter objectionable material – or people – online, and if your kids are playing with an unrestricted PC they could see inappropriate content. The other risk is that they'll mess with things they shouldn't, such as work files. While Windows 7 makes it easy to recover files, it's easier to prevent damage from occurring at all.

The answer is found in User Accounts and Parental Controls. By giving each family member their own password-protected account, you can set up Parental Controls to filter their web browsing or prevent them from running specific

programs. Best of all, the controls can be different for each account – so while you might block almost everything for young children, you can give older kids more leeway. Setting up User Accounts and Parental Controls is easy: just log in on an administrator account, open Control Panel and follow the walkthrough on page 192.

PARENTAL PASSWORDS There's no point in creating separate user accounts if your own account isn't password protected

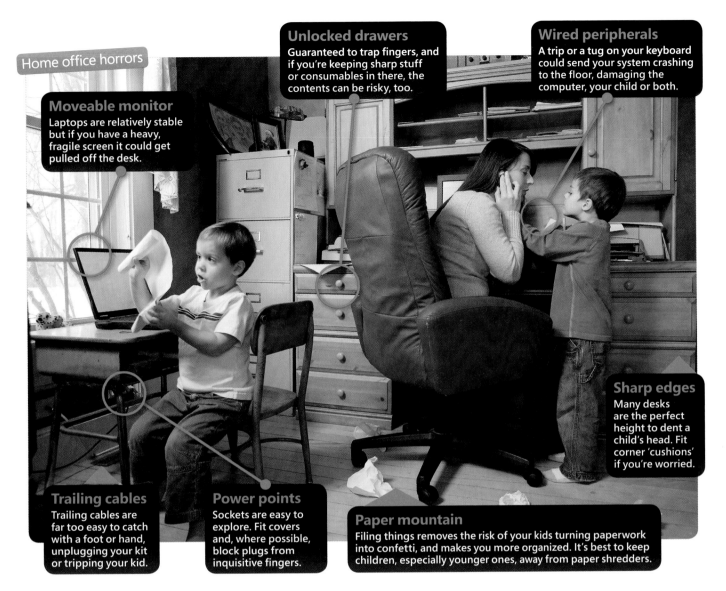

Home office horrors

Moveable monitor
Laptops are relatively stable but if you have a heavy, fragile screen it could get pulled off the desk.

Unlocked drawers
Guaranteed to trap fingers, and if you're keeping sharp stuff or consumables in there, the contents can be risky, too.

Wired peripherals
A trip or a tug on your keyboard could send your system crashing to the floor, damaging the computer, your child or both.

Sharp edges
Many desks are the perfect height to dent a child's head. Fit corner 'cushions' if you're worried.

Trailing cables
Trailing cables are far too easy to catch with a foot or hand, unplugging your kit or tripping your kid.

Power points
Sockets are easy to explore. Fit covers and, where possible, block plugs from inquisitive fingers.

Paper mountain
Filing things removes the risk of your kids turning paperwork into confetti, and makes you more organized. It's best to keep children, especially younger ones, away from paper shredders.

---

things, like keeping sharp objects out of reach, making light sockets unavailable, storing toxic substances appropriately, and so on, most of what's left is keeping your working environment safe so you don't have reasons to get mad for what really boils down to carelessness," says Jake. Of course, there are many other elements of office equipment to be aware of – paper shredders, paper cutters, electrical cables and plugs, etc. Thankfully, Jake's online advice covers everything from putting covers on sockets to choosing a chair without adjusters that a child could bang into.

Isn't there a danger that paranoid parents will go over the top though, or is it prudent to imagine worst-case scenarios? "It's prudent... but I wouldn't go overboard with it," Jake says.

No, no, no

Jake's key advice is to create a 'yes' environment. He explains: "A 'yes' environment is basically a place where you aren't constantly telling your child 'no'. If you're going to exist in a home office with your kids, you need things they can do because they are going to want to be where you are. Telling them 'no' to the point where there's nothing in the room they can do is not productive, and it's not a healthy environment for the kid, either.

"Providing solid alternatives," continues Jake, "like a small table where your kid can draw on paper – and other age-appropriate materials makes all the difference between getting work done and spending all your time giving a child negative attention."

Happy home working

Many forward-thinking companies are more parent-friendly these days, and a large number of employees are electing to become homeworkers when their little darlings arrive. We spoke to three parents and homeworkers: Patricia Kenar, Lynn Cormack and Alison Schillaci. So how do they cope?

Lynn's children – Cameron (10) and Natalie (8) – are older, so "no childproofing was really necessary, ➔

Case study: toddling traumas

The home set-up – and the changes that have to be made...

PARENTAL CONTROL Keep your home office safe for uninterrupted workflow

When Pete Boston joined web design agency Headscape (www.headscape.co.uk), working from home was entirely new to him. Fortunately, it now means Pete can spend more time with his daughter Rachel. Although Pete didn't do any childproofing to the office before she arrived, he had to make changes once Rachel began to assert her independence – and her curiosity.

"My main concerns are all the wires and plug sockets under my desk, which Rachel always heads for as soon as she crawls into the office," he says. "So I've made sure monitor cables are out of reach."

Pete will also be moving his halogen heater, which he uses instead of heating the entire house when he's home on his own in the winter." The heater is a sensible economic choice but of all the things in the office, this is probably the biggest potential hazard. So it's not just desk drawers and cupboard doors to worry about...

So is a home office more dangerous than any other room in the house? "Yes and no," Pete says. "It's more hazardous than a bedroom, but less than a kitchen – especially when I'm not there and the door is left open." For Pete, the best solution is simple: "Keep the door closed if you aren't in there!"

as my kids are at the age where they know better – most of the time," she says. There haven't been any disasters – that is, other than "the usual screaming fits while you're trying to talk to customers and the doorbell's ringing and the dog's barking..."

"The smart answer is to say 'keep them out of the office', but that isn't always possible," says Patricia Kenar. "I don't allow four-year-old Neco in my office when I'm working, but if

"I've bought Neco a little phone and he sits and copies me!"

I'm doing paperwork, or whatever, we play a game where he isn't allowed to talk to me and he'll sit quite happily with paper and crayons."

Patricia also recommends a baby gate "so you can see them but they can't get in to touch anything"; this kind of arrangement echoes Jake Ludington's comments about providing child-friendly alternatives. "I've bought Neco a little phone and he sits and copies

Keep your kids safe when using the PC
How to set up Parental Controls in Windows 7

1 CONTROL Go to **Control Panel →** **User Accounts and Family Safety →** **Set Up Parental Controls for any user**. Once you've chosen the child's account, you'll see the screen shown here. Click **Parental Controls: On** to start making the account child-friendly.

2 GAMES Windows 7 can also block games. As all games are rated, you can choose which is suitable. Click on **Games**, select **Yes**. Then either block games by age rating by clicking **Set game ratings** or block specific games by clicking **Block or allow specific games**.

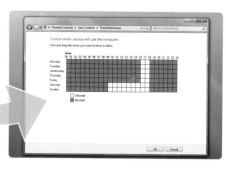

3 TIME From the main Parental Controls screen, click on **Time Limits** and you'll see a grid dividing each day into hour blocks. Use your mouse to color the grid – blue means that your PC is off-limits – if your child tries to log on Windows 7 will turn them away.

WORK & PLAY Keep your child occupied and they're less likely to interrupt your work

me," Patricia laughs. "It's hysterical."

"We use cable tidies and, while we have a shredder, we have warned both Luke (7) and Isaac (4) how dangerous it is," says Alison Schillaci. "We let them shred unwanted documents, junk mail and so on with supervision, and they don't seem to feel the need to play with it... we did tell them that they would lose a finger and it would never grow back. Shocking I know, but we find it works to be dramatic if the consequences could be dramatic."

"Children always seem to want what they can't have," Alison notes, so when Luke was three she introduced him to Paint and another child-friendly

GIVE AND TAKE It's an idea to show your children how dull office equipment really is!

website. "He doesn't touch anything – modem, wires, etc – because he's more interested in what he can put up on the screen." She found the same approach worked with other equipment: "I just demonstrated what it was and fed their appetite to play with something new, and now they don't seem to bother."

A 'yes' environment

Like Jake Ludington, Alison found that creating a 'yes' environment for your children is one of the most effective ways of childproofing.

"Feed and respect your child's curiosity," she says. "Show them how things work and give them their own time, supervised at first, on the computer, let them send a fax – it soon gets boring – and watch them learn new skills. We feel that when Luke and Isaac learn and respect what things are for and how they work, their curiosity is significantly reduced. When they don't try to go behind your back, you don't worry about their safety." So, it seems, that with a bit of forward-planning and good observation skills, a parent can work from home! ⊞

Child-friendly

Top tips for a child-safe office

1 DO THE CRAWL Explore your office on your hands and knees. Look for things that can be pulled, prodded or crashed into.

2 CUT THE CABLES Wireless keyboards and peripherals aren't tied to your PC, so grabbing hands won't pull your entire system off the desk. More expensive to start with, but could save you a fortune in repair bills.

3 TIDY THE REST Some cables – power, video and so on – are necessary; use cable tidies to keep them out of sight and reach.

4 PUT LOCKS ON Childproof locks for drawers and doors are cheap, easy to fit and prevent kids from getting their hands on dangerous or irreplaceable items.

5 COVER THE PLUGS Plug covers stop curious fingers getting into electrical sockets. Consider covering power strips and plugged-in cables to prevent accidental unplugging too.

6 MOVE YOUR PC To children, CD and DVD drives are perfect places to put toast. Move your desktop case – and monitor while you're at it – out of reach.

7 GET A LID Put a lid on your wastepaper bin to prevent potentially painful bits and bobs being grabbed.

8 MAKE SPACE Creating a kids' area in your home office will hopefully provide enough distraction to stop your little darlings tugging at power cables.

Liven up your PC with a personalized desktop

The newly-overhauled Personalization section of Windows 7 brings life to your desktop with beautiful wallpapers, sounds and themes

Windows 7 comes with the ability to create a completely individual desktop, that you can sit back and admire when you're not surfing the internet or working on your PC. Unlike Windows Vista, where you could only change the wallpaper to change the feel of your desktop, Windows 7 has many more options to adjust, including a huge range of wallpapers, sound schemes which react differently, and a choice of colors for window surrounds.

You can even choose from a pre-set desktop theme if you don't fancy adjusting the options yourself. To create your individual desktop, simply right-click the desktop area, select **Personalization** from the drop-down menu and, in the window that opens, click on one of the themes. To create a more tailored theme, follow the step-by-step walkthrough on the opposite page.

You can download even more themes at http://snipurl.com/oskt7. Once you've opened this address in Internet Explorer, find a theme you like, click **Download** then **Open**. Once it's downloaded – in a matter of seconds – it'll be added to your list of customized themes. If you decide you don't like it, just click on another theme to change it.

You can also choose from one of 36 different thumbnail pictures to suit your account (the bit you see above your username when you log in to your PC). Alternatively, you can use your own image from your hard drive. It's easy to change: in the Personalization window, click on **Change your account picture**, choose a new account picture and click **Change Picture**.

Tailor your Windows 7 appearance

Your desktop says a lot about you. As do themes and sounds...

Wallpapers
Choose a different background every day... There's the Architecture set, for a manmade look; the Characters set for something unusual, or the Regional set, which differs depending on which part of the world you bought your copy of Windows 7 in. You can also create a slide show of multiple wallpapers that your PC switches between.

Sounds
Windows 7 comes with more than just one sound scheme (15 in fact), so when you open a folder or are prompted with a message on-screen, you can get a different sound to play.

Window Color
You can change the color of your window borders, Start menu and taskbar too in the color-changing option of the Personalization window. There are 16 different pre-set colors to choose from, or there's a color mixer which allows you to exactly change the color to your liking – if you've got a favorite color then you're catered for here! You can also turn off transparency if you don't like the way that backgrounds show through the edges of windows.

Themes
When you combine the three elements – wallpaper, sound and window color – you have a desktop

CHOICE The range of desktop backgrounds is so diverse, you'll find one that suits

theme. Windows 7 comes with seven different themes as standard, each with different elements. When you want a change, just click on one of these themes or, if you want to create a completely customized theme, select which elements you like the most and save these as your own personalized theme to the My Themes area of the Personalization window.

Although Windows 7 doesn't yet have the support for animated desktops, third-party programs such as Stardock DeskScapes (from www.stardock.com/products/deskscapes) or DreamMaker (at dream.wincustomize.com/DreamMaker.aspx) may well do so in the near future – just keep checking the respective websites to find out. 🎵

ID Represent yourself with the right image

Super Tip!
Change of scene

If you want to quickly change your desktop background with an image on your hard drive, right-click it and choose **Set as desktop background** from the drop-down menu.

Dream a better dream
The easy way to create animated backgrounds

1 WHERE TO GO First of all, you need to find out where to create your customized desktop. Right-click your desktop and select **Personalize** from the drop-down menu. This will open the Personalization window.

2 NEW BACKGROUND Click on **Desktop Background** at the bottom of the Personalization window and choose a wallpaper – get one from the Picture location drop-down menu or choose one from your own folder of images.

3 SHUFFLE IT If you want to create a slide show, check **Select all images available** in a picture location. Specify how long each slide shows for by going to **Change picture every:** and changing the delay. Click **Save changes**.

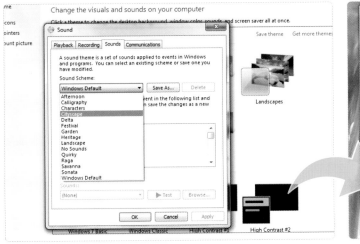

4 SOUND & COLOR Now for sounds... Click on **Sounds** and choose from the Sound Scheme drop-down menu. Finally, try adding a lick of paint to your window borders by clicking on **Window Color** (back in Personalization) and choosing a color.

5 DREAM THEME When you return to the previous screen, you'll see an unsaved theme in My Themes. Right-click the theme, select **Save theme**, choose a name, then **Save**. If you don't like what you've created, you can easily change it.

Appendix

Prepare yourself for the move to Windows 7 and keep the system in tip-top condition

Appendix

Choosing the right edition

Whatever your requirements, there's a version of Windows 7 that's perfect. Which one's best for you?

Microsoft has made not one version of Windows 7, but three main editions, as well as a 'starter' version for notebooks and special 64-bit versions of each for heavyweight PCs. Whichever edition you go for, you can easily change: Microsoft has put every version on the same disc, so if you decide you want a more powerful edition you don't need to trek to the shops. Instead, just contact Microsoft, pay for the upgrade and unlock the version instantly.

On the opposite page you'll find details of the three main Windows 7 editions. Home Premium is the best version for most people, but then the all-singing, all-dancing features of the Ultimate edition are difficult to resist...

A whole lot more

As you'll discover, it's similar enough to Windows Vista that you won't feel lost when you use it, but there are some major new features, new programs and new tools designed to make your PC more powerful and more productive. It's an impressive achievement.

Windows 7 is an operating system, acting as a middleman between your PC's hardware and software. So when you want to print a document from your word processor, Windows 7 tells the hardware what to do; when you need to find a file, Windows 7 searches your hard disk, and so on...

Windows 7 has been streamlined substantially compared to Windows Vista and, while it still enables you do to all kinds of things, you won't find it as packed with programs. Programs such as Windows Movie Maker, Internet Explorer and Windows Mail have been removed and can now be downloaded as part of Windows Live (http://get.live.com). Windows 7 also comes with a range of security tools, although you'll still need to invest in an anti-virus program.

Solid security

Iron-clad protection for your PC

Bolstered security is arguably the most important element in Windows 7. For instance, the Windows Firewall is now two-way, monitoring outbound and inbound network communications (previously it was inbound only). Windows Defender, Microsoft's anti-spyware tool, is turned on by default, offering real-time protection against malicious software. Similarly, Internet Explorer runs in a 'protected' mode that forces you to grant permission for any action that could be 'suspect', such as downloading and installing software.

Windows 7 also boasts User Account Control, which pops up whenever Windows is about to perform a process that could be damaging. The screen goes black, then freezes, and up pops a dialog box for you to choose between continuing or cancelling.

UPGRADE Windows 7 not only looks fantastic but is extremely power efficient, too

The Windows 7 user interface strikes you as soon as you switch on. The green Start button has morphed into a blue orb and the Start menu itself is organized differently. The Desktop still sports a taskbar with a Notification Area to the right and a Quick Launch area next to the Start button but it is now transparent. Icons are high resolution and 3D but the Sidebar has been removed – you can still use Gadgets though. The color scheme is subtle, soft and very easy on the eye.

As you'd expect, virtually everything in Windows 7 is customizable. Some familiar tools and shortcuts have moved though. For instance, if you right-click the desktop in search of the Properties dialog box – to adjust screen resolution, change the wallpaper or tweak the graphics driver settings – you'll find no

CLEAR VIEW Windows 7 offers you plenty of options to customize your PC to your liking

such menu. Instead, there's a Personalize option that fires up a Control Panel style window comprising seven main headings, a separate 'task' list and links.

The elements covered in this book will help you to maximize the benefits that the operating system has to offer. ⊞

Windows 7 – the three main editions compared

So what are the differences between each edition of Windows 7? Here are the salient features...

Features

Feature	Home Premium	Professional	Ultimate
HomeGroup	✔	✔	✔
Improved taskbar and JumpLists	✔	✔	✔
Advanced networking support	✔	✔	✔
Windows Mobility Center	✔	✔	✔
Aero Glass and advanced Windows navigation	✔	✔	✔
Windows Media Center	✔	✔	✔
Multi-touch and improved handwriting recognition	✔	✔	✔
Domain Join for secure server networking	✘	✔	✔
Location aware printing	✘	✔	✔
Remote Desktop Host	✘	✔	✔
BitLocker Drive Encryption	✘	✘	✔
MUI multiple language support	✘	✘	✔
Windows Search	✔	✔	✔
Windows XP Mode	✘	✔	✔

Take precautions before you install

If you're upgrading to Windows 7, a little preparation is a good idea...

Imagine being seconds away from finishing an installation and the worst happens – a power cut, lightning strikes your house, aliens land on the roof or, more mundanely, your hard drive fails. No matter how unlikely it is that anything will go wrong, you should never risk all your photos, emails and other mementos on the off-chance, particularly when it's so easy to protect them using Windows Backup.

You'll find Windows Backup in **Start ➜ All Programs ➜ Accessories**, though if you're running Windows XP Home, you need to install the utility first – you'll find it in the VALUEADD\MSFT\NTBACKUP

folder on the installation CD.

If you want an even easier option, dumping My Documents and any personal folders on a single DVD or CD takes less than half an hour.

Fight the temptation to tidy up My Documents before backing up – just be selective when you restore the data. Check where more obscure programs store files by checking their **File ➜ Save** menu, and don't forget any save points for games – they're usually in their own folders in Program Files. If you've bought online applications, grab the keys and passwords for these as well (and the actual files). And if other members of your household use the same machine,

you need to do all of this for each account. Other areas you should take note of are your internet favorites, email account settings and website passwords. It's also worth taking note of the programs in the Start Menu, because it's easy to lose more obscure utilities.

Easy transfers

The manual approach isn't the only choice, though. Like Windows Vista, Windows 7 uses Windows Easy Transfer, the program that makes it really easy to copy all the important settings over. While you can use it to get files off an old PC and on to your new Windows 7 machine – either by connecting their USB ports with an Easy Transfer cable or connecting them both to a home network – you can also use it to back up a computer before installing Windows 7 on it.

It doesn't support every program, and you'll still need to reinstall lots of stuff once you've got your new system in place, but it's a lot easier than painstakingly tracking down long-forgotten set-up details. ⊞

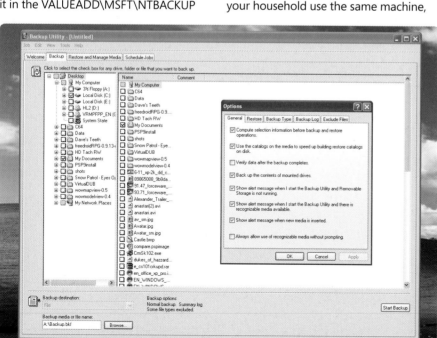

HELPING HAND If upgrading from Windows XP – let the Backup utility take the strain

If you're migrating to a new PC...

Using Windows Easy Transfer really is easy

1 GETTING STARTED Go to **Control Panel → Windows Easy Transfer**, or simply write 'Windows Easy Transfer' into the Search bar in the Start menu, and open the relevant window.

2 TO TRANSFER Click **Next** and then choose how to transfer data; an Easy Transfer cable is best, but this walkthrough shows the process for a CD, DVD or other removable media.

3 PICK A DRIVE Easy Transfer can use USB flash drives or a network drive. If you don't have either, click **CD**. Pick a CD or DVD writer from the list, and password protect your files.

4 WHAT FILES? You can click **All user accounts, files, and settings** to transfer the lot, but that requires lots of space (say, a network drive). If using DVDs, click **Advanced options**.

5 WHICH SETTINGS? You'll see a tree of every group of files and settings that Easy Transfer can move, with the size displayed. Browse the list, clearing check boxes for entries you don't need.

6 BURN DATA Place a blank, writeable CD or DVD in the drive specified, and click **Next**. Windows Easy Transfer will copy the checked files and settings – prompting you to replace it as required.

7 AT THE NEW PC Put the first disc in a drive. Click **Start → Computer**, choose the drive containing your disc; double-click on the **Migration store** file it contains to import the transferred data.

8 NAME CHECK Your PC may not have the same user account names as your old one, so you'll be asked which new accounts should be used for each old one. Pick an account and click **Next**.

9 LET'S DO IT Click **Transfer** and switch discs as prompted. When complete, click **Show me everything transferred** for a list of every file and Registry setting added or changed. Otherwise, click **Close**.

Consider the power of your PC

You need to check a few things before deciding which upgrade is best for you, and you need to maximize performance...

If you're upgrading a computer that's running Windows Vista, you can save money by opting for an upgrade rather than the full version of Windows 7. However, you can't necessarily perform an in-place or 'over-the-top' upgrade; sometimes you have to perform a clean installation of Windows 7, which means backing up and reinstalling all your current programs, folders and files. The table (right) shows where an over-the-top upgrade is possible.

In practise, a clean install means a fresh start, and anything short of this can potentially carry over all manner of problems from your old version of Windows Vista. Strictly speaking, when

Windows 7 installs itself over Windows Vista, it actually does perform a clean install and then imports all the old settings. This should help prevent problems and can even, in principle,

carry through hardware drivers that can't be installed under Windows Vista itself. However, a truly clean install is obviously the recommended option.

If you're buying a new PC with

From/To	Windows 7 Home Premium	Windows 7 Professional	Windows 7 Ultimate
Windows XP	Custom install	Custom install	Custom install
Windows Vista Home Basic	In-place upgrade	Custom install	In-place upgrade
Windows Vista Home Premium	In-place upgrade	Custom install	In-place upgrade
Windows Vista Ultimate	Custom install	Custom install	In-place upgrade

Examples listed above refer to 32-bit. For details of all upgrades/installations, including from/to 32-bit/64-bit versions, as well as from Windows Vista Starter and Business editions, go to http://snipurl.com/qtszf.

Is your PC powerful enough to install

It's easy to check your system before embarking on an installation

1 CHECK THE SPECS Get Windows 7 Upgrade Advisor from http://tinyurl.com/no4xb7. As the opening screen recommends, connect as many external devices as possible, including hard drives, then initiate a scan.

2 TAKING STOCK The Windows 7 Upgrade Advisor will scan your system thoroughly so it can establish exactly what your PC may or may not need in order to run Windows 7. This will take a few minutes.

3 THE LIST Once the program has finished scanning your PC, it will pop up with a screen that lists System Requirements, Devices and Programs. Under each of these, you'll see info about how your PC has passed muster.

	If you want to run Windows 7 on your PC, here's what it takes...
Processor	1GHz or faster 32-bit or 64-bit processor
RAM	1GB RAM (32 bit) or 2GB RAM (74-bit)
Hard disk	16GB (32-bit) or 20GB (64-bit)
Graphics	DirectX 9 graphics device with WWDM 1.0 or higher

For details of additional requirements, go to:
http://www.microsoft.com/windows/windows-7/get/system-requirements.aspx

Windows 7 pre-installed, you should have nothing to worry about with regard to performance. If you're upgrading from Windows Vista you shouldn't have any problems either: Windows 7 is, in fact, less demanding on your system so if you can run Aero in Windows Vista, you can run it in Windows 7, too.

And if you've bought a PC running Windows Vista since June this year, you may even qualify for a free upgrade to Windows 7 – just check your manufacturer's website, or www.microsoft.com/windows7 for details.

Even if you're upgrading from an older operating system, like Windows XP, you'll be surprised at how low the new requirements are for Windows 7. So long as you have a DirectX 9 compatible graphics card in your PC,

you should be able to install Windows 7 on your machine without any problems. If your graphics card is particularly old, say over five or six years, it's worth checking that WDDM (Windows Vista Display Driver Model) drivers are available. If your graphics card isn't up to speed or WDDM drivers aren't available for it, Windows Vista defaults to the Classic gray interface.

If the graphics card is compatible, does have the right drivers but doesn't have quite enough horsepower, Windows Vista displays the Aero theme but skips the transparency effects.

Windows Experience Index

If you're not entirely happy with the performance of Windows 7 on your PC, particularly following an upgrade from

Windows XP on an older machine, check out Microsoft's on-board system performance monitor. The Windows Experience Index rates the processor, memory and hard drive speeds, and checks the graphics processor's ability to render the Aero desktop theme and the demands of 3D gaming. The result is a base score of somewhere between 1 and 6, potentially going upwards as new hardware develops and is released.

The idea is that all Windows 7 compatible programs will carry a base score rating. If a box says that a base score of 4 is required (or recommended), expect sluggish performance on a PC that scores below 3. However, if this is the case it may be that just a single component, such as the memory, needs upgrading to improve performance.

To rate your hardware in Windows 7, just go to **Start ➜ Control Panel ➜ System ➜ Check the Windows Experience Index.** Use the View and print details option for the full low-down on your system spec.

Of course, it would be nice to know whether your hardware is up to the mark before installing Windows 7, and that's what the Upgrade Advisor is for. See the steps below for details.

and run Windows 7?

4 POTENTIAL PROBLEMS If your PC has any issues that may affect Windows 7 performance, they'll be clearly outlined along with possible solutions. Click on the various links to find out more about what Windows 7 needs.

5 OTHER ISSUES Upgrade Advisor flags up any devices connected to your computer that it doesn't have drivers for. It's worth checking that Windows 7 drivers are available from the manufacturers before you upgrade.

6 DOWNLOAD UPDATES Once you've assessed your system and installed Windows 7, you'll need to visit Windows Update so you can install the latest drivers and updates. Just click on **Action Center** on the taskbar to find out more.

Starting the install...

It may seem a scary thing to do but replacing the operating system of a PC isn't anywhere near as difficult as it used to be. In fact, it just takes a number of easy steps to get the job done

There's every possibility that you'll first encounter Windows 7 when buying a new PC, but you may well be upgrading from an older system. If you aren't buying a brand new PC with Windows 7 pre-installed, there are three ways to upgrade your PC to Windows 7:

1 An 'in-place' upgrade of an earlier version of Windows. This preserves your old programs, files and settings.

2 A clean installation over the top of an existing version of Windows. This erases your previous version and all of your old files, favorites and settings.

3 A clean installation on a new or freshly formatted hard disk or hard disk partition, with or without a dual boot environment.

Option 1 is not recommended as there are four main concerns. First,

there's no way back, so if you don't like Windows 7, or if it doesn't perform as you expect, that's just tough. Second, there's a risk, however small, that the upgrade will fail at some point and you'll lose your data. Third, any existing problems on your computer may be carried through, potentially including viruses and spyware. And finally, your current system may well be performing at less than peak performance due to internal clutter and conflicts, and this could affect your post-upgrade performance. There's simply nothing like a fresh, clean installation to get the best out of Windows 7.

So which of the other options is best? Well, option 2 is fine so long as you make absolutely sure that you've backed up everything you could ever need from your old version of Windows. Windows 7 formats (wipes clean) the hard disk

during installation, so your data will be gone for good. You emerge with a pristine installation of Windows 7 that's free from the performance and security issues inherent in option 1, but you have to install all your old software again... Windows Easy Transfer makes it much easier to configure your new version of Windows like the old one, though.

Option 3 is easier still. That's because Windows 7 doesn't have to delete the old version of Windows; it simply installs alongside it in a different location. If you only have one hard disk, you can either install a second disk – an easy hardware upgrade – or you can split it into two (or more) partitions. A partitioned hard disk has separate sections that behave just like physically distinct hard disks. This way, you can leave your previous version of Windows on one partition while installing Windows 7 cleanly on the

It's only 15 steps to installation heaven

Just to prove how easy it is to install, here's every major step

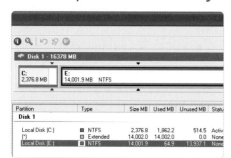

1 MAKE SPACE If you intend to install on a hard disk partition next to Windows XP, create the partition using a third-party tool. If you have a second hard disk, you don't need to worry.

2 GET STARTED The installer gets straight to work loading files. You'll see the screen change from black to the new Windows 7 start screen to a plain blue screen. This will take 5-10 minutes.

3 SPEAK TO ME Now Windows 7 will ask you to input your language preferences, time and currency format and the keyboard method you prefer. Once you've completed these, click **Next**.

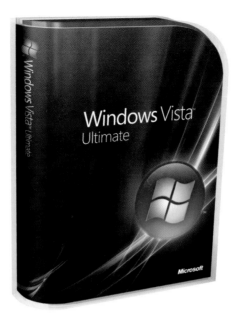

MOVING ON UP The table on p202 will tell you about upgrading or installing

other. You can also use your old version
of Windows whenever you like simply by
selecting it from a menu when you
reboot. You can launch the Windows 7
set-up routine either by accessing the
DVD from within Windows XP or by
booting directly from the DVD.

The walkthrough below looks at
option 3, accessing the DVD from
within Windows XP.

There is a point about partitioning that
needs to be taken into consideration. If
your hard disk isn't already partitioned,
Windows 7 can't do it for you without
erasing your existing data. So if you have
a PC with a 100MB hard disk and you
ask Windows 7 to split it into two 50GB
partitions – one for Windows XP and
one for Windows 7 – you get two 50GB
partitions. Unfortunately, the Windows

XP one will be completely empty.

There are two ways around this. You
can either install a second hard disk,
which removes the need for partitioning
altogether, or you can invest in a third-
party disk partitioning program. If you
use such a tool to partition your hard
disk, make sure that you choose the
more recent NTFS file system option
and not the old FAT32. ⊞

4 MORE INFORMATION You'll be taken
to the Install screen where you can
find out more about installing Windows
or repairing your computer. When you
are ready, click **Install now.**

5 PATIENCE The next screen simply
says 'Setup is starting...'; the PC will
sit at this point for another five to 10
minutes before moving on. Don't worry
if this takes a long time to prepare.

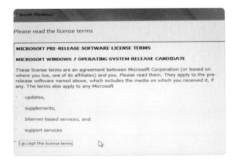

6 READ AND CONFIRM At this point
you'll be asked to read the license
terms and conditions and to click in the
box to accept. Once you've accepted
these you can then click **Next.** ➡

Installation heaven...

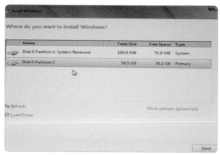

7 CHOOSE METHOD Here you can select **Custom install** or **Upgrade**. If you are upgrading from Windows XP and from various different versions of Windows Vista you will need to do a Custom install (see page 202).

8 PARTICULARS Choose which partition you want to install Windows 7 on to, if you are simply overwriting an old install then this will be simple. Check you have chosen the right system very carefully before proceeding.

9 MORE PATIENCE Windows 7 will take another 10-15 minutes to completely install on to your computer. It will move through various stages, from Copying Files to Completing Installation. Don't be alarmed if it reboots automatically.

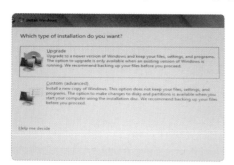

10 MARKING TERRITORY Enter in the user name and computer name for your Windows 7 install here. If you need more information, just click on account at the top of the screen. Click **Next** when you're done.

11 PROOF OF PURCHASE Windows 7 will now ask you to input your product key. You can do this now or you can do this later. Uncheck the box asking you to **Automatically Activate Windows** as you may need to reinstall later on.

12 PROTECT & SERVE Now specify some basic security settings. It's best to go for the default **Use recommended settings**, because this turns on Windows Firewall and configures automatic updates.

13 WHERE AM I? Time and date settings are the next elements on your list of things to organize while personalizing your Windows 7 set-up. Choose your settings and click **Next** to move on again.

14 FINAL STEPS Once you've filled in all of your bits of information, Windows 7 will proceed to tidy everything up, finalize your settings and get you where you need to be – inside the operating system itself.

15 HERE WE GO Finished! Your new desktop appears on your screen for the first time. Welcome to the wonderful world of Windows 7. Now you can follow the built-in guide to find out more and install all the latest drivers.

Common queries answered

Having a few problems? Check these fixes...

Q My software doesn't install. What can I do to make sure it does?

A If you put an install CD in the drive and nothing happens, right-click on it in Computer and choose **Explore**. Right-click on the installer program itself (usually called Setup or the name of the program) and choose the **Run as Administrator** option.

Q What do I do if my software installs, but doesn't work?

A Go to **Control Panel → View by → Small Icons → Troubleshoot**. Click **Next** and it will scan your computer and draw up a list of potential problem programs. Select the program from the list and then let the Program Compatibility wizard do the work for you.

Q My software *still* isn't working properly – what should I do?

A Make sure that you're running the latest version. Many programs need to have updates installed to work in Windows 7, and some won't work at all – check the official websites for their respective details.

Q Why am I having difficulties trying to import backed-up files?

A This can happen if you've transferred your files from DVD and they're set to **Read-only**. Simply select the files, right-click them and choose **Properties** – and make sure that the **Read-only** attribute is not checked.

Q How can I get my incompatible hardware to work?

A Unfortunately, not all hardware devices and components will immediately work with Windows 7. You'll need to look for a Windows 7-compatible driver at the manufacturer's website. Alternatively, try installing a Windows Vista driver instead.

Q How can I get my really old games to run in Windows 7?

A If you've got any really old software (particularly in gaming) that requires DOS, then it won't work in Windows 7. However, this can be sorted. You need to install DOSBox from Dosbox.sourceforge. net in order to run your old games on your new system.

Q Why is my PC now running so slowly?

A If you've upgraded from Windows XP and haven't made changes to your hardware or software for a while, you may find your computer only has a small amount of RAM which will cause it to struggle. If you can't add any more, plug in a ReadyBoost compatible memory stick and choose **Speed up my system** from the menu.

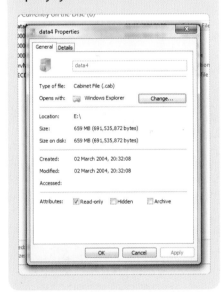

Q Why is Windows 7 taking so long to appear?

A Windows 7 is more demanding than Windows XP. Search for Aero in the Control Panel or go **Control Panel → Appearance and Personalization → Personalization**. Select **Windows 7 Basic** or **Windows Classic**.

Keep your PC as good as new

Windows 7 is packed with tools to keep your computer reliable and in top condition

The best part about a new computer is the super-fast, slick performance... Unfortunately, after a year or so, your shiny new machine may start to slow down. Thankfully, Windows 7 comes with applications designed to keep it running at its best.

Staying up-to-date is one of the best ways to keep your PC secure, and with Windows 7 it couldn't be easier. Windows Update helps to keep your PC safer and your software current by fetching the latest security and feature updates from Microsoft via the internet. In Windows 7, Windows Update is now a part of Action Center, a new tool that makes managing these updates more efficiently; security patches are updated automatically, but improved support for graphics cards and hardware are optional, so check Windows Update regularly.

THE LATEST THING Use Windows Update to keep your PC working as well as possible

In real life...
Keep it clean

**Jo Membery
Operations editor,
*Windows: The
Official Magazine***

I'm the last person in the world to look for extra work but I'm a convert to the fact that a little bit of time spent spring cleaning my PC reaps such significant performance rewards. A few checks make for a sparkling system – and Windows 7 does a lot of the hard work for me!

Also connected to the wonderfully accessible Action Center is Windows Defender – this is your first line of defense against spyware and other unwanted software. It's important to monitor the programs that are loaded when Windows 7 starts. A lot of programs automatically demand to be started up when your PC boots, and for the most part this is unnecessary – and the effort involved in opening all these programs at once can slow your boot time. Use Windows Defender (see page 30) to manage these programs and make sure that only the essential ones, such as security software, are loaded.

Driving speed

The state of your hard drive is another factor in keeping your PC running well. When your hard drive becomes cluttered, it takes longer for Windows to retrieve files. Use the Disk Cleanup utility to get rid of unwanted files.

It's also important to defragment your hard drive regularly, so that clusters of data are grouped together, and the disk doesn't have to work so hard to retrieve information. Defragmenting is time-consuming, but in Windows 7 you can schedule it to run at a time when your PC is idle.

If your PC is still suffering, try ReadyBoost to give your system extra oomph. Most USB drives and SD cards are configured for this. Just insert the drive/card, choose ReadyBoost from the auto-run menu, and you can put up to 4GB of memory aside for system processes. If you're running a system with limited RAM, you can gain a lot of speed by using the ReadyBoost feature.

Keep your PC running smoothly

Five Windows features to keep your PC happy

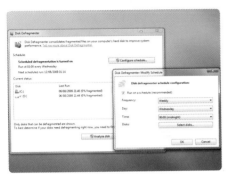

1 DISK DEFRAG The defragmenter makes sure your information is stored logically, making less work for your hard drive when retrieving and reading files. Use this regularly and schedule it for times when you won't be using your PC.

2 DISK CLEANUP Get rid of wasteful temporary files and free up space using Disk Cleanup. Making sure that your hard drive is in order will keep your PC running smoothly; you'll be shocked by how much space you can save.

3 UPDATE Keeping Windows up to date is an easy way to boost performance. Updates for drivers are released regularly but not downloaded automatically, so click on the **Action Center** icon in the taskbar to manage them.

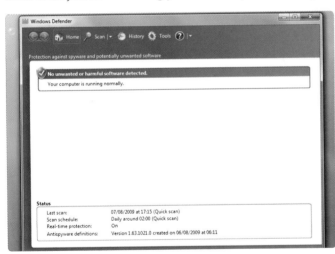

It's important to defragment your hard drive so the disk doesn't have to work so hard to retrieve information

4 WINDOWS DEFENDER As well as being your first defense against internet nasties, one of the best features of Windows Defender is its ability to monitor start-up programs. Make sure non-essential programs aren't slowing down your start-up time by disabling them here.

Stop unwanted programs

Here's another way of stopping unwanted programs at startup... Click **Start**, type 'msconfig' then hit the Startup tab; you'll see a list of programs. Uncheck next to the program's name to stop it loading at startup.

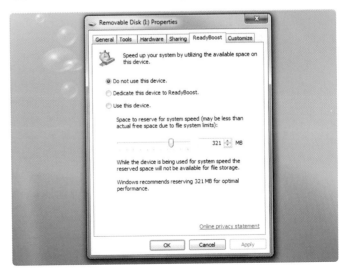

5 READYBOOST If your PC is sluggish, then ReadyBoost can provide some instant dynamism to your system performance. Plug in a USB drive configured for ReadyBoost and allocate up to 4GB of space to take the pressure off your system, and keep Windows 7 operating at its best.

Index

Index

What do you think of this book?

We want to hear from you!

To participate in a brief online survey, please visit:

microsoft.com/learning/booksurvey

Tell us how well this book meets your needs—what works effectively, and what we can do better. Your feedback will help us continually improve our books and learning resources for you.

Thank you in advance for your input!

Microsoft®
Press

Stay in touch!

To subscribe to the *Microsoft Press*® *Book Connection Newsletter*—for news on upcoming books, events, and special offers—please visit:

microsoft.com/learning/books/newsletter

Choose the Right Book for You

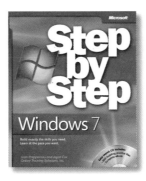

Plain & Simple

- Easy visual approach shows the simplest ways to get things done
- Full-color guide features easy-to-follow steps and screenshots
- Just the basics—no jargon, no hassle

Step by Step

- Build exactly the skills you want
- Take just the lessons you need, or work from cover to cover
- Easy-search CD includes practice files, complete eBook, and helpful resources

Inside Out

- Comprehensive, in-depth reference for intermediate to advanced users
- Features hundreds of timesaving solutions, troubleshooting tips, and workarounds
- CD packs custom resources and a fully searchable eBook

Resources from Microsoft Press

Plain & Simple

Windows® 7
Plain & Simple
978-0-7356-2666-9

2007 Microsoft® Office System
Plain & Simple
978-0-7356-2273-9

Microsoft Office Access® 2007
Plain & Simple
978-0-7356-2292-0

Microsoft Office Excel® 2007
Plain & Simple
978-0-7356-2291-3

Microsoft Office Outlook®
2007 *Plain & Simple*
978-0-7356-2294-4

Microsoft Office PowerPoint®
2007 *Plain & Simple*
978-0-7356-2295-1

Microsoft Office Word 2007
Plain & Simple
978-0-7356-2293-7

Microsoft Expression® Web
Plain & Simple
978-0-7356-2519-8

Step by Step

Windows 7
Step by Step
978-0-7356-2667-6

2007 Microsoft Office System
Step by Step, 2nd Edition
978-0-7356-2531-0

Microsoft Office Access 2007
Step by Step
978-0-7356-2303-3

Microsoft Office Excel 2007
Step by Step
978-0-7356-2304-0

Microsoft Office Outlook 2007
Step by Step
978-0-7356-2300-2

Microsoft Office PowerPoint
2007 *Step by Step*
978-0-7356-2301-9

Microsoft Office Project 2007
Step by Step
978-0-7356-2305-7

Microsoft Office SharePoint®
Designer 2007
Step by Step
978-0-7356-2533-4

Microsoft Office Word 2007
Step by Step
978-0-7356-2302-6

Inside Out

Windows 7
Inside Out
978-0-7356-2665-2

2007 Microsoft Office System
Inside Out
978-0-7356-2324-8

Advanced Microsoft Office
Documents 2007 Edition
Inside Out
978-0-7356-2285-2

Microsoft Office Access 2007
Inside Out
978-0-7356-2325-5

Microsoft Office Excel 2007
Inside Out
978-0-7356-2321-7

Microsoft Office Outlook 2007
Inside Out
978-0-7356-2328-6

Microsoft Office Project 2007
Inside Out
978-0-7356-2327-9

Microsoft Windows
SharePoint Services 3.0
Inside Out
978-0-7356-2323-1

Other Titles

The Microsoft Office Excel
2007 Toolkit: Microsoft Office
Excel 2007 *Step by Step* and
Create Dynamic Charts in
Microsoft Office Excel 2007
and Beyond
978-0-7356-2707-9

Beyond Bullet Points:
Using Microsoft Office
PowerPoint 2007 to Create
Presentations That Inform,
Motivate, and Inspire
978-0-7356-2387-3

Take Back Your Life! Using
Microsoft Office Outlook 2007
to Get Organized and Stay
Organized
978-0-7356-2343-9

The Best of Windows Vista:
The Official Magazine
978-0-7356-2579-2

Join us online

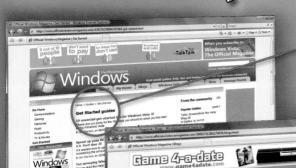

GET STARTED
How to install Windows and get to grips with all the programs and features

BLOGS
Read opinions from magazine staff and other site users – or even start your own blog

DO MORE
Discover how to use Windows to get more from your everyday interests and activities

MESSAGE BOARDS
Have your questions answered by our friendly and informed community

www.officialwindowsmagazine.com